*Cambridge Middle East Library*

Womanpower

# Cambridge Middle East Library

# *Womanpower*
## *The Arab debate on women at work*

NADIA HIJAB

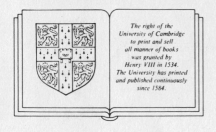

The right of the
University of Cambridge
to print and sell
all manner of books
was granted by
Henry VIII in 1534.
The University has printed
and published continuously
since 1584.

CAMBRIDGE UNIVERSITY PRESS

CAMBRIDGE

NEW YORK   NEW ROCHELLE   MELBOURNE   SYDNEY

Published by the Press Syndicate of the University of Cambridge
The Pitt Building, Trumpington Street, Cambridge CB2 1RP
32 East 57th Street, New York, NY 10022, USA
10 Stamford Road, Oakleigh, Melbourne 3166, Australia

First published 1988

Printed in Great Britain at the University Press, Cambridge

*British Library cataloguing in publication data*
Hijab, Nadia
Womanpower: the Arab debate on women
at work – (Cambridge Middle East library).
1. Women – Employment – Arab countries
I. Title
331.4′0917′4927    HD6206

*Library of Congress cataloguing in publication data*
Hijab, Nadia.
Womanpower: the Arab debate on women at work.
(Cambridge Middle East library)
Bibliography.
Includes index.
1. Women – Arab countries.    2. Family – Arab countries.
3. Women – Employment – Arab countries – Public opinion.
4. Women in development – Arab countries – Public opinion.
5. Public opinion – Arab countries.    I. Title.    II Series.
HQ1784.H54 1988    305.4′0917′4927    87–21217

ISBN 0 521 26443 X hard covers
ISBN 0 521 26992 X paperback

To A. and W., who, when our world was less
troubled, created a happy Arab family

# Contents

# Contents

# Tables

# Preface

'I have been asked to write a book on Arab women': this answer to polite enquiries on what I was doing with myself these days usually resulted in interesting (and sometimes interested) reactions. Arab women were on the whole pleased and helpful, as were many Arab men. The latter often, only half-jokingly, asked, 'Why not a book on Arab men?', and added worriedly, 'You will write, won't you, that Arab women enjoy their full rights?' As for sociologists of all nations, their reaction was somewhat disparaging: they thought the subject too general. Anthropologists tended to lose interest when it became clear I was not planning to spend several years in one village on, say, the Nile Delta.

The most frequent reaction to my statement, which showed how marginal this subject is still considered to be, was: 'Shouldn't someone in your position (I was then editor of a monthly political and socioeconomic magazine), shouldn't someone in your position be writing about something much more important?' If my interlocutor were Arab, this remark would usually be followed by a list of the problems plaguing the Arab world, from the Israeli occupation of Palestine, to the failures of economic development, to the lack of political freedom. If my interlocutor were Western, the remark might be followed by a pitying look, presumably for having fallen into some feminist trap.

It was after the first few reactions of this nature that the subject of my research began to really intrigue me. If I had described the book as being on political, economic and social currents in the Arab world today, which in fact it is, there would have been no problem. The problem was clearly the focus on women. I can understand, and sympathise with, some of the reluctance in the Arab world to 'focus on women' in the Western feminist scene. Most Arabs do not see their society as made up of individual men and women. They see the members of society as complementary; both sexes and different age groups are expected to give up some rights and to take on some responsibilities to forge a coherent community. By and large, men are seen to be as much the victims of their surroundings – family, society or state – as women, and are not viewed as public enemy No. 1.

However, women in the Arab world, as in the rest of the world, have faced one form or another of discrimination on account of their sex for centuries. This sets them apart, whether one likes it or not, and makes it important to examine their situation. Furthermore, in the Arab world today, some of the most heated debates are on women's role in society. To what extent should they be involved in the process of development and the modern work sector? To what extent will that affect their traditional roles as wives and mothers? The debate reveals the resistance of some to changing women's roles, and the conviction of others that, unless there is change, Arab society will find it difficult to move forward, at the economic and political levels as well as at the social level.

This book, then, is about the Arab world today – its society, its economy and its politics – as seen through an examination of the debate on Arab women at work. I shall speak of the 'Arab world' and of Arab women, although there is a great deal of diversity from one Arab country to the next; within Arab states between village and town; and within towns between different classes. I consider that the Arab region as a political and cultural entity has more common features within it than it has with any other grouping. The majority of its 180 million people share language, history and religion. The term 'Muslim world', for example, brings in countries that do not speak the same language, or share the same history as the Arab world. Nor do the various international geopolitical terms currently in use do the job: the 'Middle East' or 'Near East' is not sufficient to cover the Arab world, as those who add on 'and North Africa' implicitly admit; and terms like 'Western Asia' have been geographically stretched by the United Nations to include Egypt.

I shall seek to avoid generalisation by giving concrete examples and country case studies to illustrate certain trends. I shall particularly try to shed some light on the nature of the debate in the Arab world today, and to make up in synthesis what may be lacking in specifics: a good deal of material has been produced on the subject of Arab women, but a comprehensive picture of the situation has yet to emerge. I do not aim to attack or to defend the existing situation, but simply to describe and to analyse it. Nor shall I seek to show that it is better or worse than in the West, as some writing on the subject tends to do, leaving it to discerning non-Arab readers to compare the various stages of development in the Arab world to phases in their current or recent history; they may be sure that these comparisons exist.

The book is based on my observations and interviews in the Arab world and on Arab and Western writing on the subject. I should like to take this opportunity to thank those who have helped me, beginning with the following institutions: the American Middle East Peace Research Institute in Boston, whose generosity made it possible for me to take time off for research; my former publisher and colleagues at *The Middle East* magazine, IC Publications (the title 'Womanpower' was the title of a cover story I wrote for *The Middle East* in June 1983); the Centre for Contemporary Arab Studies at Georgetown University in Washington, where I spent a rewarding year as visiting scholar; and VideoArts Television and Kufic Films, for the opportunity to take part in filming 'Family Ties', the ninth programme in the 10-part series *The Arabs*, during which time some of the material in this book was collected.

I should also like to thank the Centre for Development and Population Activities (Washington), the International Centre for Research on Women (Washington), the International Labour Organisation (Geneva), the World Bank's Women in Development office, the United Nations Social and Economic Council, the *Middle East Journal* (Washington), and the Welfare Association (Geneva), for access to their resource centres; and *Forum 85*, the newspaper of the NGO Forum on women held in Nairobi in July 1985, and my fellow journalists on that short-lived but sparkling publication, for an instructive three weeks.

I should express my special appreciation to Yvonne Haddad, Doreen Hinchcliffe, Susannah Tarbush and Antoine Zahlan for their comments on specific sections of the typescript; to Amina Minns for reading the whole of it; and to Roger Owen for his valuable suggestions. (Needless to say, any mistakes are my own.)

There were many who were generous with the material at their disposal and with their advice, which was gratefully received: Laila Daoud Fanous; Sarah Graham-Brown; Walid Hamdan; Mostafa El-Hosseini; Albert Hourani; Rami Khoury; Flora Lahham and Khalil Hindi; Susan Markham; Jon Marks; Nabil Matar; Hasna Mikdashi; Muhammad al-Muttawa; Lynn Osborne; Judith Perera; Edward Said; Hisham Sharabi; and, especially, Camillia Fawzi El-Solh.

There were also many friends whose patience and understanding eased the process of writing: Riyad Abboushi; Maureen and Shafik Ali; Helga Graham and Robert Stephens, who were particularly giving during this time; Gebran Majdalany; Nayer Mikdadi; Ferial and Abdel-Ghani Mroueh; Faten Omari and Mustapha Karkouti; Zeinat and Riyad El-Rayyes; Colin Shinkin; and Ian Williams. Finally, I would like to thank my editor, Liz Wetton, for her patience.

# Abbreviations

The following abbreviations are used in the text and bibliography:

| | |
|---|---|
| AN | author's notes, based on interviews |
| MERIP | *Middle East Research and Information Project* |
| TME | *The Middle East* magazine |
| IWSAW | Institute of Women's Studies in the Arab World |
| ICRW | International Centre for Research on Women |
| ILO | International Labour Office |
| UN | United Nations |

# Introduction

We must stop considering ourselves part of the world's folklore.
*Lutfia al-Gabaili, Libyan editor*

In the 1970s, Arab governments began to talk more frequently and more eloquently about the 'need to integrate women in development'. Specialised departments were created, plans debated and women recruited. That was followed, in the 1980s, by a veritable eruption of interest at the popular level, reflected in the dozens of conferences and seminars held in the region and abroad on Arab women and their role in society.

This Arab awakening was part of a worldwide process that gained momentum when the United Nations declared 1975 International Women's Year. Indeed, two Arab countries, Egypt and Tunisia, were among the seven countries that introduced the resolution at the UN for a year to highlight women's issues. The Year became a Decade, its aim to achieve equality for women, and development and peace for the world by 1985.

## The UN Decade for Women

It could not be said, by 1985, that the aims of the Decade had been achieved, in the Arab world or anywhere else. This was admitted in the documents presented during the End-of-Decade conference in Nairobi in 1985. In spite of some progress, the UN described the overall achievement as 'modest' (UN, 1985d, p.22). It identified the obstacles that continued to block the advancement of women around the world as: deeply rooted traditions; poor understanding of the significance of women's issues; and lack of financial resources to reform the position of women (UN, 1984b, pp.21–2). It felt that world governments still lacked the political will to change the conditions which made women second-class citizens.

Clearly, it is premature for the world to pat itself on the back in the matter of human rights for women. Still, the impact of the UN Decade in the Arab world and elsewhere should not be ignored. Perhaps its major achievement was to raise awareness at the national and international levels of the

I

handicaps that women still faced on account of their sex. Governments did begin to take concrete steps to remedy the situation as a result.

This was revealed in a UN questionnaire that was sent to member states to find out whether their national development policies took women into account. Of the 92 governments that replied by 15 October 1984, 71.7 per cent said they did include specific planning for women in their national development plans – and 67.4 per cent had done so in response to the UN Decade (UN, 1984b, p.4). Furthermore, several governments had set up departments of women's affairs, to handle the integration of women in development during the Decade. Of 96 countries that had done so, 44 had established bodies between 1975 and 1985.

Of course, the efficiency of the newly created departments and ministries depended on the commitment of the governments concerned. Some simply wanted to be seen to be doing something; others wanted to look 'modern', since the status of women seemed to have become the major indicator of a country's modernity. The UN found that the work of national departments had not, in many countries, been extended to regional and local levels. A closer look at the national development plans showed that women were still seen as passive participants and consumers needing social welfare, rather than as a constituency of development that had long been denied the opportunity to develop its full potential (UN, 1984b, p.19).

In an interesting exercise, the UN undertook an examination of its own system to find out to what extent it practised what it preached. An in-house survey was conducted on the position of women working at the UN (UN, 1985a, p.6). It was found that, although UN policy makers were more aware of the need to integrate women in the system, the actual number of women employed by the UN at higher levels remained dismally low.

## The Arab world and the UN Decade

This brief background shows that the position of women in the Arab world is not unique. Women around the world are still considered to be an underprivileged group and many of the obstacles they face are the same: deeply rooted traditions, lack of finance to improve conditions, lack of political will to change the situation. This is why, in 1985, the UN conference at Nairobi adopted further strategies to achieve the aims of equality, development and peace, and extended the time limit to the year 2000.

In the period leading up to the adoption of the new strategies at Nairobi, the situation of women was reviewed in each UN region. For an indication of how Arab governments viewed the situation in their region by the mid-1980s, it is instructive to look at the recommendations of the UN's Economic and Social Commission for Western Asia, which groups 13 Arab countries: Bahrain, Democratic Yemen, Egypt, Iraq, Jordan, Kuwait, Lebanon, Oman, Qatar, Saudi Arabia, Syria, the United Arab Emirates and the Yemen Republic (UN, 1985b). The ESCWA recommendations reveal, perhaps unintentionally, some of the reasons why women in the Arab world have not yet achieved the elusive goal of equality and why their involvement in the modern work sector is as yet limited.

There were two striking things about the approach of the Arab region as compared to that of the other regions – Africa, Asia and the Pacific, Europe, Latin America and the Caribbean. First, the ESCWA report started with a cultural definition of the region that none of the other regions had felt necessary: 'The Strategy for Arab Women in Western Asia to the Year 2000 is based on the heritage of Arab–Islamic civilization and the religious and spiritual values of this region, the cradle of the messages of God which affirm the dignity and freedom of all human beings in this universe' (p.40).

This statement was a clear indication of the Arab attachment to a shared heritage; but the fact that it was felt necessary to assert this so categorically indicated an uneasy awareness that this ideal was under threat. Moreover, the statement immediately defined the framework for any discussion of women in the Arab world today: such a discussion had to fall within the framework of 'the heritage of the Arab–Islamic civilization', a phrase we shall come across again and again in the course of this book.

The second most striking thing about the ESCWA recommendations was the dedication of a whole section to the family. Other regions mentioned the family, but not to the extent that ESCWA did. The ESCWA report underlined that 'Constitutions, charters, and legislation in the region have asserted the role of the family as the nucleus of social organization in Arab societies. It is necessary, therefore, to make available to the family the economic, social, cultural and psychological conditions that would ensure its stability and satisfy its needs' (p.46).

The Arab family, then, was at the core of Arab society, and there was a clear determination to preserve it, but not, in theory at least, at the expense of women's role in society. This section of the ESCWA recommendations supported 'the right of women to choose their roles in and out of the family' and considered 'family responsibilities as developmental activities' (p.46). A paragraph in another section, however, accorded 'priority to the work of women who devote their time to family and home affairs and hence ensure the continuity of generations, the cultivation of values and the transmittal of knowledge and expertise from one generation to another' (p.43). This indicated that there might, in reality, be a difference between theory and practice.

In the other sections of the ESCWA report, the approach was similar to that of other regions. The recommendations emphasised the need to ensure women's 'participation in decision making . . . and in the benefits produced by development' (p.41). It proposed reviewing labour laws and taking the necessary measures to provide women with guidance on their rights. The recommendations on education proposed the review of 'school curricula, teaching methods and textbooks to provide boys and girls with a common culture . . . This review should also be directed towards correcting the traditional stereotyped image of women' (p.44). The recommendations on the role of the media urged the development of 'an alternative image of women that stresses the productive aspects of women's work instead of women's consumption activities' (p.46).

Thus, there was a clear awareness at the regional level of what remained to be done for women. In some instances, the thinking behind the ESCWA report seemed to be quite revolutionary. However, while the recommendations were laudable, the actual extent to which they could be implemented was in fact circumscribed by the cultural framework that had been drawn up at the start.

## The Convention's rocky road

The difference between government theory and practice is also sharply illustrated through a look at another Decade activity, the ratification of the Convention on the Elimination of All Forms of Discrimination Against Women. This was adopted by the UN General Assembly on 18 December 1979; it entered into force on 3 September 1981 when 20 countries ratified it. The 30-article convention sets out the internationally accepted principles on equal rights for women. It becomes legally binding on the states that sign it, although they can attach reservations to certain articles they do not intend to abide by.

Of the Arab states, Egypt had ratified the Convention by 13 June 1985, Democratic Yemen had acceded to it, and Tunisia and Jordan had signed it. As for reservations, Democratic Yemen, for instance, said it would not be bound by the article 'relating to the settlement of disputes which may arise concerning the application or interpretation of the Convention' (UN, 1985g, p.7).

Egypt had more serious reservations. It took exception to 'article 9, paragraph 2, concerning the granting of women of equal rights with men with respect to the nationality of their children' (p.7). The Egyptian statement explained, 'It is clear that the child's acquisition of his father's nationality is the procedure most suitable for the child and that this does not infringe upon the principle of equality between men and women, since it is the custom for a woman to agree, on marrying an alien, that her children shall be of the father's nationality' (p.7).

Another serious reservation was to article 16, 'concerning the equality of men and women in all matters relating to marriage and family relations during marriage and upon its dissolution. This must be without prejudice to the Islamic Sharia provisions whereby women are accorded rights equivalent to those of their spouses so as to ensure a just balance between them. This is out of respect for the sanctity deriving from firm religious beliefs which govern marital relations in Egypt and which may not be called in question' (p.7). The Egyptian statement explained that, because the husband was obliged to support the wife financially and to make payment in case of divorce, whereas the wife had no such obligation, 'the Sharia therefore restricts the wife's rights to divorce by making it contingent on a judge's ruling, whereas no such restriction is laid down in the case of the husband' (p.7).

Thus, it can be seen that, on the one hand, women were entitled to full equality with men since Egypt had ratified the Convention. On the other hand, when it came to the detailed application of the Convention, the women's rights were restricted on grounds that no one 'may call in question'. The cultural framework described above meant that Arab women could be equal outside the home but not within it.

The Arab states were not unique in their approach to the Convention. Some world governments did not sign at all, and many others took their time about signing and attached detailed reservations once they had signed. By 13 June 1985, neither the US nor the UK, which had signed the Convention, had yet ratified it. When the UK eventually ratified it, it did so with several pages of reservations, a move criticised by British women's groups that had hoped for unconditional ratification.

Some states which signed the Convention attached so many reservations that they made a nonsense of the whole exercise, and were taken to task by other countries. For example, three signatory countries, Bangladesh (a non-Arab Muslim country), and Jamaica and Mauritius (both non-Arab and non-Muslim countries) attached such comprehensive reservations to the Convention that Mexico took it upon itself to protest. 'These reservations', the Mexican government declared, 'if implemented, would inevitably result in discrimination against women by reason of their sex, contrary to the entire intent of the Convention' (p.13).

## Change at the grassroots level

The ambivalence of world governments on the question of the human rights of women, as outlined above, would probably have held up progress indefinitely, had it not been for the activism of women at the grassroots level. The development of the political will for change at this level was apparent during the meetings of non-governmental organisations (NGOs) that took place alongside the official UN conferences during the Decade. It was at the NGO meetings that the most interesting debates on women's issues were conducted. Indeed, it was initially as a result of NGO lobbying that the UN conferences were held at all.

The NGO meetings were open to all, and were organised so that anyone could hold a workshop on any topic that concerned them. Some 14,000 women from all over the world converged on Nairobi to attend the NGO meeting Forum 85 – about 5,000 more than at the mid-Decade conference in Copenhagen in 1980, and 9,000 more than at the start of the Decade conference in Mexico in 1975. They participated in or organised workshops on law, society, religion, health, education, work, politics and many other subjects.

More women from the Third World participated in the Nairobi Forum than previously, and there was a noticeably active and energetic Arab representation. Some of the world's women taking part in the Forum were 'hardline' feminists or Marxists; thousands were not. They simply shared a determination to change the status quo on their roles as women, which made even the political conservatives among them social radicals. Thus, they could be said to pose as much of a challenge to the political and economic establishment worldwide as, say, communism poses to capitalism, and vice versa.

Perhaps the most striking thing about Forum 85 was the extent to which an understanding had grown up between women from the First (the Western bloc), the Second (the Eastern bloc) and the Third (the 'developing' nations) Worlds. There seemed to be a clearer understanding in the West that the problems women faced because of their sex could not be isolated from the problems they faced as a result of military occupation, apartheid or famine. At the same time, there was a stronger feeling in the Third World that women should not wait for a solution to political and economic problems to achieve their human rights.

Those taking part in the Forum could not help being carried away by the sheer energy and creativity expressed; it was difficult to imagine that the impetus of the Decade would not carry women forward. But there was some pessimism as well. The feeling that women now had 'enough rights' was, according to some participants, being expressed more frequently in government circles. Projects to integrate women in development were beginning to be seen as a pretext to raise funding from international agencies. There were fears that the rest of the century might see a backlash that would reverse the advances made in the position of women around the world.

## Tough times ahead

In the Arab world, there is no doubt that the process of 'integrating women in development' – the catchphrase of the 1970s and 1980s – has produced mixed results. Arab women's involvement in the modern work sector remains limited and their entitlement to equality under the law remains ambivalent. Naturally, the reasons are complex, and will be elaborated during the course of this book. The first major reason is that the debate on women's role in society is taking place within the framework of the 'Arab–Islamic heritage'. As was noted earlier, this has resulted in a somewhat schizophrenic approach, which both encourages women to join in the process of development as equal partners and holds them back in their place as secondary actors within the family context. This dilemma will take time to resolve, because the debate on the role of women in society is caught up in the larger debate on the role of religion in society. Men and women from all walks of life are taking part in this intense debate, which will be covered in chapters 1 and 2.

The second major reason is that the process of development itself has been a poorly defined and ill-executed venture in the Arab world, as in other parts of the Third World. The efforts of the Arab nation states to produce and distribute wealth, health and education have not been particularly successful, partly because of inexperience, and partly because of apathy, since the majority of the people have been excluded from the decision-making process. Thus, those who argue that the opportunity for education and work in the modern sector will of itself liberate women's capacities ignore the fact that the capacity of Arab society as a whole is largely unliberated. Having started out in second place, women have further to go to catch up, but fewer opportunities to do so.

The partial successes and the failures of Arab development since independence will be examined in chapters 3, 4 and 5. Here, it will be argued that it is not enough to blame 'the Arab–Islamic heritage' for the fact that women's involvement in the modern sector has been limited. Other factors must also be taken into account in examining how far women have been integrated in the development process: economic need, opportunities for women in the workforce, and their ability to carry out the task. Chapter 3 will give an overview of Arab women at work; chapters 4 and 5 will further clarify the point by focussing on Jordan and the Gulf states as case studies.

What power do Arab women have at their disposal to bring about appropriate change and to achieve equality? This is the focus of chapter 6, for, as was noted in a UN document presented at Nairobi, 'success will depend in large measure upon whether or not women can unite to help each other to change their poor material circumstances and secondary status and to obtain the time, energy and experience required to participate in political life' (UN, 1985d, p.21).

To sum up, this book seeks to explain why Arab women are not yet fully involved in the modern sector by showing how the question of the role of women in society is inextricably linked to the issue of the role of religion in society, and how both are tied up with the quest for national political and economic independence and development. The Arab world is caught up in the struggle to solve all of these major questions at one and the same time. If the Arabs are to survive as a cultural group and to develop independent political and economic unity, they must solve these questions quickly, although this means achieving within decades what other societies have taken centuries to accomplish. The task is so enormous that, at times, the goal seems to be out of reach.

# Chapter 1

# The great family law debate

The problem of women in the Arab world is that we don't know our legal rights – and that's very dangerous. If you don't know your rights you can't protect yourself. One reason why women don't know their rights is because they have not participated in the process of making law or enacting legislation.

*Badriya al-Awadhi, Kuwaiti lawyer*

Rarely a day went by, in the 1970s and 1980s, when an Arab newspaper or magazine appeared without an article on a 'first Arab woman' who had successfully entered a new field. Sample headlines ran like this: 'The first woman broadcaster in Qatar' (who joined the staff in the early days of Qatar radio in 1970, and who soon became head of section); 'The youngest deputy in the Tunisian parliament' (who was elected in the early 1980s); 'The first Kuwaiti woman publisher' (who began publishing political, general interest and sports magazines in 1970); 'The first Jordanian woman pilot' (who was reportedly the first woman in the world to pilot a Tristar); 'The first Sudanese woman marine biologist'; 'The first Egyptian woman film director'; 'The first Arab woman earth satellite station manager'.

The pride and respect with which these Arab women were welcomed into the professional world was not restricted to the press. Any amazement that greeted their success was more likely to be expressed by non-Arabs than by Arabs. As the Jordanian pilot, Taghreed Akashah, said, her Arab colleagues 'simply accepted me as one of them. In fact, I am much more likely to hear comments from the German or American pilots working for [the Jordanian airline] than from the Arab personnel' (TME, 1980, p.50).

The ease with which Arab women enter the professions, often climbing to the top of the ladder, is partly due to the respect that they carry with them from the private domain of the family to the public domain of work for wages. Of course, the professions are the most problem-free area for working women worldwide, as their colleagues are more likely to be well-educated and liberal in outlook. In addition, the number of women involved in the modern sector is still small in the Arab world, so that they are not yet much of a threat to those already in place. Nevertheless, the traditional respect that Arab women enjoy in society should not be under-estimated, and it has practical value in that it is respect not only for a woman's person but also for her ability to do the job.

Indeed, when it comes to Arab society, it is important not to interpret the lower profile women still have in the public sphere as meaning that they lack respect and power. This was noted by the sociologist Nadia Haggag Youssef, who defined 'women's status' as having two different components:

the *rights* given to women and the *respect* given to them. Confusion ensues because the two distinct factors are erroneously used interchangeably, when in reality they are often inversely correlated. Thus, women receive great respect in certain societies that give them few rights; they receive equality of rights in societies in which they compete with men but have relatively low respect. (1978, p.76)

Interestingly, the Moroccan sociologist Fatima Mernissi arrived at a somewhat similar conclusion, although by different means, in her book *Beyond the Veil*. Mernissi wrote,

At a deeper level than laws and official policy, the Muslim social order views the female as a potent aggressive individual whose power can, if not tamed and curbed, corrode the social order. It is very likely that in the long run, such a view will facilitate women's integration into the networks of decision-making and power. One of the main obstacles Western women have been dealing with is their society's view of women as passive inferior beings. (1981, p.108)

## A slow pace of change

While Arab women receive respect and encouragement when they are embarking on new careers, there is some resistance to this becoming a permanent feature of Arab society, partly because of the impact this would have on the family. Not only is the number of women involved in the modern sector small, but there is one piece of information that stands out in most of the writing on Arab women: the Arab region, often incorporated into the Middle East, or the Muslim world in the literature, appears to have the lowest women's labour force participation rates (economically active women over 15 as a percentage of all women over 15) of any region in the world.

For example, a report in 1980 estimated that

women's reported labor force participation rates in the 1970s are highest in Africa (45.8) and Asia (42.9) and lowest in the Middle East (11.4) with Latin America (26.8) falling midway between. All regions have experienced a rise in the rates of labor force participation since the 1960s with the largest proportionate increase being reported for the Middle East (53%). (ICRW, 1980, p.9)

Why were Arab women's labour force participation rates so low, at least in the 1970s? To answer this question, a good many writers on the region, including economists, have automatically turned to Islam and to religiously inspired cultural attitudes, the conservative nature of which, they feel, is responsible for holding women back. However, the approach of 'blaming Islam' for keeping women out of the modern sector ignores the fact that many attitudes to women are shared worldwide. As Beck and Keddie noted in their introduction to *Women in the Muslim World*: 'In the light of patterns that are found in many traditional societies around the world, although with numerous variations, one comes to question the view that attributes these patterns to Islam or its laws and customs' (1978, p.25). Moreover, 'blaming Islam' ignores the fact that cultural attitudes, including Islamically-inspired ones, change remarkably quickly when the need and opportunity arise, as will be shown in chapter 4 on Jordan. Indeed, religion is frequently drawn on to justify new attitudes which may be radically different from previous ones.

Beck and Keddie posed another question: 'The real question . . . is why Islamic society has been more conservative in its maintenance of old laws and traditions in this area than have other societies – although the others have not lacked conservatism' (p.28). In the Arab world, the reason for the slow pace, as was mentioned in the Introduction, is that so many different issues have to be resolved at one and the same time: the role of women in society – whether they should be out at work as equal partners or stay at home to rear the family; the role of religion in society; the struggle for an independent political and economic identity *vis-à-vis* the rest of the world; and the establishment of a sound mode of development. These issues have become inextricably tied together, and the attempt to solve them all at once is holding up the resolution of any one of them.

The Arab world is a society in transition, and it is during periods of transition that contradictions are at their most severe. Traditional definitions and methods of operating are no longer completely valid, but new ones have yet to take shape. Thus, on the one hand, women are respected and encouraged to embark on new careers; on the other, there is an unwillingness to accept that this will mean change in other spheres, particularly in the area of relations within the family. It is possible, in some states, for an Arab woman to be the chief executive of a company, and yet not have equal rights with her husband when it comes to guardianship of their children – an inequality enshrined in the law of the land.

It could fairly be said that, of all members of society, women suffer the most from the tensions of the transitional phase. The question of changing their roles lies at the base of the intricate pyramid of problems that the Arab world is seeking to solve. They are the key to maintaining the traditional family unit, and in this transitional phase the family is the only security against the nebulous future. There is most resistance in the Arab world to change in anything to do with the family, although it is unrealistic to believe that there can be change in the political and economic interactions of society without change in social relations.

## The Arab family: the key to society

What is so special about the Arab family? According to the ideal concept of the Arab family, the responsibility of the man for his wife, his children and his female relatives is accepted by all concerned. Similarly, the eldest son is responsible for his parents, and his brothers until they are old enough to stand on their own feet; brothers are responsible for their sisters should their marriages terminate in divorce or widowhood, and for other stranded female relatives throughout their lives.

Arab families are still fairly large. Members of the extended family do not necessarily share the same household, but close links continue to tie the strands of the extended family together. This involves the parents, their children and their children's spouses, as well as dozens of cousins, uncles and aunts. The family defines the status of individual members in the community, hence the importance of preserving family honour. It provides its members with warmth, companionship and moral support; equally importantly, it is the main social security centre, caring for the old, the infirm and those whose luck has run out.

The family is also the major job-hunting centre. Many, if not most, business concerns in the Arab world are family-run and it is taken for granted that bosses will appoint, or help to appoint, family members in gainful employment, just as civil servants will seek to advance the appointment of family members in their own or other departments. In rural areas, the family's subsistence depends on the work of all its members – husband, wife and children – either in the field or in food-processing and other agriculturally related activities. The same is true of small, family-run business concerns in urban areas.

Although the state has become one of the biggest employers in Arab countries, few Arabs have been involved in meaningful political institutions, or in decisions on the running of their countries. Thus there is little loyalty to the state, and the family continues to dominate individual loyalties, in turn holding up the establishment of effective political and social institutions. This has been shown to be the case in sociological studies. For example, Halim Barakat's data on university students in Lebanon indicates that they 'are least likely to be alienated from their families, while they are often alienated from religion, politics, and society' (Barakat, 1985, p.36).

## Women: the key to the family

Within the family, the father has the final say, which in theory gives him ultimate power. Nevertheless, the woman's role is the key to maintaining the family. Not only does she reproduce successive generations, ensuring family continuity, size and power, but she is also responsible for the new generations' informal education. It is the mother who transmits the cultural and religious traditions that reinforce solidarity and loyalty to the family. It is not surprising that there has been such strong resistance, from men and women alike, to change in women's roles.

Those who argue against any change in women's roles express themselves in religious terms (God willed it so), in appeals to 'reason' (women are naturally, biologically, unsuitable for any function other than mother-hood), and in appeals to nationalism (feminism is a form of neo-colonialism developed by the West to subvert the Third World). Underlying all the arguments is the very real fear that, if women allow their key role in the family to be overtaken by other roles, then the whole social system will fall apart. The proponents of these arguments find conclusive support for their stand in what they see as the breakdown of society in the West. They hold the erosion of family ties responsible for a range of social ills in the West, from the loneliness of the old to drug addiction among the young, from violence and crime to immorality.

It should be restated that resistance to change in women's roles does not break down along sexual lines. Within each Arab family or community, there are liberal men who are open to new ideas and methods, and conservative women who resist change, and vice versa. Some daughters will find support from their fathers for pursuing their education, careers or travels, in the face of unyielding mothers. Some sisters will find their strongest allies in their brothers when they need to lobby their parents for more freedom.

Over the last few decades, much energy and ink have been expended on debating the 'harm' that change in women's roles would do to the family. However, less time has been spent on assessing how much change has in fact already taken place. Nor have the protagonists paused to question how they can maintain what is good about the Arab family (the sense of security it offers, the warmth, the way it ensures that people have more time for one another and more of a share in material goods), while shedding the negative aspects (its domination over its members, its sacrifice of the individual for the general good, its stifling of initiative and, often, its tyranny regarding its female members and its youth).

The Arab world has begun to acquire the worst of both worlds: family links are loosening under the pressures of modern life, resulting in what Arabs view as the negative facets of Western society – the nuclear family and individualism; but few of the positive contributions of Western development in terms of democratic social, economic and political institutions have been transplanted along the way.

As the reality of the Arab family becomes distanced from the ideal, the accepted roles are changing, and men are no longer seen as solely responsible for women's financial up-keep. Women's traditional economic safety net is growing threadbare: widowed or divorced sisters can no longer rely on brothers as before; a husband is beginning to offer less economic security than a job outside the home. One would expect these changes to increase women's participation in the wage labour force, and this is indeed happening, as was noted in the ICRW report mentioned above. Whether the mode of development followed in the Arab world can provide opportunities for men and women seeking paid employment is another question.

### 'Equivalent' under the law

Although change is taking place in the content of social and economic relations, it has yet to take place in form. The rest of this discussion will focus on the resistance to change in family structures and laws, and on how the debate on the role of women is conducted within the broader debate on the role of religion in society. This will perhaps help to explain what lies behind the contradictory sets of attitudes whereby women are respected as equal partners at work but remain unequal within the family under the law.

Needless to say, many Arabs lead happy and contented lives. It is when situations of conflict arise that people resort to the courts, and that matters of law become important. Conflicts relating to marriage, divorce and custody are among the most difficult issues that face legislators in modern nation states. In the Arab world, personal status codes – or family laws – deal with these and other questions such as inheritance. The laws are drawn from the Sharia (Islamic law) in all the Arab countries; in those countries where no family laws have been passed, judges simply apply the Sharia.

The articles of personal status codes generally conflict with constitutions in the region. Constitutions, in the Arab countries that have them, guarantee equal rights for all citizens; under personal status codes, men and women have 'equivalent' rather than equal rights. The fact that this is one of the most sensitive subjects in the region is clear from the way Arab governments have tried to legislate or reform family laws. Such attempts are frequently abandoned in mid-stream.

Examples will be given, over the next few pages, of how different Arab countries have acted on the issue: how Tunisia and the People's Democratic Republic of Yemen managed to pass the most progressive codes; what problems were faced in Bahrain and Kuwait; and the arguments used in the heated public debates in Algeria and Egypt. As will become clear, the debate on the personal rights of women is conducted almost entirely within an Islamic framework, both by the conservatives who oppose change, and by the liberals who want to see the law reformed.

Conservatives and liberals, men and women alike, believe that Islam brought about a real revolution when it was revealed in the seventh century, and both argue that rights for women will be ensured if the precepts of Islam are followed correctly. The difference, of course, arises over how they define these rights. Opposing groups draw on different verses from the Quran (the word of God as revealed to mankind through the Prophet Muhammad), the main source of Islamic law, to prove their point; or they quote from the sayings of the Prophet Muhammad, the Hadith, another major source of Sharia; or they draw examples from the Sunna, the way of the Prophet. The other bases of the Sharia include *ijmaa* (consensus), *qiyas* (analogy) and *ijtihad* (independent reasoning), although *ijtihad* is not encouraged because it is feared that it will lead to deviations fom orthodox Islam.

Four main schools of Sunni (orthodox) Muslim law developed in the first centuries of Islam: the Maliki, after Malik Ibn Anas who died in Medina at the end of the eighth century; the Hanafi, after the Persian Abou Hanifa who settled in Iraq and died at the end of the eighth century; the Shafi'i, after Ash-Shafi'i who died in Egypt at the beginning of the ninth century; and the Hanbali, after Ibn Hanbal, who died in Baghdad in the middle of the ninth century. The main school of Shia law is the Jaafari. Some schools are more liberal than others on certain matters; under the Maliki school, for example, a woman can petition for divorce.

## The early days of Islam

In the debate on women's rights under Islamic law, both liberals and conservatives hasten to point out that the revelation of the Quran ensured the basic human right to life for women by putting an end to the Jahiliya. This was the 'time of ignorance', the days before the revelation of Islam when female babies could be buried at birth. Both also point out that the Quran gave women full rights to hold property in their own names, and to inherit and to bequeath wealth, adding for good measure that Muslim women enjoyed this right long before women in the West. There were already businesswomen around at the time of the Prophet. His first wife, Khadija, was a successful merchant, and the Prophet had worked for her before their marriage – as liberals never cease to point out in arguing women's right to work. The Quran began to be revealed to Muhammad during his marriage to Khadija and it was only after her death that he remarried.

As for women's rights in marriage, liberals and conservatives agree that marriage is a contract between two parties (see Appendix p. 36 for verses from the Quran on spouses' rights within marriage). According to the Quran, the man is to pay the bride a *mahr* (dowry), which is to be her property. Traditionally, half the dowry is held back, to be paid in case of divorce, which acts as a financial restraint on the husband's right to divorce. Husbands must financially support their wives; wives have no financial obligation to the family, but must obey husbands. Divorce is permitted if the marriage has become impossible and after attempts at arbitration by members of the two families have failed. Divorce is nevertheless, in the words of the Prophet, of all permissible things the most hateful in the eyes of God.

Polygamy, which was reportedly widespread in pre-Islamic Arabia, is limited by the Quran to four wives. Liberals stress the fact that polygamy is only allowed if certain conditions prevail like the loss of large numbers of men through war. The verses in the Quran that allow polygamy begin by referring to the problem of orphans. Moreover, polygamy is only permitted if equality between the wives can be ensured. If not, the Quran enjoins monogamy. In many of the verses on women and family relationships, the Quran urges that all dealings be conducted with kindness and fairness, as do many of the Prophet's sayings.

As for women's public and political rights, liberals point out that the Prophet accepted the *baya* (pledge of allegiance) from a group of women who had come, on their own, to join the ranks of the first Muslims. Liberals note that women even joined in battle in the early days of Islam. Liberals also point out that Aisha, beloved wife of Muhammad and daughter of his closest friend Abu Bakr al-Siddiq (the first caliph), played a prominent political role after Muhammad's death and was one of the major transmitters of his sayings.

It should be noted that there is disagreement among historians and anthropologists as to what social systems actually prevailed in pre-Islamic Arabia. Some social historians insist that a matriarchal system existed in various parts of Arabia at the time of the Prophet, and that in certain tribes women had more than one husband; the 'husbands' travelled with their tribes while the women and children remained with their tribe. These other systems, they believe, disappeared under the weight of the family system favoured by Islam.

## Restrictive interpretations

Although little is known about pre-Islamic times, the legislation on women became more restrictive in the centuries after Islam was revealed. This was pointed out by Stowasser in her study of the process of change in women's status in early Islamic society. Stowasser made a comparative study of Quranic interpretation (*tafsir*) and the science of Hadith criticism (exegesis) which developed over the centuries to put an end to the proliferation of sayings attributed to the Prophet (Stowasser, 1984).

Stowasser took as one example the fourth *sura*, 'Women', and the following verse (a difficult one for liberals), 'Men are the managers of the affairs of women for that God has preferred in bounty one of them over another, and for that they have expended of their property. Righteous women are therefore obedient, guarding the secret of God's guarding. And those you fear may be rebellious admonish; banish them to their couches, and beat them' (35, Arberry's translation).

Stowasser noted that one early interpretation (Tabari, d. 923) held simply that men had authority over women in the family setting and that they had an obligation to provide material support (p.26). However, she said, some 350 years later another interpretation (Baydawi, d. 1286), which was to hold thereafter, was that men were in charge of women as rulers were in charge of their subjects, and that women were unfit for public duty.

There is no doubt that by the nineteenth century there were several abuses of the rights of women in marriage and at divorce, some as a result of restrictive interpretations of the Quran and Hadith, and some which had no basis in the Quran. Some of these 'traditions' are carried on to this day in parts of the Arab world. For example, parents matchmake on behalf of their children, male and female, without seeking the contracting parties' consent. Further, children can be betrothed to each other at very young ages, even at birth. It is accepted, in many parts of the region, for the father to pocket the dowry, on the grounds that he is losing his daughter, and thus to attempt to 'sell' his daughter to the highest bidder. Nor are the stipulations on polygamy observed, although this represents only a small proportion of marriages in the region, ranging from 2 per cent in North Africa to 10 per cent in the Gulf.

In case of divorce, men do misuse their right to divorce, by simply stating 'I divorce thee' three times, effectively casting off, or repudiating, their wives and following none of the stipulations in the Quran, which provides for arbitration, and for a period of reconciliation. In some states, they are not obliged to divorce in court, and in some cases the divorce is not registered in court. While men have the right to divorce, women have to petition for divorce. In practice, women have little or no right to divorce as they have to prove that they have legitimate grounds for divorce. (See Algeria and Kuwait in Table 1, for a list of the traditional grounds on which a wife can request divorce.) They have to go before a judge in court to do so, a procedure both discouraged and considered shameful. This is one reason why families often prefer to marry their daughters to relatives, as they can

Table 1    *Personal status laws on divorce, custody, polygamy in selected Arab countries*

| | Tunisian personal status code, 1956, amended, incl. 1964, 1966, 1981 | Moroccan personal status code, 1957–8 | Democratic Yemen family law, 1974 |
|---|---|---|---|
| DIVORCE | *can take place only in court, by will of husband, at request of wife, by mutual consent; judge to decide compensation to either side; [1981] in case of harm to wife by divorce, wife to be maintained, with housing, unless remarries* | | *unilateral divorce prohibited; men and women to petition before courts on the same grounds* |
| requested by husband [*talaq*] | | absolute right if in full possession of faculties; maintenance according to husband's circumstances | |
| request by wife [*tatliq*] | | can petition judge on traditional grounds [see Kuwait, Algeria for such grounds] wife has *usma* [i.e. wife's right to divorce on her own behalf is written into marriage contract] by *khalei* [mutual consent and repayment of dowry; i.e. wife 'redeems herself']; wife to keep custody | |
| POLYGAMY | prohibited; bigamous man liable to prison, fine or both; bigamous woman also punishable | restricted; forbidden if unequal treatment feared; first wife can claim harm; if wife puts clause in marriage contract against polygamy, it is grounds for divorce; second wife to be informed of existence of first | restricted; only if written permission from courts, only if wife sterile or incurably ill |
| CUSTODY | in best interest of child | mother keeps boys until puberty, girls until marriage | with mother, even if she remarries, boys to age 10, girls to age 15 |

*Note:* This table is based on Badriya al-Awadhi's *Selected Questions*, 1982; on the Algerian famil[y] code, *Journal Officiel* 12 June 1984; and other sources; it is meant to give an indication of th[e] different approach of various countries, and not as a legal reference.

18

| Egypt personal status law, 1979, amending law of 1929[a] | Kuwaiti draft personal status law, 1982[b] | Algerian family code, 1984 |
|---|---|---|
| absolute right if in full possession of faculties; maintenance minimum two years; wife to keep home so long as children being reared [similar to Moroccan law] | absolute right to divorce if in full possession of faculties; maintenance 1 year | by husband's will, by mutal consent, at demand of wife; judge to try conciliation for maximum 3 months; if husband judged arbitrary, wife to be compensated and housed if raising children |
| | can petition judge on grounds of: non-maintenance; no physical union for over 4 months; harm by word or deed not bearable to one of her kind; absence or imprisonment | grounds of non-maintenance; infirmity; no physical union for over 4 months; imprisonment or absence; prejudice; immorality |
| | by *khalei* | by *khalei* [mutual consent], judge to decide if disagreement; wife to observe *idda* |
| husband must inform previous wife; this to be considered legitimate grounds for divorce even if not in marriage contract [under 1985 law, judge to rule if wife harmed by second marriage] | unrestricted; a man may not marry a fifth until he divorces one of four and her *idda* ends | restricted by limits of Sharia; if justified, if equal treatment possible, and after informing wife; can be grounds for divorce |
| mother keeps boys to 10, girls to 12; can be extended to 15 and until marriage | mother keeps boys until puberty, girls to marriage | mother keeps boys to age 10, girls to marriage; can be extended to 16 for boys |

[a] New law passed in 1985, with amendments of 1979 law.
[b] Passed in 1984.

arbitrate moral and material disputes within the family, and exercise some influence over those in dispute.

In case of divorce, a mother loses custody of her children when they are young (see Table 1 for the ages in different countries), and in many places is not entitled to be their legal guardian even if the father dies. Indeed, in some countries the woman can be considered to be a legal minor throughout her life, in need of her father's or husband's or male relative's permission to travel or work.

In the case of inheritance, a female inherits half the share of her brother, the argument being that men are obliged to spend of their property on women, whereas women have no such obligation. The shares of inheritance of parents, children and other relatives are set out in the Quran. The problem for Sunni parents arises if they have only daughters, who then traditionally share their inheritance with the closest male relative (uncles or cousins). However, under Shia Jaafari law, the children receive their full share, even if there are only daughters; if there are sons and daughters, the daughters receive half the share of the sons, as in Sunni law. It is not unknown, for instance in Lebanon, for a Sunni father to turn Shia on his deathbed so as to ensure his only daughter's full share.

## The secular approach: Turkey

Of course, the Arab world is not unique in restricting women's rights, and similar restrictions existed or still exist in other parts of the world. What is interesting, for the purposes of our discussion, is the inordinate amount of time and anguish that is still going into the process of changing and reforming family law. Before we turn to the Arab nation states of today, it is worth looking briefly at the approach adopted by Turkey, the only state in the Middle East to break completely with religious law and adopt a secular code.

When Mustafa Kemal Ataturk became the leader of the new state of Turkey, he was determined to give women equal rights under the law. Ataturk began by arguing that there was nothing in the religion that required women to be inferior to men, and appointed a committee in 1923 to review the family law. When it became clear that the committee's work would not achieve the results he wanted within the framework of Islamic law, Ataturk decided on a complete break. Turkey became a secular state and a civil code was issued in 1926 modelled on the Swiss civil code (see Ahmed, 1984, for a full account).

Men and women were equal under the new code, except that the man was still the legal head of the family, a stipulation found until recently in family laws around the world, and one of the main issues raised by feminists in

Latin America. The Swiss, for example, only amended this part of their law in 1985. It took time for the new law to become known or accepted by the population in Turkey, particularly by the vast numbers living in rural areas. For example, Turkish law only recognised civil marriage, and banned polygamy, but the Government found itself facing a serious problem as a result: many children were being born who were legally illegitimate. By the 1950s, the state had to legitimise some eight million children. The secular law is still not completely accepted by all sectors of the population, and there is a strong current of opinion that wishes to see the restoration of religious law.

Ataturk's approach is an example of what a strong national leader can achieve when he comes to power on a wave of revolutionary fervour and popular support. A similar approach was adopted by Tunisia's president Habib Bourguiba, who presided over the passage of a personal status code in 1956, shortly after Tunisia's independence from the French. However, Tunisia was careful to stay within the framework of Islamic law. The code is the most progressive in the Arab world; it provides for equality in all fields except inheritance, and except for the fact that the man remains the legal head of the family.

Table 1 shows how selected Arab countries treat the problems of divorce and polygamy in their family laws. It is interesting to note the differences between the laws, although all are based on the Sharia. Many countries have drawn on more than one of the four Sunni schools of law and in some cases on all four, irrespective of which one was common in their country; they thus took advantage of the fact that some schools are more liberal than others.

None of the Arab states broke with Sharia law in the case of the personal status codes, although some have completely secular civil, commercial and penal codes even though the Quran contains some detailed regulations in these areas as well. Why is it that Turkey, the seat of the Islamic caliphate for four centuries, managed to go secular? And why did none of the Arab countries do so, even though Tunisia managed to go quite far in equalising treatment of men and women under the law within the framework of the Sharia?

For one thing, the Islamic religion is intricately tied up with the history and culture of the Arabs, more so than is the case with the Ottoman Turks. The Quran was revealed in the Arabian peninsula and in Arabic. Islam is part of the Arab identity, both national and personal: Christian Arabs are often as attached to Islam, as part of their culture and identity, as are Muslim Arabs. For another, most Arab states had to try to preserve and defend their identity against foreign colonisers, unlike the Turks, who indeed dominated much of the Arab world in their heyday.

The main European colonisers were the French in the Maghreb countries, Lebanon and Syria, the Italians in Libya, and the British in Egypt, Palestine, Jordan and Iraq, with British influence holding sway in the Arab Gulf states. The colonisers sought to control material resources and trade routes; to achieve their aims they tried to dominate the occupied areas' social and legal systems.

The colonisers made small improvements in the subject people's situation, by building some schools, for example. They also expressed their distaste for what they saw as the low status of women in the region, and suggested that women should unveil and imitate European dress. As this concern was accompanied by the rape of the people's resources and in extreme cases by such measures as forbidding them to speak their own language in school, these suggestions were not only looked upon with suspicion but were strongly resisted. Indigenous people who adopted the ways of the coloniser were also suspect. Many Arabs held on even more firmly to tradition and to what they believed was the Islamic way of life.

## Nationalism vs reform: Tunisia's 'Islamic secularism'

Even Bourguiba, who is now looked upon as the liberator of Tunisian women, refused to hear of any changes in women's position during the struggle for independence. This was noted by Norma Salem in her study on the status of women in Tunisia. At a nationalist meeting in 1929, a woman had taken off her veil, but Bourguiba declared, 'Is it in our interests to hasten, without caring for any transitions, the disappearance of our ways, of our customs, bad or good, and of all those little nothings which as a whole – whatever one might say – constitute our personality? My answer, given the very special circumstances in which we live, is categorical: NO!' (Salem, 1984, p.149). While Tunisia was occupied, it was to maintain its personality as part of the struggle against the French.

Indeed, severe criticism was aimed at those seeking reform at this time. In 1930, a great storm erupted when the Tunisian religious scholar, Al-Tahir al-Haddad, published a book on the status of women, *Imara'tuna fil sharia wal mujtama* (our woman in law and society). The fact that Al-Haddad was passionate in his defence of Islam did not appease his critics. He had written:

I believe, without the shadow of a doubt, that Islam is innocent of the accusation of arresting reform but that, on the contrary, it is the . . . inexhaustible source of reform. The collapse of our (social) structure is but the result of illusions we have believed in, of pernicious and terrible customs we have tied ourselves to.

He added,

There is nothing which states or indicates that the stage achieved during the Prophet's lifetime was the hoped-for final (stage). (Salem, pp.143–4)

Al-Haddad said Islam considered the sexes equal because the rights and duties of men and women were balanced. However, no one else agreed with him, and he was stripped of his religious degrees, lost his job and died a broken man (p.148).

After independence, Bourguiba felt that Tunisia could tackle the question of women. According to Salem, the reasons Bourguiba gave for seeking women's equality were: so that Tunisia did not remain an abomination among the civilised nations of the world; the need for social justice; and the need for a rational effort at adjustment to Islam (p.156). There was criticism by the conservatives of the new personal status code, but this was nothing as ferocious as the attack on Al-Haddad.

In her work on Tunisian women, Souad Chater wrote that Bourguiba had succeeded, not only because of the euphoria following national independence, but also because the conservatives had been seriously weakened and discredited during the struggle.

The 'shaikhs' who officially represented religion and who could have, in the name of Islam, vetoed every change, were not in a very good position to do so. The nationalists among them were mostly active, because of their social position, in the ranks of the 'Vieux Destour'. The others were not engaged in political activity, and some had been very complaisant with the authorities under the Protectorate. (Chater, n.d., p.92)

She added that the highest religious authority at that time, the Mufti, who is responsible for religious decrees or *fatwas*, was happy that at least Islamic law had not been thrown out altogether as it had been in Turkey.

Naturally, Bourguiba used his popular support as leader of the revolution to lobby for the code. Religious leaders had been consulted to make sure that the code stayed within the general framework of the Sharia, and they too took part in the public campaign to ensure that the code was accepted and understood. In 1956 and 1957, all religious courts – Muslim and Jewish – were dissolved and matters of personal status became civil matters. August 13th, the day the code was passed, was declared 'Women's Day' and a national holiday in Tunisia.

The code's provisions on divorce and polygamy are given in Table 1. Among its other provisions are the following: marriage could only be performed with the consent of both spouses, and the dowry had to be fixed; women had the right to contract marriage on their own behalf and did not need a guardian; custody was decided in the interests of the child, and mother and father had equal claims. In a 1981 amendment, the mother was automatically given guardianship over her children if the father died, rather than this going to another male relative.

Tunisia is also in the forefront of other Arab states along with Iraq, Morocco and South Yemen, because women judges serve in the courts; many Arab states have women lawyers, but not necessarily judges. This is significant because traditionally, women were regarded as legal minors, and two women were needed as witnesses in place of one man. This stems from the Quranic verse 280 in *Sura* 2, 'The Cow', 'And call in to witness two witnesses, men; or if the two be not men, then one man and two women, such witnesses as you approve of, that if one of the two women errs the other will remind her.'

## An 'Islamic Marxist' approach: Democratic Yemen

As can be seen from the above, the Tunisian code goes a long way in providing for equal rights within the family context, although complete equality has not yet been reached. (However, as in Turkey, there is a strong Islamic current in Tunisia that would prefer a conservative religious interpretation of the law.) Another Arab country that has reformed its personal status laws in quite a revolutionary way is the People's Democratic Republic of Yemen, which also kept within the Islamic framework, although the revolution that led Yemen to independence in late 1967 was a Marxist one.

The Yemeni Family Law was passed in 1974 following extensive debates in what was a very conservative society. The provisions for divorce and polygamy are given in Table 1. As can be seen, the law restricts but does not ban polygamy. Men and women have equal rights when it comes to divorce. Other provisions include: both spouses' consent to the marriage; setting a limit to the dowry; sharing the cost of running the household between husband and wife; and favouring the mother for custody of the children even if she remarries, although in the end the court has to decide in the child's best interests.

A Yemeni public health official admitted that there was a rise in the number of divorces immediately after the law was passed, because it had become easier for women, but she insisted that the situation had soon stabilised. Officials from the Women's Union had acted as marriage counsellors to try to reconcile couples before a divorce (AN, 1984). A women's conference was held in April 1984, a decade after the family law had been passed, to see whether it needed any changes. The women concluded that there was nothing wrong with the law as it stood, but that there were still some problems in implementation. No date was set for another review.

## Leaving the law to the courts: Bahrain and Kuwait

Tunisia and Yemen have the most progressive state laws on the family, which are based on a liberal interpretation of Sharia law and which have to be applied by judges in the courtroom. What of countries where the Sharia continues to be applied without intervention by the state? By the mid-1980s, this was still the case in Bahrain, where in practice much depended on the nature, tolerant or otherwise, of the judges in Sharia courts. According to a remarkably frank interview with a Bahraini woman lawyer which appeared in the government-owned magazine *Al-Bahrain* on 2 May 1984, women submitting a request for divorce to the religious courts had a difficult time.

Traditionally, a man can initiate divorce, but a woman has to be divorced, either by her husband or by the judge, if she petitions for divorce. The woman lawyer, Haya Rashid al-Khalifa, said Bahraini religious scholars did agree that women could petition for divorce on certain grounds (see Table 1 for traditional grounds). Nevertheless, Al-Khalifa noted that, in most of the cases she had studied, the judge did not use his authority to divorce the woman without conditions. Instead, judges tended to divorce a woman by *khalei* (literally, casting off), so that she had to repay the husband what he had spent on her, sometimes including the dowry. Effectively, women bought their freedom.

This, Al-Khalifa declared, was not legal in Islam (see Appendix 1 for spouses' rights in the Quran). Nor, she added, was it legal to force the woman to give up her custody rights. With the system in force in Bahrain, she pointed out, it could take the woman a long time to get a divorce. If the husband did not show up in court when ordered to, the case could be continuously postponed. Al-Khalifa noted that the family laws of other Arab and Islamic countries had instituted safeguards for women, and urged that similar steps be taken in Bahrain.

In Kuwait, a state family law was finally promulgated in 1984. Years were spent drafting a personal status code, which was ready for debate in the National Assembly in 1982. While the Assembly debated the law, the Kuwaiti lawyer Badriya al-Awadhi published a comparative study of Arab and Islamic family laws, since she felt that it was important for those taking part in the debate to look at other laws before finalising the Kuwaiti one. The other laws were, in her view, more progressive than the Kuwaiti draft law, although all had remained within an Islamic framework.

For an illustration of the contrasts that exist in the Arab world, it is interesting to note that Al-Awadhi was actually the Dean of the College of Law and Islamic Sharia at Kuwait University for some years – in a country where women had not yet acquired the right to vote by mid-1986, or equal rights in matters of personal status. During the debate on giving the women the right to vote, Al-Awadhi used to embarrass her male students by asking them if they did not feel uncomfortable being taught by a woman who did not have the right to vote (AN, 1982).

In her study, Al-Awadhi urged that men's unconditional right to divorce be restricted. She suggested that the husband be made to pay more compensation than usual to the divorced wife, as was already the case in some other Arab states. This was necessary, she said, because the number of divorces in Kuwait had risen in the previous five years.

The preparatory committee which had drafted the law had originally planned to give women the right to insert whatever clauses they wished into their marriage contracts, but had later decided against this. Such a stipulation would have enabled women to insert a clause denying the husband the right to take another wife, and so have served to restrict the practice of polygamy. Al-Awadhi wondered why the committee had changed its mind. In any case, Al-Awadhi's efforts to draw the legislators' attention to other, more liberal, laws were in vain. When the National Assembly eventually passed the law in 1984, the amendments proposed by various women's groups were largely ignored.

## The debate on identity, religion and rights: Algeria

The most interesting recent debates on family law took place in Algeria and in Egypt. In Algeria, a personal status code was finally passed in 1984. Until then, there had been great gaps in legislation. There were some laws on marriage dating back to colonial times, but these were abrogated in 1975. According to the civil code of 1975, the judge was expected to act in accordance with the principles of Muslim rights, or according to custom, in the absence of any legal regulations.

Writers on the status of women in Algeria frequently remark on the irony that women were pushed back into the home once the struggle for independence was won in 1962, although the new regime was determinedly socialist and although women had played an active and prominent role in the revolution. Women immediately received full civil rights like the right to vote and to be elected, but personal rights remained a grey, uncharted area.

The issue of personal rights was not high on the agenda of the country's post-independence governments. The Algerians were materially very badly off at the time of independence, and their country had been shattered by the long years of struggle. They lacked an infrastructure, and had not been able to develop facilities such as education. There were only some 20,000 secondary school students out of a population of 12 million.

More importantly, a major aim of the revolution against the French occupation for both men and women had been to restore the Algerian way of life, which the occupier had sought to fragment. In order to preserve their cultural identity from the French onslaught on their language and traditions, the Algerians had clung even more closely to Islam and Islam-based traditions. The problem arose after independence; it was all very well to define an Algerian identity in reaction against the French, but what constituted an independent Algerian identity? According to statements by Algerian officials over the years, Algeria was an Arab–Islamic country, with an Arab–Islamic identity. Thus, any social changes had to remain faithful to the Arab–Islamic heritage.

Attempts to pass family codes were made in 1963 and 1966, and during the 1970s, but the issue was so sensitive that it was abandoned each time. Finally, in 1981, a working group was formed of the attorney general, the religious affairs minister and a number of religious and government figures, in order to formulate a draft law. The committee went about its work in the strictest secrecy, but word leaked out. Algerian women were particularly upset by reports that they would become perpetual legal minors under the law, and would need the permission of male guardians to work or travel. It was said that polygamy would be somewhat restricted, but women would not have equal rights to divorce.

The women rose up in protest. Respected militants from the days of the revolution – like Jamila Bouhired whose story of resistance and steadfastness under torture had become the stuff of legend throughout the Arab world – led a march in December 1981 to protest the secrecy surrounding the subject. According to *Le Monde* in its 9 January 1982 edition, about 100 women gathered in the Algiers town centre carrying banners reading 'No to silence, yes to democracy' and 'No to socialism without women's participation'. In the end, the police broke up the demonstration. There were reportedly three other demonstrations in 1982 and a few more in 1984. Although the numbers were small, it was significant that the demonstrations took place in a country where there was only one legal political party, and where dissenting opinion outside the party was not encouraged.

An Algerian feminist interviewed in the March 1985 edition of a Washington-based radical American feminist newspaper, *off our backs*, described the secrecy that had surrounded the subject:

We had friends who were ministers – they had only two sessions to discuss this project. They told us that a copy of it was given to them when they entered the room, and taken back when they went out of the room . . . We had to steal this proposal. Then we duplicated 25 copies on an old alcohol machine . . . Only one of these copies reached the target – it was veteran women, women who fought in the Liberation struggle and who are legally organised . . . They understood the situation, and they called a demonstration . . . The woman veterans also wrote to their Minister, the Minister of Veterans, saying that they hadn't fought for such a result. They also wrote to the Minister of Justice and to the President.

Even the single-party parliament was sharply divided over the 1981 draft law. One school of thought was that women had done enough to earn full equality during the revolution. The other school insisted that Algeria must remain faithful to its 'Arab–Islamic heritage'. Interestingly, the government newspaper *El Moudjahid* campaigned against the draft that would have restricted women's rights. In its 8 June 1983 edition, *Le Monde* quoted an *El Moudjahid* editorialist as saying, 'To want, in the name of Islam, to push an important part of the population out of the production process is to ignore the realities of today'.

Emotions were running so high that the president withdrew the draft bill. This, one Algerian official said, was the first time in the history of modern Algeria that a bill was withdrawn from parliament (AN, 1984). A commission was set up to redraft the bill, and a woman minister (of social affairs) was appointed to the cabinet for the first time, as was a woman vice-minister of education. Some radical feminists criticised this as a sop to women's feelings. An Algerian woman psychiatrist wrote that the woman minister should have turned down the post: if Algerian women accepted being treated like minors for life, she declared, this would be a betrayal of women past and future. The psychiatrist said that she worked as a single woman in Algerian towns and villages and that she received every respect; the government and the law, she declared, were well behind the reality on the ground.

After the formation of the National Assembly Commission to study the matter, the national debate initiated by the president took a different and somewhat healthier tone. The deputies who were on the commission, and who included the handful of women deputies in parliament, talked to lawyers, representatives of the women's union and others. The draft was amended accordingly. In the 22 April 1984 issue of *El Moudjahid*, the minister of justice was reported as telling the deputies that the law would fill a clear judicial void. It would, he said, preserve the 'authenticity and identity of our Arab–Islamic values', taking into account the correct Islamic traditions of the people and rejecting certain ways of thinking alien to Algerian ethics.

On 29 May 1984, the Family Code was finally adopted by the Assembly; it became law on 9 June 1984, 22 years after independence. At a press conference reported in the 19 June 1984 edition of *El Moudjahid*, the minister of justice declared that the Family Code should not be thought of as a code for women; it was a law for the family in its entirety; indeed, Article 2 declared that the family was the basic unit of society. The promulgators of the law, he said, had been guided not by so-called religious experts, but by the true principles of Islamic law in the Quran and the correct traditions of the Prophet.

The 1984 code defines marriage as a contract between a man and a woman, undertaken with their consent, and in the presence of the woman's legal guardian. The guardian cannot prevent marriage, which can be authorised by the judge if the guardian is opposed. The dowry has to be fixed and is the woman's property. The marriage has to be registered, and both parties can insert any stipulations they wish into the contract. A widow or divorcee has to wait out the legal period before remarrying (the *idda*, set at three months, to ensure that the woman is not carrying the former husband's child). A Muslim woman cannot marry a non-Muslim unless he converts to Islam, although a Muslim man can marry a non-Muslim woman. This is the case throughout the Arab world.

Under the code, mothers have first right to custody of their children, and become the children's legal guardian in case of the father's death or disappearance. This is an important move away from the concept that women are legal minors. The mother has custody of boys until they are 10 years old, and of girls until the age of marriage; this can be extended to 16 years for boys if the mother does not remarry. The interests of the children are to be taken into account when deciding custody. Any matter not covered by the code is to be resolved by recourse to the Sharia. Clearly, the Algerian family law is very much a compromise between tradition and modernity; it seeks to prevent abuses of rights within the family, but not that seemingly elusive concept of equality between men and women.

## The Egyptian family law saga

Until 1979, family matters in Egypt had been regulated by a series of laws amended in the 1920s. Like Turkey and Tunisia, Egypt produced a strong and popular leader, Gamal Abdel-Nasser, who was bent on making his country a socialist state after the 1952 revolution. However, Nasser did not really concern himself with the issue of personal status codes, although Egyptian women were granted civic and political rights a few years after the revolution.

Some writers have attributed this to Nasser's somewhat conservative outlook in his personal life; his wife and family, for instance, were kept out of the public eye. Others argued that Nasser believed change would come gradually in this sphere once people had wider access to education and more women worked outside the home. Certainly under Nasser the state made every effort to provide educational facilities for boys and girls, and all university graduates, male or female, were guaranteed a job in the civil service if they could not find one elsewhere.

Be that as it may, steps were taken to extend state jurisdiction over the religious courts soon after the revolution. The religious courts (Islamic and non-Muslim) were incorporated into the state's National Courts in 1957. The personal status matters of Egypt's Christians were covered by a section in the personal status laws entitled 'Personal Status Laws for Non-Muslims', which was stricter in matters of divorce. The procedure generally followed in Christian divorce cases was for the National Courts to record recommendations made by church councils (Hill, 1979).

There were several efforts in the 1970s, some more timid than others, to reform the personal status laws. According to Hill,

The first proposal was couched in terms of needing to 'reopen the door of *itjihad*' (independent reasoning) and of using 'creative thinking' to solve modern problems. The second proposal emphasised that the proposed amendments to the personal status law were completely in harmony with the Islamic Sharia. Nevertheless, the opposition to both was vigorous. The 1974 proposal even elicited a protest march from the Al-Azhar community of *ulama* (religious scholars) and students upon the People's Assembly and President Sadat promised in a public speech that no action on the proposal was presently contemplated. (p.89)

Another proposal in 1977 also came to nothing.

In 1979, as a result of some efforts by women's organisations and the interest taken in the subject by Jihan Sadat, the late president's wife, further amendments were made to the personal status laws of the 1920s. Law No. 44 of 1979 became known as 'Jihan's law', and this came to be used in a derogatory sense as the Sadats became increasingly unpopular in Egypt. Egyptian feminists, many of whom opposed Sadat's 'open-door' economic policy with the West and Egypt's peace treaty with Israel, found themselves in an ambivalent situation. They wanted nothing to do with the works of the Sadats, but, at the same time, the family law was of some benefit to women.

The 1979 Law restricted polygamy by obliging a man to declare the presence of another wife to both existing and future spouses. Further, it made the contraction of a second marriage grounds for divorce by the first wife. A more practical economic aspect was the article obliging men to provide housing for a divorced wife so long as she had custody of the children. The mother had custody up to the age of 10 for boys and 12 for girls, which could be increased by the judge to 15 for boys and marriage for girls. Given the severe housing crisis in overpopulated Cairo, the impact of the new stipulation on housing can be imagined.

As in all the cases where Arab governments had attempted to amend or promulgate family laws, a number of religious scholars and experts were involved in drafting Law No. 44 of 1979. In an interview with the magazine, *Akher Saa* on 6 March 1985, the former minister of *waqf* (Islamic trusts) noted that the draft of Law No. 44 had been presented to a committee composed of himself (then minister), the former and the present sheikhs of Al Azhar, and the minister of justice. This committee had reviewed the draft and deleted some articles which it felt contravened Islamic law. One draft article stipulated that divorce could only take place before the judge; the committee felt two witnesses of the husband's pronouncement was sufficient. Another draft article concerned women's work outside the home; the committee insisted that woman's first priority was work within the home, and she could only go out to work with the explicit or implicit permission of her husband.

Clearly, the 1979 Law was more restrictive than the draft had been. Nevertheless, no sooner was it passed than the sniping began. Some people attempted to have it repealed on the grounds that it contravened the Sharia, since Sadat had made the Sharia the main source of law in a constitution passed in the early 1980s. They failed to have the Law repealed on these grounds because it had been passed before the new constitution had come into effect.

Finally, in 1985, the very constitutionality of the Law was challenged. Sadat had used his presidential privilege to pass Law No. 44 by decree shortly before parliament reconvened, presumably to avoid the kind of debate that would arouse religious emotion. However, the privilege to pass laws by decree was only meant to be resorted to in case of emergency. The Law's opponents argued that the promulgation of a family law could scarcely be considered an emergency; on 4 May 1985, the higher constitutional court agreed. Law No. 44 was repealed, and the country was suddenly thrown back on the 1929 Law.

## Egyptian women argue their case

Egyptian feminists again found themselves in an ambivalent position. On the one hand, they applauded the fact that Egyptians were availing themselves of their rights as citizens and challenging the highest authority in the state. On the other, the improvement in their legal status had just been dealt a major blow. The press was full of heart-rending stories about women and children who suddenly faced eviction from their homes. Journalists at the law courts reported that men were busy engaging lawyers to file suits against their ex-wives to regain their homes.

So, Egyptian women went into action. At one meeting on 9 May, women activists decided to form a delegation to go to parliament. The meeting was attended by women from the Wafd, the right-of-centre opposition party represented in parliament; from the Tagammu, the coalition of leftists, Nasserists and 'enlightened Islamists' who won no representation in parliament during the 1984 elections; from the women's committee in the Arab Lawyers' Union; from the Arab Women's Solidarity Association, a group that had recently won legal status; from the Family of the Future Association in Cairo; and concerned individuals.

The meeting issued a statement, reproduced in the 15 May 1985 edition of *Al-Ahali*, the Tagammu party newspaper. It affirmed the women's belief in the constitution and in the democratic process, and insisted that other unconstitutional laws should be thrown out as well. The statement said, 'Although Law No. 44 of 1979 does not fully achieve the interests of Egyptian society, the stability of the family, or the hopes of Egyptian women, its cancellation at this time will cause grievous damage to the Egyptian family unit and the stability of relations between its members. It is not possible to return to the laws of 1920 and 1929 which were in force half a century ago in social, political and economic conditions radically different from those of today.' It called for a family law that would meet the needs of the times, without conflicting with the Sharia, and urged an open debate on the subject.

In an editorial in the same edition, *Al-Ahali* condemned the

attacks by reactionary circles, and those whom they call men of religion – although there are no priests in Islam. They want to prevent woman from working and want her to return to the harem, or restrict the type of work she is allowed to undertake or cut back her wages. The strange thing is that many of these 'men of religion' were loudly in favour of women's rights and the amendments of the 1979 personal status code, but they quickly changed when the circumstances and regime changed.

There was some criticism of the role of the women deputies in parliament, who, many writers said, had remained strangely silent. Under the electoral law in force at the time, there had to be a minimum of 30 women in parliament, in addition to others who might be elected. Some of the women deputies defended themselves by saying that they were working behind the scenes, and had left the talking to the men so that they would not be accused of defending the law simply because it was a woman's law.

Meanwhile, the debate about women's rights in Islam heated up. The respected columnist Ahmad Bahaeddin wrote in the 8 May edition of *Al Ahram*,

The articles of the law should be taken up by a deputy and presented to parliament anew, and woman, who has the right to vote and be elected, and to serve as minister, must give her opinion on such a law.

He added on 12 May,

Those who interpret the rulings of Islamic Sharia are men, and those who pass laws of all description are men. The world has been a man's world for thousands of years, and even if the message of heaven comes to bring women justice, the world of men listens a little, then goes back to its previous ways.

Not all writers were so liberal. Ahmad Bahgat said, in the 6 May edition of *Al Ahram*, that he had had objections to the law from the start: 'The amendments did not bring justice; indeed, they brought unintended injustice. The amendments were contrary to Islamic Sharia in more than one area.' He added on 7 May, 'What Almighty God has allowed should not be described as harmful', referring to the article whereby polygamy was judged to be harmful and grounds for divorce.

Another columnist declared in the 18 May edition of *Al Gumhouriya* that there was a

difference between women's freedom and women's liberation. Islam gives women many rights, and more freedom and respect. But it does not recognise the wave of liberation which some ladies are calling for. Islam protects the Muslim woman who is decent and who respects her home, her husband and children. Islam does not give rights to the woman who rebels and who is *nashez* [who leaves her husband's house and refuses to return]. Islam protects the veiled woman, but it does not look at the woman in a bikini.

Some writers were critical of what they saw as women's half-hearted efforts to remedy their position. In the 17 May edition of *Al Mussawar*, Hussain Ahmad Amin, a columnist noted for his liberal Islamist views declared,

As for our women, in spite of my sympathies for their plight, I say frankly I am not sorry to see them lose rights that were not the fruits of real efforts on their part. How easy it is to lose rights that come without struggle. The conditions of women all over the world were similar at one time, no better than those of slaves. The European or American woman only got her rights after a bitter fight and as the fruit of centuries of development and struggle. As for our society . . . these rights came because of two or three books written by men earlier this century, because of the struggle of some wives of prominent men, and because our governments want the West to look upon them as enlightened. They are always rights that are given, not rights that are taken.

Addressing himself to the dozens of women who had urged him to write in favour of restoring the law, he declared,

Crying and complaining never won rights, nor does wailing and breast-beating ever erase injustice. Organise yourselves; register your objections; raise your voices so that people may know you have voices. Write to your deputies in parliament; convince one of them to present the law anew. Above all, let the educated among yourselves, and this should be easy, strive to prove that the rulings of this law are not in conflict with the Sharia as some claim. Let them try, and this is harder, to put an

33

end to this miserable holier-than-thou bargaining and trading with religion that has become such a heavy nightmare.

In fact, there were divisions in the women's ranks, and personality and political clashes surfaced at meetings. One columnist wrote in the 16 May edition of *Al Gumhouriya* that the cancellation of the law 'revealed the lack of unity in women's ranks and the absence of an organisation to speak in women's name'. Referring to a women's meeting that had taken place, she said sarcastically that nothing had come of it but the decision to hold another meeting. 'If the women of Egypt cannot unite over this question which affects the life and future of each and every one of them, they will never unite', she declared.

As the days passed, Egyptian women began to work together a little more effectively than before, according to several women who were involved in the campaign to restore the law. As Aziza Hussain, a long-time campaigner for women's rights described it,

We decided we had to get this law back because the decision was a setback and other setbacks would follow if we did not act, although most of us did not think the law was good enough. We went to the head of the constitutional court, and to everyone involved including the minister of social affairs. We dug out copies of the 1979 law with the accompanying explanations from the Sharia and passed them round so everyone could understand it.

The most important thing, she felt, was that the issue had been brought into the arena of public debate.

Before we acted you heard only the conservative reaction. We said: the public has to listen and to get into the debate, and all the mass media picked it up and began giving wonderful arguments in support of the law. (AN, July 1985)

Malak Zaalouk, a social scientist who had also been active in the campaign, said,

We learned to work together. We worked round the clock to educate people. At one meeting we drafted a law and were careful not to be too extremist. Some of the men and some religious scholars said we were being too careful; they said polygamy should be abolished completely, without beating about the bush. We formed a committee to defend the Egyptian woman and family, and we have decided to continue its work. We will not be restricted to this issue but will take up political rights and consciousness-raising. The people on the committee are not narrow feminists but can make the link between the political, economic and social spheres. (AN, 1985)

How much the women would have achieved, and how much further they would have been prepared to go, had the Government not been on their side is another matter. The Hosni Mobarak regime, which replaced Sadat's in

1981, clearly wanted to see the law restored. The woman Minister of Social Affairs, Amal Othman, was most active in this respect. An official committee was formed within days of the constitutional court's decision to conduct a quick study on the rights of women in Islam. Some days later, the parliament speaker convened a meeting of women deputies to discuss preparing a new personal status draft law.

Just weeks after Law No. 44 had been scrapped, a new personal status code was passed by parliament for the first time in Egyptian history: the 1929 and 1979 amendments had been passed by royal and presidential decrees. The new law was passed just in time for the UN End-of-Decade conference in Nairobi in July 1985. This, cynics said, was deliberate so that the Egyptian Government would look 'modern' at the meeting. The 1985 Law kept the basic amendments of the 1979 Law, with some changes. For instance, it made the judge responsible for deciding whether a wife had been harmed by a second marriage; in Law No. 44 this had automatically been grounds for divorce. On the other hand, the new law provided for penalties to enforce its provisions, which the 1979 Law had not done.

## A small step for womankind . . .

As can be seen from all of the above, the issue of family law and of women's personal rights is debated almost entirely within an Islamic framework by both conservatives and liberals. What should be noted is that, in the case of Algeria and Egypt, it proved difficult for the Government to ignore both the need for reform and the number of people seeking reform, even if this displeased the conservatives.

Significantly, in many of the debates we have examined above, women were fairly vociferous, and female lawyers were able to argue the issue of women's rights on solid grounds. As Al-Awadhi declared, women must know their legal rights as a first step towards achieving them. Moreover, people were willing to go public with their grievances, and to organise demonstrations, petitions and media campaigns. True, this was done on a limited scale, but considering that most serious political opposition has been crushed in the Arab world, the extent of the response was dramatic.

Through the debate, citizens were learning to use political tools other than outright rebellion or assassination to bring about change. The debate on women's roles should be followed with interest by those seeking indicators of the nature of political development in the Arab world; it is certainly one of the major indicators of such development, as will be seen in chapter 2.

# Selections from Arberry's translation of the meaning of the Quran on issues relating to the family

### Sura II – The Cow

Verse 225   For those who forswear their women a wait of four months; if they revert, God is All-forgiving, All-compassionate; but if they resolve on divorce, surely God is All-hearing, All-knowing.

Divorced women shall wait by themselves for three periods; and it is not lawful for them to hide what God has created in their wombs; if they believe in God and the Last Day. In such time their mates have better right to restore them, if they desire to set things right. Women have such honourable rights as obligations, but their men have a degree above them; God is All-mighty, All-wise.

Divorce is twice, then honourable retention or setting free kindly. It is not lawful for you to take of what you have given them unless the couple fear they may not maintain God's bounds; if you fear they may not maintain God's bounds, it is no fault in them for her to redeem herself.

Verse 230   When you divorce women, and they have reached their term, then retain them honourably or set them free honourably; do not retain them by force, to transgress; whoever does that has wronged himself.

Mothers shall suckle their children two years completely, for such as desire to fulfil the suckling. It is for the father to provide them and clothe them honourably. No soul is charged save to its capacity; a mother shall not be pressed for her child, neither a father for his child.

Verse 240   And those of you who die, leaving wives, let them make testament for their wives, provision for a year without expulsion; but if they go forth, there is no fault in you what they may do with themselves honourably; God is All-mighty, All-wise. There shall be for divorced women provision honourable – an obligation on the godfearing.

### Sura IV – Women

Mankind, fear your Lord, who created you of a single soul, and from it created its mate, and from the pair of them scattered abroad many men and women; and fear God by whom you demand one of another, and the wombs; surely God ever watches over you.

Give the orphans their property, and do not exchange the corrupt for the good; and devour not their property with your property; surely that is a great crime. If you fear that you will not act justly towards the orphans, marry such women as seem good to you, two, three, four; but if you fear you will not be equitable, then only one.

And give the women their dowries as a gift spontaneous; but if they are pleased to offer you any of it, consume it with wholesome appetite.

Verse 5    To the men a share of what parents and kinsmen leave, and to the women a share of what parents and kinsmen leave, whether it be little or much, a share apportioned.

Verse 10    God charges you concerning your children: to the male the like of the portion of two females.

Verse 20    And if you desire to exchange a wife in place of another, and you have given to one a hundredweight, take of it nothing. What, will you take it by way of calumny and manifest sin?

Verse 35    Do not covet that whereby God in bounty has preferred one of you above another. To the men a share from what they have earned, and to the women a share from what they have earned. And ask God of His bounty; God knows everything.

And if you fear a breach between the two, bring forth an arbiter from his people and from her people an arbiter, if they desire to set things right; God will compose their differences; surely God is All-knowing, All-aware.

Verse 125    You will not be able to be equitable between your wives, be you ever so eager.

# Chapter 2

# Cross-currents conservative and liberal

If we go back to the early days of Islam, we will find it was a real revolution. Why should I go against a real revolution?

*Arab woman student wearing Islamic dress*

The public debate on women's roles began in the nineteenth century, alongside the slow spread of formal schooling for boys and girls. It was conducted within the larger debate on reforming society as a whole in order to lift the Islamic world out of the centuries of stagnation that had afflicted it under Ottoman rule. With the growth of Turkish and Arab nationalism, the reformist debate gradually became more boundary-conscious.

The major issue for the reformists was how to reconcile the precepts of religion to the needs of the modern age. The great liberal Islamic reformists of the nineteenth century, such as Rifaa al-Tahtawi, Jamaleddin al-Afghani and Muhammad Abduh, believed that Islamic traditions had been corrupted over the centuries. A proper understanding of Islam's message would reconcile the demands of the modern age with the principles of faith. (For the best account of Arab thought in the nineteenth and early twentieth centuries see Hourani, 1983.) The need to resolve this question and to set about strengthening Arab society became more pressing as the nineteenth century wore on and the Arab world found itself an easy prey for Europe's growing appetite for new colonies.

It was clear to Muslim liberal thinkers early on that the status of women was the key to the question of reforming society, just as it was clear to the conservatives that women were the key to maintaining social customs unchanged. Women were responsible for the family, the basic unit of society, and for transmitting culture from generation to generation; if their position was not improved, society would suffer and ignorance would be perpetuated.

Tahtawi was one of the first nineteenth-century reformists to write about the need for women's education; he was also in favour of work for women since, he said, idleness was a lamentable state. There were those who believed that women's minds were incomplete or that they might start writing love letters if they learned how to read and write; these people should be ignored, Tahtawi believed.

These arguments were followed up by Muhammad Abduh, who became Mufti of Egypt, the highest religious authority. In 1899, one of Abduh's disciples, Qassim Amin, brought out a book outlining these and other ideas, and this has generally been taken as the date when the call for women's emancipation in the Arab world was formally 'launched'. Qassim Amin's *The Liberation of Women* caused an uproar in Egyptian circles, although he had phrased his arguments cautiously and drawn on Islamic texts to prove his point. He published another book a year later, *The New Woman*, in order to answer his critics.

Amin declared, as so many were to do later, that Islamic law had been the first to provide for equality between men and women, but that it had been corrupted. Women should be educated, if not as highly as men, then enough to enable them to run proper households, bring up the children, and work, since they would always be at the mercy of men unless they could support themselves. Women could not play their part in society if they were veiled and secluded. (Amin was really talking about the upper classes; as he and other writers noted, women in other sectors of society and in the countryside were not veiled, and shared in productive output.) He said there was nothing specific in the Quran telling women to cover their faces, while seclusion was mentioned only with regard to the Prophet's wives. As for polygamy, this had only been permitted in very special circumstances. Divorce should be a matter for the courts, and should be regulated according to Islamic procedure.

## 'Cultural loyalty' and the limits of debate

The early reformists debated the role of women within the Islamic framework – and there the debate has largely remained for the past century. The reason why this has been the case is bound up with Arab political and economic development, and the search for identity. A hint of the answer can be found by looking more closely at the development of Qassim Amin's views, which were radically different in 1894 from what they were to become in 1899. In 1894, Amin wrote a book in French called *The Egyptians*. In an analysis of Amin's writings, the Egyptian writer Muhammad Amara commented that Amin's later critics could have used his own remarks in *The Egyptians* against him. These had been amazingly conservative for a man who was later to be credited with launching women's liberation. Amara wondered why no one at the time, or even in recent times, seemed aware of the views Amin had expressed in *The Egyptians* or of how conservative these had been (Amara, 1976).

Amin's *The Egyptians* had been written in response to a Frenchman's attack on the Egyptian way of life. Clearly incensed that a foreign visitor should criticise Egyptian manners and mores, Amin responded with an attack on what he saw as the excesses and corruption of French society. Amin also defended Arab and Islamic traditions. Seclusion did not imply inequality between men and women: everything forbidden to men was forbidden to women; they were exactly alike in this respect. As for divorce, this could not possibly be a matter for the courts; it was a personal issue between husband and wife. Polygamy was only meant to be practised in times of need; in any case it was not harmful to family life. Nor, as some claimed, did the children of different wives grow to hate each other, since people soon adapted themselves to their situation (Amara, pp.45–71).

Clearly Amin's thinking had changed between the time he wrote *The Egyptians* ánd 1899. Amara believed that this change of heart could not be explained away as a natural development in Amin's thinking. Amara argued that Amin was not just influenced by Muhammad Abduh's liberal outlook, but that Abduh had himself written parts of *The Liberation of Women*. Be that as it may, it is very likely that, when Amin wrote *The Egyptians*, he was suffering from an attack of 'cultural loyalty'. He may well have expressed himself more strongly in defending Arab traditions against foreign criticism than he really felt, although he considered it possible to criticise these same traditions among his own countrymen.

'Cultural loyalty' has played a major part in setting the limits of the debate on the roles of women in the Arab world, as the academic Leila Ahmed has pointed out. She believes that cultural loyalty explains

the persistence with which reformers and feminists repeatedly try to affirm (with remarkable tenacity and often too with ingenuity) that the reforms they seek involve no disloyalty to Islam, that they in fact are in conformity with it, and if not in conformity with the letter and actual text of the culture's central formulation, then in conformity with what nevertheless is still there somehow, in the spirit not quite caught by the words. (1984, p.122)

Cultural loyalty, Ahmed insists, accounts for Islam's hold over the members of its civilisation.

Naturally, members of all civilisations will feel some loyalty to their cultures. However, these feelings are particularly strong in the Islamic world, Ahmed believes, because

the Islamic civilisation is not only a civilisation unambiguously on the defensive, emphasizing and re-affirming old values, but also a civilisation that finds itself re-affirming them the more intransigently and dogmatically and clinging to them perhaps the more obstinately because it is re-affirming them against

an old enemy. She adds,

it is only when one considers that one's sexual identity alone (and some would not accept this) is more inextricably oneself than one's cultural identity, that one can perhaps appreciate how excruciating is the plight of the Middle Eastern feminist caught between those two opposing loyalties, forced almost to choose between betrayal and betrayal. (p.122)

## Cultural colonialism

The 'old enemy' of Islam, of course, is the West, which until the twentieth century meant Europe to the Arabs and Muslims; America was added to the list later in the twentieth century. Neither Europe nor the Islamic world could forget their major confrontations over the centuries, when each had threatened to overrun the other. During the nineteenth century, there was one of those brief pauses in world conflicts that allowed for the exchange of ideas, and much of the renaissance in Arab thought and culture at this time took place because the Arabs travelled to Europe, particularly France, and came into contact with the concepts of freedom, equality and progress based on science and reason.

In the Arab world, some of the first formal schools were established by Christian missionaries, European and American. While religion was often used by European powers as a ploy to stake out spheres of political influence, some of the missionaries were sincere in their belief that knowledge should be shared among mankind. Thus during part of the nineteenth century, there was admiration for Western thought and progress in the main Arab centres of culture at that time, Cairo and Beirut, and a feeling that the Arab world could learn from Europe, much as Europe had learned from the Arabs during the Middle Ages.

The admiration for values and concepts emanating from the West began to fade as Europe embarked on the outright colonisation of the Arab world. The colonisers were often contemptuous of Islamic traditions. Although they were determined to exploit the colonised country's people and resources, they sometimes expressed their concern about the well-being of the colonised, particularly about the status of women. They had much to say about seclusion, veiling and circumcision where this was practised. This made the Arabs defensive about traditions they might have changed more rapidly on their own. The Arab feeling that knowledge could be shared on a basis of mutual respect was gradually replaced by the feeling that the Arabs had to reform their society in order to survive the European onslaught. They had to take what was good from Europe, that is, what had enabled Europe to become superior and more powerful than the Arabs, and to adapt this to Arab and Islamic values.

As the twentieth century wore on, the Arabs became increasingly disillusioned with the West. Certain acts stood out in bold relief from the unappealing record of colonialism: the double-dealing of the British in promising Palestine to the Zionists in 1917, although it was not theirs to promise, while at the same time promising the Arabs independence; and the brutality of the French in Algeria. The Americans, seen as the 'good guys' during the early part of the twentieth century, soon lost that image. When the days of outright colonialism drew to a close, the Americans assumed the mantle of leader of the 'Free World'. The Arabs, and the rest of the Third World, rapidly found out that this meant keeping repressive regimes in place so long as these served Western economic interests.

Moreover, there was America's unquestioning commitment to the survival of the Israel Britain had helped to create. As the Arabs saw it, Israel was not just the brainchild of a group of Zionists who had made their dream come true by occupying Palestine and by dispossessing the Palestinians. The Jewish state had been deliberately implanted by Europe and maintained by America in order to divide the Arab Maghreb physically from the Mashreq, keep the Arab world in constant turmoil and achieve what the Crusades had failed to achieve. By the second half of the twentieth century, the Western way of life had been almost completely devalued in the Arab world, and each succeeding conflict between the Arabs and Israelis drove another nail into the coffin. How could those Westerners, the Arab man in the street wanted to know, who were so duplicitous and who had brought so much destruction, be the source of any good at all? Many came to believe that if the Arabs were to regain their strength and to recover their territory and dignity, they had to seek their sources of strength in their own religion and cultural values, and nowhere else.

The extent to which the Arab world remains defensive about its values and traditions is the clearest indication of the extent to which it still feels threatened by the West. Given the death and destruction visited on the region to this day, the strength of that feeling is not surprising. The defensiveness also reflects an awareness that, although national independence has been achieved in form, the Arab world remains colonised in reality. Given the region's economic dependency on the West, this is not surprising either. Thus, while there is currently a good deal of lively debate and criticism in the Arab world, those who carry this debate into a Western arena (as does this book) lay themselves open to accusations of cultural betrayal. By the same token, Westerners, however well-meaning, who express criticism of certain Arab traditions, will face a vehement reaction, even if they use arguments used by the Arabs themselves against those traditions.

## Cultural loyalty and the status of women

Although, or perhaps because, the West is seen as the 'enemy', it is particularly important to present an unblemished Arab image for its consumption. Two examples will serve to illustrate the sensitivity in the Arab world to the opinion of the West. Both examples have to do with the position of women in the Arab world, which has traditionally been the area where Arabs feel most defensive. As has been pointed out, this is partly because any change in the role of women threatens the structure of society, and partly because the status of women is so often the focus of Western interest.

The first example comes from my own experience, and the second from the experience of the American black activist Angela Davis during a visit to Egypt. In the first case, the debate in the Arab world about a variety of issues – democracy, development, women – was carried to a Western audience by the 10-part English-language television series, 'The Arabs'. This was produced by a British company and was screened on British television in the autumn of 1983. The series producers and directors had wanted to break with the pattern of Europeans commenting on and perhaps misrepresenting the Arabs, and thus invited Arabs to comment on their own culture. Each programme in the series had an Arab scriptwriter/ presenter, and there were several Arabs involved in off-screen research. Criticism could be made about some aspects of the series' structure and content, but it could certainly not be accused of being anti-Arab.

The reaction to the series among the Arab community in Britain was interesting. Arab residents who had lived in the West for many years found much to enjoy, particularly as they compared the picture that emerged to that in other programmes on the Arab world, which they felt were biased. On the other hand, some of those who had not lived abroad very long were appalled. Why should the Arabs wash their dirty linen in public? they asked. Why not show the West the bright picture of Arab achievements instead of discussing the problems? The most sensitive programme was, naturally, the one on the position of women for which I was the scriptwriter/presenter.

Since a great deal had already been done on the veil, female circumcision, crimes of honour and other subjects that Arab culture shared with non-Arab but that were made to seem peculiarly Arab and Islamic (or so it seemed to my, perhaps culturally loyal, eyes), the film team decided to focus instead on family ties in the Arab world. Our aim was to show the warmth and strength of the Arab family through the story of the Jordanian woman recounted in chapter 4, while illustrating some of the difficulties in the search for more personal freedom, as in the story of the Tunisian girl recounted in chapter 3.

43

However, some people did not find this acceptable. Why, for example, had we chosen a family with ten children to film, when two children seemed much more 'normal'? Why had the family been shown eating a chicken dish with their fingers (the only way to eat this particular dish), which would just reemphasise the Western view of Arabs as barbarians? Why had some aspects of the Islamic revival been shown, such as women wearing the Islamic headdress, which made the Arabs look odd? The most negative aspect of the film for this group was the portrayal of some of the difficulties of family life – the rising incidence of divorce and the growing generation gap – although the major focus of the film had been the warmth and strength of family ties. The editor of the Arabic-language newspaper *Asharq al-Awsat* devoted a column to an attack on the film and on me as its presenter. In my defence, he said that he was sure I had not really understood the script I had been given to read, and had been tricked into saying what I had said.

In the second example, from the experience of Angela Davis in Egypt, Western ideas were carried into the debate in the Arab world. Davis had agreed to write a piece in the book *Women: a World Report*, a project undertaken by a group of feminists to see where women stood at the end of the UN Decade (Davis, 1985). The project organisers invited prominent feminists to investigate the position of women in a country other than their own. Thus, for example, Egyptian feminist Nawal Saadawi was assigned the topic of women and politics in the United Kingdom, while Davis was given the very tricky subject of women and sex in Egypt. There was another study on women and sex in the book, by a feminist sent to Australia, and another example of women and politics from Cuba. Angela Davis could not be accused of being a 'racist' Westerner; not only was she black, but she was much admired by Arab radicals. Moreover, she was aware of the sensitivity created when an outsider examined another people's culture.

Indeed, she had wondered about going ahead with the project when she realised she had been assigned the topic of sex, since

I was very much aware of the passionate debate still raging within international women's circles around the efforts of some Western feminists to lead a crusade against female circumcision in African and Arab countries. Being an African–American woman myself, I was especially sensitive to the underlying racism characterising the often myopic emphasis on such issues as female circumcision – as if women in the twenty or so countries where this outmoded and dangerous practice occurs would magically ascend to a state of equality once they had managed to throw off the fetters of genital mutilation . . . In lecturing on various university campuses throughout the United States, I have encountered not a few women who know nothing at all about women in Egypt or in the Sudan except the fact that they suffer the effects of genital mutilation. (pp.325–6)

None of this saved Davis from a heated reaction at the start of her visit to

Egypt, before she could explain the approach she wanted to take. 'Angela Davis', one Egyptian woman declared, 'in the Third World your name, your personality is known because of your struggle. [Yet] You can be used by your society, a wealthy society, which is trying to exploit our country.' A respected Egyptian writer and activist, Latifa Zayyat, told her, 'I have come to see you this evening because you are Angela Davis. If you were simply an American research worker, I wouldn't have come to see you . . . I would boycott any American who is doing research on Arab women because I know that we are being tested, we are being listed in catalogues, we are being defined in terms of sexuality for reasons which are not in our own interests.' A third woman said, 'You would be doing a great service . . . if you tell people that women in the Third World refuse to be treated as sexual objects' (pp.329–30). Later, several women argued that sexuality could not be ignored by those concerned with the emancipation of women, and the discussion during the rest of Davis's visit settled down to a calmer, more productive, debate, which discussed the issue without isolating it from other feminist or political issues.

## Feminism vs nationalism

From the above discussion, it should be clear that, in the Third World, cultural imperialism is seen as the other side of the coin of political and economic imperialism. Thus, not only is the issue of women's rights a very sensitive one, but proposals to change the status of women are seen as particularly suspicious if they are expressed in Western terms or if they emanate from the West, to the extent that Western family planners are seen by some Third Worlders as part of a plot to control their populations and to prevent them from threatening the West. Such proposals might be more acceptable if they are framed in Islamic terms – and this is what most Arab liberals, and even Marxists, have done since the early days of the debate.

Proponents and opponents of equality for women can be divided into two camps, the liberal nationalists, and the conservative nationalists, a division as valid in the 1980s as it was in the 1890s. The liberal nationalists followed Amin's arguments, and believed that to liberate itself the Arab world had to take from Europe the things that made it strong – democracy, freedom, and equality of rights under the law, especially for women. The liberal nationalists used Western concepts intermingled with quotations from Islamic texts, and added that these concepts could be achieved within an Islamic framework.

Conservative nationalists, on the other hand, believed that Arab society could only face the foreign invaders by conserving its traditions; indeed, many conservative nationalists believed that the concept of 'women's liberation' had deliberately been introduced by foreign colonisers with the aim of weakening Arab society by attacking its core, the family. (See Gran, 1977; Philipp, 1978 for the expression of these trends in Egyptian political parties in the early twentieth century.) The need to conserve tradition during the struggle for liberation was certainly a major element in the Algerian struggle, as was noted in chapter 1, and was an argument used by even Bourguiba, the man who was responsible for the most progressive family law on women within an Islamic framework but who had no time for 'women's liberation' while Tunisia was under occupation.

In this context, Philipp noted that many of the women's magazines that began to appear around the turn of the century were published by Egyptian Christian women and Syrian Christian women in Egypt. This, he argued, could have been a further factor in confirming the conservative nationalists' worst fears, that the West was using the women's issue to subvert social structures. In fact, because of their earlier access to formal education in Christian missionary schools, Christian Arabs, particularly women, had a head start when it came to articulating issues such as the role of women. The Christian Arabs, descendants of the first Christians, for the most part lived in harmony with their Muslim neighbours (as did Arab Jews until Zionism penetrated the region). Western 'concern' for the well-being of Christian Arabs made certain sectors of Muslim opinion feel that they were too close to former crusaders and present-day colonisers for comfort.

Thus, nationalism has dominated the Arab debate on women since its earliest days. It could even be argued that the more dominated the Arab world feels, the stronger the conservative nationalist trend. The more independent it feels, say in the days before European colonialism really took hold, or during the first flush of independence in the 1950s and 1960s and before the defeat of the 1967 Arab–Israeli War, the stronger the liberal nationalists. So far, in the Arab world, the majority of feminists have belonged to one or the other of the two camps, and those seeking equal rights for women have had to argue their case as nationalists who do not seek to betray cultural values shaped by Islamic traditions.

Because the 1970s and 1980s have been characterised by what is loosely described as the 'Islamic revival', it would seem that the conservative nationalists have the upper hand. According to the line of argument set out above, the Arab world is therefore feeling particularly dominated and infiltrated by the West. Examples will be given below of the ideas expressed by conservative nationalists as they relate to the position of women, to show how their views reflect a sense of domination by the West and to assess just how much of the Islamic revival is religious and just how much is nationalist.

## The establishment outlook

Perhaps the most conservative views on women's roles in society are expressed by the religious establishment in Saudi Arabia. For instance, in a pamphlet on the question of veiling, the head of the Saudi religious establishment Sheikh Abdel-Aziz Bin Abdullah Bin Baz stated that Almighty God had, in His Holy Book, ordered women to keep to their homes, to veil and to mind the word of men. He quoted from the verse on the Prophet's wives, who were told that they were not like other women and should keep to their homes and mind the words of the Prophet. He pointed out that if Almighty God had admonished the wives of the Prophet, who were known for their strong faith, their purity and their goodness, then how much more necessary it was to warn other women about their behaviour and about the need to abide by these rules.

Liberals arguing within an Islamic framework insist that, precisely because other women are not like the wives of the Prophet, such rules are not meant to apply to them. In any case, as will be seen in chapter 5, thousands of Saudi women do go out to work, and, in some parts of Saudi Arabia, do not cover their faces in spite of the religious establishment's views. Still, there are often lively debates in the Saudi press on the question of women's work. For instance, the letters of one Mr Haroon Basha to the English-language Saudi daily *Arab News*, attacking women's work outside the home, were answered equally sharply by a Saudi woman.

In his letter of 1 December 1984, Mr Basha had declared,

Women are to be blamed for their provocative and revealing dresses, their artificially decorated rosy lips which lead innocent men to become lecherous with such women. After all, women, 'the last thing civilised by men', are perhaps the weakness of men and so we cannot expect all men to be pious. The *purdah* [seclusion] serves as a protection to both. Of course, work always brings self-respect – to a man, rarely to a woman. Sometimes it brings shame to her family if she forgets the immaculate religion. I am not against women's employment as all religions, including Islam, permit it. But such an employment should not betray the moral laws.

In a letter in the same edition, the Saudi woman, Mrs S.F., retorted,

As a Saudi working woman I felt indignant by what Mr. Basha wrote. To me it is very easy to label him as a male chauvinist. But perhaps he is more than that. Mr. Basha belongs to a very small group of individuals who profess to know everything and wish to impose their own ridiculous ideas upon others . . . Let me say this to Mr. Basha: Please keep your nonsensical ideas to yourself, we Saudi women don't want your sermons. Saudi women are playing a positive role and their contribution to society is increasing. One last word of advice to Mr. Basha: Please don't stare so hard!

The influence of the religious establishment in the Arab world differs from country to country. In the Gulf, it generally manages to impose its views on governments; in the rest of the Arab world, it can generally be brought to support changes governments wish to make. However, there is a large number of religious groups active outside the official establishment, and it is their growing strength that has led to what is known as the 'Islamic revival'. There are several reasons for the growth and strength of these Islamic groups.

### Defining the role of religion in society

The first is simply that people are in the process of analysing religion and its role in society, an activity common to all cultures. This movement in the Islamic world deserves to be treated seriously, as the Arab–American professor and Islamic scholar Yvonne Haddad, herself a Christian, never tires of pointing out. Why was it, she asked at a lecture at Georgetown University on 19 September 1984, that when Christians reflected on their religion this was called 'theology', but when the Muslims did so this was called 'apology'? No one said that the Christians who went back to the first century when they analysed their religion were fanatics. But when Muslims did so they were treated as fanatics who wanted to turn the clock back to the seventh century. The Islamic revival deserved to be treated with respect, she said.

Moreover, the issues being tackled were of major significance, involving change, modernisation and development. From a reading of the literature of Islamic groups and through discussions with the 'Islamists', Haddad outlined the 'Islamist' approach to change, and compared it to the liberal and socialist approaches. The liberal approach and the ideas of the reformist thinkers dominated the first part of the twentieth century, she noted; this was followed by the socialist approach under such leaders as Nasser, and finally by the Islamist approach. The liberals believed in the equality of all citizens; the socialists believed in the equality of all people; and the Islamists upheld the equality of all believers.

The major arena for the liberals was the political, she went on, and they demanded democracy, constitutions, and so on; the socialists focussed on the economic, and there were experiments with nationalisation, industrialisation, etc; while the Islamists focussed on the social, with the emphasis on the family and the role of women. The liberals defined man as a citizen; the socialists defined man as a revolutionary worker; and the Islamists defined him as a revolutionary missionary. The liberals took the French revolution as their model; the socialists took Russia and China as theirs; while the Islamists saw Japan as a model, since they felt it had industrialised without compromise and had taken the technology of the West without its ideology. As for women and their role in society, Haddad summed up, the liberals defined women as mothers and daughters; the socialists saw them as workers, as partners in development; and the Islamists saw them as the repository of religion, culture and tradition.

## Organisational strength

There are also several other, more prosaic, reasons for the strength of the Islamic revival, not least of which is the organisational capacity and financial power of some of the groups. Many of these, particularly the Muslim Brotherhood, enjoy support and funding from governments such as the Saudi Arabian Government, which takes its role as the guardian of the Muslim holy places very seriously, and which also wants to prevent the spread of communism in the region. Groups receiving such material support operate in the Arab world, and in Muslim communities around the world.

Occasionally, Islamic groups are supported by their own governments, whenever these feel that leftwing movements are gaining the upper hand; the governments then turn on the Islamic groups if they become too strong. Ironically enough, the two most disciplined groups in the Arab world are the communists, which have largely been crushed by governments, and the Islamists. The late Egyptian President Anwar Sadat gave Islamic groups a good deal of leeway in Egypt during the 1970s, in contrast to Nasser, who had suppressed the Muslim Brotherhood. The Brotherhood was noticeably more active in Jordan during the 1970s and up to the mid-1980s, during which time relations between Jordan and Syria were at rock-bottom, and when the Brotherhood posed a serious threat to the Syrian regime.

Finally, it is quite common for a leader who has lost all vestiges of popular support to pose as the defender of the faithful. It is a useful rule of thumb that the more Islamic pronouncements pepper an Arab leader's speech, the more insecure he feels in his position. For example, in Sudan, ex-President Nimairi imposed Islamic law, as his Muslim Brotherhood advisers defined it, in order to shore up his position in the months before he was finally toppled in 1985, having managed to grind Sudan's economy into the dust before departing.

It should also be noted that, since independence, the democratic process has barely scratched the surface of the Arab world, and there is little power-sharing between rulers and ruled. Arab citizens who are genuinely concerned about improving their nation and sharing resources have no real outlet in Arab parliaments. As has been pointed out, it is possible to close political offices, but it is politically impossible to close down mosques. The mosque has thus become almost the only rallying point for many of those seeking to restore the nation's moral and physical strength.

Because of government financial support, some Islamic groups could afford to spread the message as widely as possible by publishing books, by offering allowances to needy students and to young couples looking for housing, by offering low-priced Islamic clothing. In short, they had at their disposal not only the message with which to sway the faithful, but also financial inducements to equal those that government parties in the Arab world use when recruiting members to their ranks. Certainly, the ability to disseminate information is a source of power, and books by members of Islamic groups are readily available in the markets of the Arab world. Many of these books are aimed at women.

## Reaching out to women

An 'Islamic novel' called *O Sister, O Hope,* written by one Mr Ahmad Badawi, is a good illustration of the kind of message going out to women from groups such as the Muslim Brotherhood. By 1981, the novel, published by Muassassat al-Rissala (the Message Establishment) in Beirut, was in its third edition. It began with a description of the heroine, Nour, a pretty girl dressed in the latest fashion, standing before the mirror for a final check on her appearance. The members of a loving and supportive family gathered round Nour, for whom this was to be the first day at university, to wish her good luck. Nour planned to study medicine and her excitement at going to university knew no bounds. During the first lecture, a young man embarrassed her by trying to strike up a conversation, but soon three nice girls rescued her from his unwelcome attentions by asking her to come and sit with them.

The lecturer began the course with an attack on Darwinism, which he said, with a heavy heart, he was forced to teach his students although it was against his beliefs and although scientists themselves agreed that Darwin's theories could not be proved. Enthralled by what she had heard, Nour was made even happier when her new friends invited her to tea at their home. She wondered how they could want to be her friends when she was dressed so differently from them, for they were wearing Islamic dress (headdress like a nun's, and a loose, long-sleeved gown down to the ankles). They replied laughingly that this did not matter, and that when Nour's parents saw how they were dressed, they would know that their daughter's new friends were serious and well-brought-up girls; this, indeed, came to pass.

At the tea party, the girls discussed political matters and delved into the causes of social evils. The Muslim world was weak and had lost so much of its land to its enemies because, they said, its society was corrupt and its people had fallen into bad ways. Girls were harassed if they just went out for a walk. Soon, Nour was 'converted' to the Islamic way of life. She appeared on campus wearing the Islamic dress, radiant, happy and proud, showing by her dress and in her manner that she was a true Muslim whom others had to respect accordingly.

It is easy to imagine the impact such a novel might have on young university and high school students. There are real economic and social ills to provide a responsive audience for such ideas: the occupation of Arab land, the growing economic disparities, and the fact that men and women are leaving a world, perhaps the village, the neighbourhood, or the extended family, where everyone knows and respects everyone else, to enter a world of strangers. An Islamic community offered the chance to be like everyone else, irrespective of economic background, and the opportunity to rebuild community ties that had suffered during the process of urbanisation. The men who joined the community also adopted a form of Islamic dress and trimmed their beards differently. However, as the Islamic groups grew more powerful and governments grew more worried, men abandoned forms of dress that gave away their politics. Women, who were taken less seriously as a political threat, were able to continue with their new way of dressing.

## The uses of veiling

The 'veil' is, to Western and Arab observers, the most obvious sign of the Islamic revival. The older generation of Arab women are particularly taken aback that younger women should return to the veil when the removal of the veil by the Egyptian feminist Huda Shaarawi in 1923 on her return from a women's conference in Rome had heralded the start of the women's liberation movement in the Arab world. However, as some writers have noted, the 'veil' brought in by the Islamic revival is quite different from the one that Shaarawi removed in the early 1920s.

The word 'veil' in English is loosely used to refer to a wide variety of head and face coverings. In Saudi Arabia, for instance, women use a gauze-like type of black material that covers the face and body. Women of the younger generation in the rest of the Gulf cover the hair and body with such a veil, but leave the face free; women of the older generation in the Gulf use a leather mask to hide the face, a type of 'veil' that is dying out. In Arab North Africa, some women use the traditional type of 'veil' there, a white sheet-like material that envelops nearly all the face and body. Throughout the Arab world, older women feel more comfortable with a scarf covering their hair; and many younger women have never dreamt of wearing a scarf or a veil.

What the Islamic revival has introduced is the Islamic headdress, the *hijab*, which covers the hair and neck like a wimple. It is worn with a long loose gown. Thus, there was an interesting crossing over of eras in the Gulf, for example, during the late 1970s when the Islamists grew particularly strong: some girls were gradually letting the black gauze veil slip to their shoulders as a first step towards removing it altogether, while others were taking up the Islamic headdress.

The difference between the old veil and the new headdress is not just one of form, but also of content. The black face and body veil that Shaarawi removed did symbolise seclusion which, in fact, only the wealthy classes could afford to practise. The Islamic headdress, on the other hand, is used by students at university, as the Islamic novel shows, and by women who are out at work. It serves, in this sense, as a useful off-limits sign: it tells the public, particularly the male public, that although a woman has left the house to study and work, she is respectable and does not expect to be harassed. It is a useful mechanism for societies in transition, where such off-limits signs have not yet had time to take root internally.

In her study of the Islamic movement, El Guindi wrote that 'to understand the new reality these women represent we cannot focus on single [exotic] elements such as the "veil" or the "new woman" without considering the totality in which they fit' (1981, p.465). She said that observers generally dated the beginning of the Islamic revival to 1967, following the shock of defeat in the Arab–Israeli war. However, El Guindi differentiated between the 'Islamic movement' and what she called a general religious revival. In Egypt, she said, the 1967 war did bring on a religious revival, but this affected both Muslim and Christian Arabs alike. The most significant example of this was the fact that, following the war, some people in Cairo believed they saw the image of the Virgin Mary, and large crowds of people flocked to see it; the Virgin Mary is an article of faith for both Christians and Muslims.

The Islamic movement was a separate phenomenon, El Guindi said. She traced this phenomenon back to the 1973 Arab–Israeli War. The religious revival that took place after 1967 affected the whole *umma*, the community of believers, while the revival of the Islamic movements concerned only the *jamaa*, those belonging to Islamic groups. The first *jamaa* (group) to be established in Egypt was the Muslim Brotherhood, which was set up in 1927, and which was eventually forced underground by Nasser, after an attempt on his life. When Sadat gave the Muslim groups a freer rein, 'alternative Islam reappeared in the '70s as *al-Jama'a al-Islamiyya* – organized and strong, "having learned from the mistakes of the past" . . . and with strong nonelitist youth appeal' (p.473).

Thus members joined a community of believers where everyone was equal, irrespective of social and economic background, but where the sexes were segregated. Far from forcing women into seclusion, the Islamic headdress enabled them to study and work without harassment. Indeed, El Guindi noted that the biggest concentration of *mitdayyinin* (religious ones) in university was to be found in the practical divisions of medicine, engineering and pharmacy. She noted that in Egypt a woman at work does not face a problem – 'a woman can become an engineer without losing her identity as a woman. No assertiveness is necessary on her part to prove herself, nor discrimination on the men's to reaffirm the separate identities' (p.482). However, women do face a problem in the rest of the public sphere, as will be noted in chapter 3. 'Therefore, a woman in public has a choice between being secular, modern, feminine and frustratingly passive (hence very vulnerable), or becoming a *mitdayyinan* (religieuse), hence formidable, untouchable and silently threatening' (p.481).

Other research has shown that the adoption of Islamic dress, for example in Cairo universities, is linked to families' social and economic back-grounds. Most students wearing the dress coming from families whose education was limited to the intermediate stage. This seems to indicate that the revival is strongest among the petty bourgeoisie, and it is interesting that the strands of conservative nationalism can be traced to this class through the decades. (See Gran for an account of the economic impact of Western capitalism on the Egyptian small farmer, merchant and artisan, which she traced from the late nineteenth century to Sadat's open-door policy.) For this class, modern life brought the opportunity and the need to educate daughters who, in previous times, would have shared in farm-based production or handicrafts and so would not have had to mingle widely in society.

Girls wearing the Islamic dress give revealing answers in interviews in newspapers and magazines: 'I feel comfortable and much more free in these clothes'; 'I wear the Islamic dress because it shows me to be a Muslim Arab woman, of which I am proud'; 'Many men treat women as objects, look at their beauty; the Islamic dress allows a woman to be looked upon as a human being and not an object.' Girls who do not wear the Islamic dress were also interviewed: 'I don't wear the Islamic dress because what I understand from God's words is simply that modesty is required, and therefore veiling is a way of behaviour, and not a way of dressing'; this is clearly a woman who has been able to internalise her off-limits signs.

## Islamic liberation

Thus, the uses of Islamic dress, that is, the outward appearance of an inner faith, are varied; they include political, social and economic causes, as well as religious ones. The radical nature of some of these trends was clearly expressed in an article by a Lebanese woman in the 31 March 1985 edition of the Beirut daily *As-Safir*. The piece was entitled 'The liberation of women and the role of the *hijab*'. The writer, Mona Fayyad Kawtharani, began by noting that the Iranian revolution had been marked by the widespread participation of women, and by the widespread use of the *hijab*.

Kawtharani pointed out that the nationalist uprising against the Israeli invaders of Lebanon in 1982 was similarly marked by a large number of women wearing a *hijab*. It should be noted that several Lebanese groups which emerged in the 1970s and 1980s looked to Iran for inspiration, partly because its revolution was a source of inspiration for many people in the region, especially in its earlier days, and partly because the large Shia Muslim community in Lebanon has traditionally had religious links with Iran's majority Shia community.

To explain the phenomenon of the use of *hijab*, Kawtharani began by recalling a study trip to Belgium that she had gone on in the early 1970s with some other girls. The Lebanese girls were wearing the latest fashions, to the surprise of the Belgian girls, who wondered if they also dressed like that back home. The Lebanese girls were proud of the fact they were just like Western women, since this proved they were as 'liberated' and 'advanced'. This had been misplaced pride, Kawtharani later decided. The incident also showed, she wrote, that European women still had no idea how their countries had kept up the pressure on the Third World until they had managed to flood it with Western commodities.

The women's liberation movement in the region had gone wrong, Kawtharani believed, from the day that Huda Shaarawi removed her veil in the call for the restoration of women's legitimate rights. The movement had adopted the Western woman as its model and blamed Islam for the low status of women; this was why they had failed to reach the majority of women. In fact, Islam gave women full rights, to education, to vote, to enjoy economic freedom. Western women themselves suffered from low status and had only managed to achieve the rights given in Islam, were it to be properly followed, after a long and bitter struggle. As recently as 10 years ago, women in Belgium could not open a savings account without their husbands' permission. Had work freed women, or had it simply added another burden to their lives in the West? And as for Soviet women, who were supposed to have reached the acme of liberation, they remained without representation in the upper echelons of power; there was not even a token woman, Kawtharani declared.

The truly liberated woman, East or West, was the woman who had liberated her potential as a human being, who was confident in herself, her independence, her personality, her culture, and her loyalty to the cause of her people, Kawtharani wrote. Thus women in Israeli-occupied South Lebanon were truly liberated in spite of, or because of, the *hijab*, because they adhered to their culture and civilisation. The *hijab* was one of the weapons of resistance to the West, which had found that the

best way to control us was by destroying our cultural and religious beliefs, so that the believer came to be defined as a 'fanatic'.

And this was done to enable the West to invade our lands and to penetrate with its consumer commodities, to transform our countries into markets. This led to political and economic dependency and to loss of cultural identity, which was replaced by 'modernisation'. The Easterner would not buy these diverse commodities – clothes, cars, electrical appliances, processed foods, furniture, etc – unless he was convinced that he was in need of a culture other than his own, and that this culture represented 'modernity' whereas his own represented backwardness.

As for the Eastern woman, Kawtharani wrote, she came to believe she would not be liberated unless she imitated the Western woman in all things, including women's groups that separated her from her own sisters. Such a woman had only become liberated by enslaving another woman to do her housework for her and bring up her children. What was needed, Kawtharani said, was a redefinition of work. If work outside the home brought self-reliance and freedom, fine; if not, then work at home was as valuable.

The concept that working outside the home for wages is a liberating factor for women is related to the traditional view that does not see housework as productive labour that contributes to economic development. But this is because the capitalist definition of commodities predominates; a commodity must be given monetary value.

A housewife could save her family the money wasted on buying ready-made goods by making these at home, which in turn was a contribution to the national economy, and should be valued as such.

The problem is the linkage between buying ready-made goods and the concepts of progress and backwardness: a modern woman is supposed to buy ready-made goods, while women who prepare these at home are considered backward.

Kawtharani concluded that the liberated woman was a woman who had discovered her humanity, not a 'commodity woman'; and Islam guaranteed women's humanity. The statement that the *hijab* covered a woman's mind and prevented her freedom of movement was given the lie, she declared, by the brave deeds of the women of South Lebanon.

The *hijab* is a symbol of a woman's faith and of her loyalty to her culture; it is one of the weapons of resistance, of *jihad* [holy war] and of brave confrontation. The enemy understands the meaning of the *hijab* full well and fears it as much as it fears the cry *Allah akbar* [God is great, the cry used in battle].

What is particularly interesting about this analysis is not Kawtharani's fierce attachment to her culture, which is natural in a people whose country was occupied, as South Lebanon was by Israel. It is the assessment that cultural invasion is a necessary precondition for economic invasion, and that this is the whole purpose of the West in the region. Indeed, if one removes the references to Islam, Kawtharani's argument is similar not just to that of Arab nationalists, but also to that of Arab Marxists.

Kawtharani also used accepted feminist arguments in her analysis – the need to redefine work, the need to recognise the contribution of household work to the national economy – while questioning the accepted definitions of liberation, again on economic grounds. An interesting area for research would be the comparison of such ideas with those of the leftwing Islamists in pre-revolution Iran, who were in the vanguard of the struggle against the Shah, but who lost out in the struggle for power after the Shah was toppled in 1979.

## How to define the role of women

The 'Islamic revival', therefore, clearly has strands that are politically, economically, and socially conservative, and others that are radical. The different approaches to economic and political issues are matched by different outlooks on the role of women. Interestingly, women define their roles much more aggressively than men, even in the more socially conservative groups. In the Muslim Brotherhood, for example, the role of woman is considered to be primarily that of wife and mother. Education is considered essential both for the woman's sake and so that she can bring up the family. Work is allowed if necessary and if it does not affect a woman's role in the family. However, women are not seen to be fit for leadership positions, except of other women. Those who argue this way base themselves on the Prophet's saying that a nation will not prosper if it is ruled by a woman.

It is instructive to see the way these positions are defined by a leading woman in the Muslim Brotherhood in Egypt, Zeinab al-Ghazali. Al-Ghazali, who became one of the top leaders of the Brotherhood, began by working with Huda Shaarawi's movement for women, but soon established her own Muslim Women's Association. She had direct contacts with the founder of the Brotherhood, Hassan al-Banna, and frequently gave her opinion on how things should run. She was so active that she spent some time in prison under Nasser. She divorced her first husband, who disapproved of her work in the movement. She was able to get a divorce because she had stipulated in the marriage contract her right to do so. She insisted on written agreements from her second husband that he would not interfere with her work for the cause, nor question her movements, which frequently involved meeting Brothers at the dead of night (Hoffman, 1985).

In an interview in the 25 July 1983 edition of *Sayidaty*, Al-Ghazali insisted that the 'West has invented the women's issue. We are in a weak position and have become imitators of the West because it has overtaken us economically. Awed by its materialism and failing to properly understand our Islamic teachings, we imitate the West like monkeys, saying that women have an issue and we want women's rights.' She went on to outline women's rights in Islam, which were equal to those of men in all respects, except that some things had been organised so that life could proceed more smoothly. For instance, men's work took them outside the home and women's work was home-based. However, if a woman had to go out to work, there was nothing wrong with this, so long as she wore the proper dress. Education was a duty, and work was optional. A husband should either provide his wife with household help or help her with the housework himself, as indeed the Prophet used to do in his own household, she said.

Further, there was nothing to stop women having a public life. The first Muslim women were fighters and nurses and social workers. They had held seminars and opened their homes for learning and as schools. Similarly, they had taken part in politics, and done then what was now called voting. Could a woman be a head of state or a company director? Women had the right to become judges and ministers, and even prime ministers, she declared; it was only the caliphate which was restricted to men. Women could also be preachers, and could teach, judge, discuss and question. It was clear that Al-Ghazali's views, while still falling within the framework of the Muslim Brotherhood, had pushed to the limits of the frame, especially with regard to the question of women's public roles.

## The liberal nationalists

As can be seen from the views expressed above, there is a powerful strand of nationalism underlying the 'Islamic revival'. Constant reference is made to the weakness of the region, and to the political and economic domination it suffers. Thus, conservative nationalists are determined to ensure that the process of change and reform maintains Islamic traditions. They believe that the West is seeking to undermine the region's Arab and Islamic identity in order to control it.

Some of these views are shared by the liberal nationalists. The difference is that the latter seek to reform society by applying concepts drawn from European liberalism to Arab and Islamic traditions. They are willing, effectively, to be more 'Western' in their approach to issues like equal rights for women. It should be kept in mind that the majority of the Arab population is not organised into groups, whether Islamic, rightist, leftist or otherwise. However, many are ordinary, believing Muslims, who would naturally refer to examples from the Quran, the sayings of the Prophet and the actions of the faithful in the early, therefore more pure, days of Islam. Thus, it is sometimes expedient for liberal nationalists to express ideas for reform using Islamic terms of reference. It is, in any case, out of the question for a group seeking mass support to criticise the religion itself.

A good example of a liberal nationalist argument can be found in the document prepared for the 25 February 1985 First International Conference on Arab and African Women. This was organised in Cairo by the Arab Lawyers Union, to prepare a position paper for the UN End-of-Decade Conference and Forum in Nairobi. The Arab Lawyers Union, an active socialist body, is one of the few really independent professional organisations in the Arab world. It is also unusual in that it has a women's section.

In its analysis of the situation of Arab and African women, the February 1985 document began by reviewing the history of colonialism and the role of the coloniser in transforming Arab and African colonies into one-crop, export-oriented countries. The colonisers had also further developed the class structure so as to strengthen the capitalist class and make it their ally. The position of women deteriorated under the coloniser as the national economy was transformed from a subsistence economy in which women played a major part to a market economy from which they were excluded, according to the document.

Women's conventional roles were further reinforced as a result of the adoption of the Western brand of development, the document continued. This was followed by the appearance of new intellectual and political trends which attempted to counter Western concepts by basing themselves on traditional ideology. In the absence of a strong, organised liberation movement, women were faced with contradictory choices: the first was dependence on the Western cultural heritage; the second was acceptance of the traditional trend that secluded them and excluded them from participating in the affairs of their country.

This analysis sidesteps the prickly question of religion: it criticises traditional ideology without going into the extent to which religion is responsible for religious tradition. Indeed, feminists like the Egyptian Nawal Saadawi have often warned that Arab feminists should not fall into the trap of opposing religion. This, Saadawi says, is a trap set by the imperialists. In her published work (see, for example, *The Hidden Face of Eve*), Saadawi gives political, economic and social reasons from a leftwing perspective to explain the current position of women, focussing on the absence of democracy in the Arab world, and the economic exploitation and dependency of the region. Of the social traditions, she has harsh words for the patriarchal structure of the family, which she says should be changed without destroying the strength of the Arab family.

Saadawi's writings have helped to shape the debate among liberal feminists, particularly as she has treated the issues of sex and sexual oppression with a frankness unwelcome to the official establishment. Her books have been banned in a handful of Arab countries and once, at a Gulf conference on women in 1981, there was a bomb scare just as she was scheduled to speak. She was among the women imprisoned by Sadat during his campaign of arrests in 1981, which jailed some of Egypt's most respected leftists, liberals and Islamists.

## Questioning the framework

The Moroccan sociologist Fatima Mernissi has also influenced the debate among Arab feminists through her work. She does, however, examine the link between the 'ideology' of Islam and the status of women, as well as the connection with capitalism and the class structure. The key to male–female relationships in Islam, in her view, is that women are seen as very powerful beings who need to be controlled in society as well as in the family. In *Beyond the Veil*, Mernissi pinpointed a central issue in the debate on Islam – indeed, the key dilemma that all reformers have faced – when she noted that the 'fact that God is the legislator gives the legal system a specific configuration' (p.xvii). She also referred to the strong feelings of cultural loyalty in the region, which she said emerged after every attack by the 'infidel' and which, rather than pushing society to strengthen itself, drove it further back on its traditions.

As noted earlier, cultural loyalty is the main reason why calls for a more secular approach have been few and far between, and are rarely articulated long and forcefully enough to muster support. Nevertheless, some Arab intellectuals have questioned the need to keep within an Islamic framework when discussing social reform. Most have sought to find ways whereby Islam can continue to be a primary element in Arab identity, but not the only one. For example, a Tunisian sociologist speaking in a workshop at the 1985 Nairobi Forum urged that the distinction be made between Islam as a religion and Islam as a civilisation that is capable of change and new interpretations, which would allow its adherents to live in changing times.

Indeed, according to Hourani, a similar argument was made by Qassim Amin, as his views on the role of women in society developed. Hourani has pointed out that Amin's first book, *The Liberation of Women*, phrased the arguments within an Islamic framework, while his second, *The New Woman*, based itself almost entirely on European concepts.

In other words, Amin has dissolved the relationship established by 'Abduh between Islam and civilization, and created in its place a *de facto* division of spheres of influence. While treating Islam with all respect, he claims the right for civilization to develop its own norms and act in the light of them . . . Qassim Amin was not alone in developing 'Abduh's thought in this direction. A number of others, while remaining loyal to their master in thought, began in fact to work out the principles of a secular society in which Islam was honoured but was no longer the guide of law and policy. (1983, pp.169–70)

This was echoed in the argument put forth by the Tunisian Al-Tahir al-Haddad in 1930, as was noted in chapter 1. As Norma Salem pointed out, the most significant aspect of Al-Haddad's book on women and society was not what he had had to say about women but what he had had to say about Islam: he stated that there was nothing that indicated that the stage achieved during the Prophet's lifetime was the hoped-for, final stage. The significance of this intellectual argument was missed by his critics, who attacked him on the grounds of what he had said about women.

Some intellectuals believe that the conflict between change and tradition can be resolved if a distinction is made between the specific procedures for day-to-day life laid down in the Quran and the sayings of the Prophet, which they believe are meant to apply to the time and place in which Islam was revealed, and the overall moral guidelines that apply to all times and places. This argument was recently used by an Islamic scholar who argued that women should be appointed to serve as judges. He said that the Prophet's saying – that a nation would not prosper if ruled by a woman – applied specifically to the conflict with Persia at that time and was not meant as a general statement on the nature of women.

It is ironic that, in fact, the conservative nationalists are more rational in their approach than the liberal nationalists who try to wed European ideals and Islam. This point emerged from a carefully argued paper, 'The contemporary discourse on Islam and the position of women', presented by Maha Azzam to a seminar on women in the Arab world organised by the Oxford Arab Committee in March 1985. Azzam reviewed the arguments of modernists and traditionalists on the roles of women within an Islamic framework, and noted the mistake made by the modernists: 'The Quran does have something to say about women, something that may be valid for many women, but if the latter [the modernists] seek the ideals of Western provenance, and even if they manage to assert that they exist in the Quran, they will nevertheless not experience those ideals that are part of a liberal and secular milieu', because the Quran had been specific on men's authority over women except in the spiritual sphere.

Azzam was also well aware of the strength of feelings of cultural loyalty, of the political and economic dimension of the Islamic revival 'which should be viewed as one response to the status quo that is no less modern than other responses, except in its use of language and religious symbolism'. The Arabs were aware and proud of an Islamic heritage . . . [however,] So long as religion remains an inherent criteria of reference in Arab Muslim countries, then we can expect to find the question of Islam and women coming up again and again in various forms and moulded into new interpretations, constantly in tension with Western ideas and the changing economic set-up, trying to reach a *modus vivendi* with Islam, while women themselves will continue to be the standard bearers of one or another interpretation of Islam.

The debate should be moved beyond this framework:

This would not necessarily undermine the importance of Islam, but it would allow us to analyse the role of Arab Muslim women with the use of analytical frameworks that, for example, draw on the sociology of religion and on the political and economic dynamics of nationalism and dependency . . . By showing some of the contradictions that arise from remaining solely within the Islamic discourse, perhaps we can begin to answer some of the questions relating to Arab women.

In the final analysis, the conservatives are more rational in their approach to the role of women than liberals arguing within an Islamic framework because they know that European concepts are not in accordance with Islamic ones, and this does not worry them. While the liberals have to go through mental contortions to prove that women and men are equal in Islam, the conservatives see men and women as having been created complementary rather than equal, and this is not, for them, a bad thing.

## The debate goes on

As the foregoing discussion has sought to show, the debate on women in the Arab world is not just a debate on the role of women; it is also a debate on the role of Islam in society. The two issues are inextricably tied; without resolving the question of the role of Islam in society, the question of women cannot be resolved. It is difficult to see how the debate on women can be moved outside the framework of Islam, although most modern Arab nation states have moved outside this framework in such matters as commercial codes and constitutions. In the Arab countries that have them, constitutions include almost verbatim the European concepts of liberty, equality and fraternity, and are at odds with the personal status codes.

Moreover, the debate on the role of women, is inextricably tied to the Arab quest for national independence. This is something of a vicious circle, for the question of the role of Islam in society, and the role of women, can only really be solved when the Arab world becomes politically and economically independent; and the Arab world cannot become politically and economically independent until the questions of the role of women, and the role of Islam in society are settled. So, the Arab world has to handle the crucial issues of the role of religion in society and the role of women, at the same time as it tries to complete the process of political and economic independence. No wonder developments in the Arab world seem so complex, and, at times, for Arabs struggling to reform and strengthen their nation, so hopeless.

However, the passion and long duration of the debate is not a cause for hopelessness, but an indication of the significance of the issues at hand – modernisation, independence, and the relationship between religion and state – issues which have taken centuries to resolve in other societies, and which have not yet been completely solved. The separation of church and state, for instance, is supposed to have been resolved in the West. Nevertheless, to this day there are efforts to relink the two as, for example, in the persistent calls to reintroduce school prayers in American government schools.

The key change in the Arab world from the nineteenth century to the present time is that many more people, and many more women, are involved in the debate. Unlike the early reformers who came from the upper classes because they had access to education, today's debaters cut across the class barriers. They have also all familiarised themselves with the texts and spirit of their religion, the better to do battle. As Yvonne Haddad pointed out, the Quran is now the property of every human being – and the feminist movement in the United States began in the nineteenth century when women began to read the Bible.

# Chapter 3

# Arab women in the workforce

Integration of women in the development process is now considered an essential first step toward their liberation . . . Yet the process of development itself has been little discussed or explained. *Rose Ghurayyib, Lebanese editor*

The Arab debate on women has focussed on the same issues for nearly a century. This is partly because of the complex nature of the issues at hand, as has been shown earlier, but also because there has not been a strong enough need for change to force the pace. Western nations might still be arguing about equal rights had the integration of women in the modern work sector not been speeded up by industrialisation and two world wars.

The Arab world has not been through a similar process, although it is, in theory, seeking to industrialise in order to modernise, and although there are plans to integrate women in development. Had the need for women in the modern sector been overwhelming, then much of the Arab discussion about roles and identity would have been shelved. In actual fact, the modern Arab sector can hardly provide enough opportunities for men, let alone for women. What are the dilemmas of development in the Arab world? And what are the prospects of overcoming the obstacles that exist?

## Redefining development

The attempt to develop from the traditional to the modern has had mixed results in the Arab world. Traditional socioeconomic systems that work, such as the Arab family, are slowly fading away, without really being replaced by others. One reason for this state of affairs is the fact that 'modernity' has not been clearly defined by those Arabs aspiring to it: it was generally assumed that modernity was everything that tradition was not. Arab social scientists have recently been questioning this view, in the search for more appropriate definitions.

A paper by Farida Allaghi and Aisha Almana (1984) at a meeting of Arab women social scientists in Tunisia in 1982 noted that

emerging theoretical perspectives on the nature of modernization and its impact on the traditional social structure refute the notion that traditionalism and modernism each stand at opposite poles of a continuum with no convergence between them.

### There was growing interest in recent social science literature

which demonstrates that modernization and development may further lower, rather than elevate, the status of women, especially those in rural areas and in poor urban slums.

### Allaghi and Almana criticised the belief

that modernization (the Western way) is the ideal that Arab women should strive to achieve. These writings also imply that the optimum stage of egalitarianism has been achieved by Western women. Western literature and the women's movement in the West greatly weaken this argument, demonstrating the inequalities and disadvantages of women. (pp.16–17)

An edge was given to the questions Arab intellectuals raised about development by the oil boom of the 1970s, when the region was flooded with easy money. At a Gulf conference on women in Kuwait in 1981, participants rejected the definition of development as an improvement in material conditions. They criticised the failures of development policies in the Arab world, noting the weakness of the economic base, the reliance on imports and the spirit of consumerism that had been unleashed throughout the land.

At the conference, the Qatari economist Ali Khalifa al-Kuwari suggested that a definition of development appropriate to the region should go as follows:

Comprehensive socioeconomic development must be a conscious social operation . . . to develop a self-reliant productive capacity that will lead to an orderly increase in real per capita income over the medium term; and to develop political–economic relations that link rewards to productivity and effort, and that will secure an individual's basic needs and rights to participation, security and stability in the long term. (1982, p.247)

By the 1980s, there was an international consensus that development should focus less on industrialisation and more on human resources. For the purposes of the 1975–85 UN Decade for Women, development was defined as a process involving total development – in the political, economic, social, cultural, and other dimensions of human life as well as in the physical, moral and intellectual growth of the human person (UN, 1984b, p.8).

It is difficult, of course, to measure development in human terms, although some indicators for education and health can be used. It is even more difficult, however, to understand how human resources can be developed when Arabs have no control over their political destiny and little freedom of expression. This is the main obstacle to successful development in the Arab world, and a key reason for the serious brain drain suffered by the region, which has lost thousands of the best and brightest products of its schools to the West. Manpower expert Antoine Zahlan estimated that up to 1976 'the percentage of outflow of Arab medical doctors, engineers and scientists to Western Europe and the US was 50, 23 and 15 per cent respectively of the total Arab pool' (TME, 1982, p.29).

The statements of Arab governments when the present-day nation states were just hatching earlier this century made it clear that political freedom would have to wait until economic development was achieved, and the Arab people were 'mature' enough for democracy. In turn, economic development had to wait until the Arabs completed the process of national liberation by liberating Palestine from Israeli occupation. Certainly, many of the scarce resources at the disposal of the emerging Arab nation states were channelled into the battle to liberate Palestine. None of these aims had been achieved by the 1980s: political freedom was still a rare commodity, economic growth had yet to take a self-reliant form, and the rest of Palestine had been occupied by Israel.

## Some positive indicators

The picture is not, of course, one of unrelieved gloom; there are some achievements, particularly in the fields of health and education. Arabs can look forward to a longer life span in the 1980s than they could in the 1970s. Much remains to be done, and Table 2 illustrates the gap between the poor and rich states in the Arab world, with the life expectancy at birth in 1980 ranging from as little as 40.4 years for men (42.2 for women) in the Yemen Arab Republic to as high as 66.9 years for men (71.6 for women) in Kuwait.

As for education, it is now generally accepted in the Arab world that this is a right, and a need, for boys and girls. Some two-thirds of Arab school-age children were enrolled by 1983. Table 3 shows how much of an improvement there has been between 1970 and 1980, particularly in the ratio of girls to boys in the total school population. This is a far cry from the days, in some cases only a generation ago, when parents were reluctant to let girls go to newly established schools for fear they would use their skills to 'write notes to boys' (a comment frequently made by the older generation, from the Maghreb to the Gulf).

There is also evidence of a change in attitude regarding the purpose of women's education, as was shown in a survey on 1,109 female students at the primary, preparatory, secondary and technical secondary levels in 18 schools in lower-middle and lower socioeconomic classes in Cairo in June 1980 (Khattab and El Daeif, 1984). The researchers found that the 'overwhelming majority of the parents (94.5%) intend to allow their daughters to pursue their education'; the majority of girls (94 per cent) also

**Table 2** *Arab population: household size, life expectancy*

| | Average household size, 1980 | Life expectancy at birth | | | |
|---|---|---|---|---|---|
| | | 1970 | | 1980 | |
| | | Female | Male | Female | Male |
| Algeria | 6.14 | 52.4 | 50.4 | 56.3 | 54.4 |
| Bahrain | 6.4 [1971] | 62.0 | 58.1 | 68.1 | 64.1 |
| Egypt | 4.85 | 49.5 | 48.9 | 55.6 | 53.9 |
| Iraq | 5.83 | 54.6 | 51.5 | 60.9 | 57.2 |
| Jordan | 5.69 | 53.2 | 50.2 | 62.0 | 58.3 |
| Kuwait | 6.5 [1975] | 66.4 | 62.5 | 71.6 | 66.9 |
| Lebanon | 5.25 | 64.8 | 61.1 | 67.0 | 63.1 |
| Libya | 5.11 | 51.8 | 49.0 | 57.0 | 53.8 |
| Mauritania | 5.5 [1976] | 40.6 | 37.5 | 43.6 | 40.4 |
| Morocco | 5.91 | 51.8 | 49.0 | 57.0 | 53.8 |
| Oman | 5.52 | 43.3 | 41.4 | 48.4 | 46.2 |
| Qatar | NG[a] | 64.4 | 60.7 | 71.6 | 66.7 |
| Saudi Arabia | 5.53 | 48.3 | 45.8 | 54.6 | 51.5 |
| Somalia | 5.09 | 40.5 | 37.4 | 42.5 | 39.3 |
| Sudan | 5.29 | 42.1 | 39.8 | 46.4 | 43,9 |
| Syria | 6.0 | 56.2 | 53.8 | 65.6 | 63.2 |
| Tunisia | 5.28 | 52.6 | 51.6 | 58.6 | 57.6 |
| U.A.E. | NG | 64.4 | 60.7 | 71.6 | 66.7 |
| Yemen A.R. | 5.78 | 38.7 | 37.3 | 42.2 | 40.4 |
| Yemen P.D.R. | 5.84 | 40.0 | 38.5 | 45.1 | 43.0 |

[a] NG = not given. (See Table 4 for key).
*Source:* United Nations, *Report of the Secretary General: selected statistics and indicators on the status of women*, 1985.


**Table 3** *Arab population: enrolment rates*

| | Total enrolment, all stages [1000s] | | % female to total | % of secondary vocational[a] | |
|---|---|---|---|---|---|
| | | | | F | M |
| Algeria | 1970 | 2149.5 | 36.3 | 18 | 20 |
| | 1980 | 4271.0 | 40.9 | 1 | 2 |
| Bahrain | 1970 | 52.0 | 41.9 | 1 | 11 |
| | 1980 | 76.5 | 45.2 | 8 | 13 |
| Egypt | 1970 | 5515.0 | 35.5 | 18 | 19 |
| | 1980 | 8001.0 | 38.3 | 22 | 21 |

Table 3    *continued*

| | | Total enrolment, all stages [1000s] | % female to total | % of secondary vocational[a] | |
|---|---|---|---|---|---|
| | | | | F | M |
| Iraq | 1970 | 1455.4 | 28.8 | 2 | 3 |
| | 1980 | 3761.0 | 42.0 | 5 | 6 |
| Jordan | 1970 | 379.5 | 41.1 | 2 | 4 |
| | 1980 | 726.0 | 46.2 | 4 | 7 |
| Kuwait | 1970 | 149.7 | 42.2 | 2 | 3 |
| | 1980 | 351.7 | 46.7 | 0 | 1 |
| Lebanon | 1970 | 644.0 | 42.3 | NG | |
| | 1980 | 744.0 | 45.1 | | |
| Libya | 1970 | 410.2 | 34.2 | NG | |
| | 1980 | 974.3 | 44.9 | 3 | 7 |
| Mauritania | 1970 | 35.4 | 26.2 | NG | |
| | 1980 | 112.2 | 34.4 | 2 | 5 |
| Morocco | 1970 | 1490.1 | 32.5 | 1 | 3 |
| | 1980 | 3086.0 | 36.8 | 3 | 3 |
| Oman | 1970 | 3.5 | 16.6 | | NG |
| | 1980 | 108.0 | 33.4 | | NG |
| Qatar | 1970 | 19.1 | 41.8 | | NG |
| | 1980 | 47.4 | 49.7 | | |
| Saudi Arabia | 1970 | 520.5 | 28.9 | 4 | 1 |
| | 1980 | 1361.0 | 37.9 | 0 | 3 |
| Somalia | 1970 | 57.8 | 22.3 | 2 | 3 |
| | 1980 | 338.8 | 36.0 | 13 | 19 |
| Sudan | 1970 | 972.3 | 36.0 | | NG |
| | 1980 | 1929.5 | 39.6 | 2 | 5 |
| Syria | 1970 | 1294.7 | 33.1 | 1 | 4 |
| | 1980 | 2311.0 | 40.4 | 3 | 5 |
| Tunisia | 1970 | 1138.3 | 36.9 | 10 | 12 |
| | 1980 | 1367.0 | 40.2 | 22 | 30 |
| U.A.E. | 1970 | 30.9 | 33.3 | | NG |
| | 1980 | 123.0 | 47.1 | | |
| Yemen A.R. | 1970 | 94.0 | 9.1 | | NG |
| | 1980 | 509.4 | 12.5 | | |
| Yemen P.D.R. | 1970 | 152.7 | 20.0 | | NG |
| | 1980 | 365.7 | 35.4 | 4 | 17 |

[a] Percentage of secondary school enrolment that is vocational: dates for Kuwait, Morocco and Saudi Arabia are for 1978, 1978 and 1975 respectively.
NG = not given
*Source:* United Nations, *Report of the Secretary General: selected statistics and indicators on the status of women,* 1985.

planned to continue (pp.180–1). As regards the purpose of education, 93 per cent of the girls believed that once a 'young woman completes her education, she must work' (p.183).

When women study for a career, many still go into the 'traditional' fields of teaching, health and clerical work seen, as elsewhere, as the natural extension of their roles as wives and mothers. However, as mentioned earlier, quite a few Arab women do go on to unusual and challenging careers, and are encouraged to do so. A study by Nagat al-Sanabary (1985) found that

thousands of Arab women have disregarded society's expectations and have ventured into educational and occupational fields previously dominated by men. Thus, probably the most remarkable achievement over the past twenty-five years has been women's increased access to engineering and the natural, physical, and medical sciences, which, in several Arab countries, are superior to those in many advanced Western nations. (p.108)

## And some negative indicators

In spite of the advances in education and health, the challenges are enormous. The most serious is keeping up with the rapid growth of the population. The region has one of the highest growth rates in the world. Industrial market economy countries, for example, showed an average annual population growth rate of 0.7 per cent between 1973 and 1983, whereas the lowest for any Arab country during the same period was 1.9 per cent, with the exception of Lebanon (see Table 4). It has been estimated that, according to the present rates of growth, the Arab world would double its population in just 23 years.

The second problem is the youth of the population. Whereas in the industrial countries the proportion of the population under 15 years of age averages around 22 per cent of the total, it was over 40 per cent in most Arab countries in 1980. Obviously, both the rapid growth rate and the youth of the population place severe strains on the facilities in health, education and welfare that the state has been able to provide, as well as on the ability of family wage earners to make ends meet.

The situation is exacerbated by the rapid flow of humanity from the countryside to the city. The Arab world boasts many ancient, continuously inhabited cities, so that urban life is not a new phenomenon; what is new is the sheer size of the population converging on the urban areas. Arab government planners initially believed that industrialisation, along Western lines, would bring prosperity, so the development of rural areas was neglected. More recently, a large proportion of investment budgets has been allocated to agriculture, but the damage may have been done. The

Table 4   *Arab population: size and rate of growth*[a]

|  | Population [millions] 1980 | [1983] | % below 15 1980 | rate of change % 1980 | % of rural population 1980 | [Average annual growth rate of urban population % 1973–83] |
|---|---|---|---|---|---|---|
| Algeria | 18.7 | [20.6] | 47 | 3.1 | 40 | [5.4] |
| Bahrain | 0.35 | [0.4] | 34 | 4.9 | 22 | NG[b] |
| Egypt | 41.3 | [45.2] | 39 | 2.6 | 54 | [2.9] |
| Iraq | 13.2 | [14.7] | 47 | 3.6 | 28 | [5.3] |
| Jordan | 2.9 | [3.2] | 50 | 2.3 | 44 | [4.8] |
| Kuwait | 1.4 | [1.7] | 43 | 6.2 | 6 | [7.8] |
| Lebanon | 2.7 | [2.6] | 40 | −0.7 | 24 | [1.6] |
| Libya | 2.97 | [3.4] | 47 | 4.0 | 48 | [8.1] |
| Mauritania | 1.6 | [1.6] | 46 | 2.8 | 64 | [4.6] |
| Morocco | 20.0 | [20.8] | 46 | 3.0 | 59 | [4.2] |
| Oman | 0.97 | [1.1] | 44 | 4.9 | NG | [17.6] |
| Qatar | 0.25 | [0.3] | 33 | 7.3 | NG | NG |
| Saudi Arabia | 9.2 | [10.4] | 43 | 4.8 | 33 | [7.4] |
| Somalia | 4.6 | [5.1] | 44 | 7.8 | 70 | [5.5] |
| Sudan | 18.7 | [20.8] | 45 | 3.1 | 75 | [5.5] |
| Syria | 8.8 | [9.6] | 47 | 3.4 | 50 | [4.2] |
| Tunisia | 6.4 | [6.9] | 42 | 2.6 | 48 | [3.7] |
| U.A.E.[c] | 1.0 | [1.2] | 29 | 13.3 | NG | [11.2] |
| Yemen A.R.[d] | 5.8 | [7.6] | 46 | 1.9 | 90 | [8.8] |
| Yemen P.D.R.[e] | 1.9 | [2.0] | 46 | 2.3 | 63 | [3.5] |

[a] The Palestinian Arab population is estimated at 4.5 million, about 2 million of whom live in historic Palestine; the majority of the rest live in neighbouring Arab countries.

– No figures were available for Djibouti.

[b] NG = not given.

[c] U.A.E. = United Arab Emirates.

[d] Yemen A.R. = Yemen Arab Republic.

[e] Yemen P.D.R. = People's Democratic Republic of Yemen.

Sources: United Nations, *Report of the Secretary General: selected statistics and indicators on the status of women*, 1985.

World Bank, *World Development Report*, 1985 [figures in brackets].

major cities in the heavily populated Arab countries are ringed by belts of poverty, and the strain on services is tremendous. The neglect of the countryside, along with the rapidly growing population, has meant big food import bills and increased reliance on food aid. To make matters worse, industry has not yet properly taken off, and the region imports many manufactured goods.

The trade imbalance in the Arab world (see Table 5) is quite serious, with countries like Egypt, Syria and Tunisia importing nearly twice the value of their exports in 1983. In those countries that seem to have a healthy trade balance, the major, indeed almost the only, export is oil, which is highly vulnerable to the state of the world market. The external public debt of the poorer Arab countries has reached alarming levels. The World Bank figures given in Table 5 are in fact quite conservative estimates; the International Monetary Fund, which relies on its own calculations rather than on government figures, puts Egypt's external public debt at some 150 per cent of GNP, making it almost impossible to repay (AN 1985). More worrying is the fact that the oil boom, which helped to shore up Arab economies during the 1970s, was over by the early 1980s.

Intra-regional trade and other forms of regional cooperation would be an effective strategy for survival for the Arab world. The capital-poor, heavily populated countries, like Morocco, Tunisia, Egypt, Sudan, Syria and Jordan, could develop a solid, diversified economic base with the right investment and planning, while the capital-rich, under-populated countries, which have oil but few other natural resources, could provide the investment and share in the output.

Cooperation between Third World countries is a solution recommended by the UN for their economic woes, because 'when entering into the world market competitive struggle, which is fully dominated and controlled by developed countries, developing countries have little or no choice in selecting partners for trade or other forms of cooperation' (UN, 1984a, p.223). And, in fact, non-oil trade between Third World countries grew at an annual rate of 26.7 per cent between 1970 and 1975 and 20.6 per cent between 1975 and 1980.

However, in spite of some regional cooperation, the Arab world has not turned to this remedy with the seriousness it deserves. Inter-Arab trade consisted of only 5 to 6 per cent of total Arab trade in the 1970s (Sayigh, 1984). Some money did flow from the rich Arab states to poorer ones through workers' remittances, aid and investment, but this diminished as oil revenues dropped. The cash produced during the 1970s and early 1980s was not effectively transformed into renewable resources in either the oil-producing or the non-oil Arab states; much of it went into consumption and foreign banks.

Therefore, the weakness of the productive sectors and the limited nature of regional cooperation are also serious obstacles to development opportunities for men and women alike. Arab governments should increase sound investment in the productive sectors so as to lessen the dependency on

Table 5 *Economic indicators: GNP, inflation, public debt, trade*

| | Per capita GNP 1983 ($) | Average annual inflation rate % 1973–83 | External public debt as % of GNP | | Merchandise trade (mn $) | |
|---|---|---|---|---|---|---|
| | | | 1970 | 1983 | a. 1983 exports | b. 1982 imports |
| Algeria | 2,320 | 12.8 | 19.3 | 28.0 | a. 11,158 | 10,332 |
| Bahrain | 10,510 | NG | NG | NG | NG | NG |
| Egypt | 700 | 13.2 | 23.2 | 49.4 | a. 4,531 | 10,274 |
| Iraq | NG | NG | 8.8 | NG | b. 10,250 | 21,280 |
| Jordan | 1,640 | 10.0 | 23.5 | 47.9 | b. 739 | 3,217 |
| Kuwait | 17,880 | 10.2 | NG | NG | b. 10,447 | 8,283 |
| Libya | 8,480 | 11.6 | NG | NG | b. 13,252 | 9,500 |
| Mauritania | 480 | 7.8 | 13.9 | 158.2 | a. 246 | 227 |
| Morocco | 760 | 8.4 | 18.0 | 69.6 | a. 2,062 | 3,599 |
| Oman | 6,250 | 17.9 | NG | 16.1 | a. 4,058 | 2,492 |
| Qatar | 21,210 | NG | NG | NG | NG | NG |
| Saudi Arabia | 12,230 | 16.5 | NG | NG | b. 79,125 | 40,473 |
| Somalia | 250 | 20.1 | 24.0 | 62.0[b] | a. 163 | 422 |
| Sudan | 400 | 18.0 | 15.2 | 77.8 | a. 624 | 1,354 |
| Syria | 1,740 | 12.7 | 10.6 | 13.7 | a. 1,875 | 4,180 |
| Tunisia | 1,290 | 9.4 | 38.2 | 42.4 | a. 1,851 | 3,117 |
| U.A.E. | 22,870 | 12.7[a] | NG | NG | a. 13,950 | 8,120 |
| Yemen A.R. | 550 | 13.9 | NG | 38.4 | b. 204 | 1,521 |
| Yemen P.D.R. | 520 | NG | NG | 118.5 | b. 449 | 1,010 |

No figures were available for Lebanon or Djibouti. NG = not given.

[a] 1973–82.

[b] 1982.

*Source:* World Bank, *World Development Report*, 1985.

imports and alleviate the problem of unemployment in the heavily populated states. This did not happen during the boom years of the 1970s, when the cash was available, and it is hard to see it happening in the 1980s, with funds running low.

With such mixed results for the Arab development process, neither men nor women can be fully integrated into the modern economic sector. The debate on women's roles in society could have been more speedily resolved – or rendered academic – if women had entered the wage labour force in large numbers, but the growth of the wage labour force itself is restricted by the weakness of Arab economic development. It is not therefore enough to turn to religiously inspired cultural factors to explain why women's participation in the wage labour force remains low in the Arab world, as so many writers on the region have done. Economic factors must also be taken into account.

It is important to establish why female participation in the wage labour force is low, and whether this can be increased. In my view, this is now the key to women becoming equal partners in society. Of course, guaranteed wages at the end of the month do not necessarily guarantee independence: a woman in paid employment may have to hand over her earnings to her father or brother. On the other hand, a woman who is not in paid employment may have a good deal of personal wealth at her disposal, through inheritance or through gifts and dowries, and so enjoy much power. Nor is money the only measure of economic transactions. In transitional societies, a great deal of economic activity, particularly women's, takes place without money changing hands. However, this situation is, precisely, transitional.

The Arab world, whether one likes it or not, is developing along Western lines, and increasingly in the West men and women are responsible for earning their incomes as individuals in paid employment. It is likely that the 'modern' economic system which values and rewards labour in monetary terms will become, and in many areas has become, the dominant system in the Third World. Women are often glorified for their self-sacrificing work without remuneration; one cannot simply continue to praise these unwaged labourers, but must try to establish whether they are likely to receive monetary reward for their efforts.

## Working women: unreliable statistics

It should be noted that the total labour force as a proportion of the population in the Arab world is low. It has variously been estimated as ranging between 20 to 30 per cent of the Arab population in the early 1980s, as compared to some 40 per cent in Western Europe and more in other parts of the world. The reasons for the small Arab labour force include the youth of the population and the fact that women constitute a very small proportion of the labour force.

The small proportion of women in the labour force in official statistics does not mean that few Arab women work, or even that few earn money. Third World statistics rarely reflect the real number of economically active men and women, although methods are improving. Ironically, while many researchers have pointed out the unreliability of available statistics, they have nevertheless gone on to build theories or to make recommendations based on these same statistics. It would be as well to get a clear picture of how limited official statistics are before going further.

Official statistics tend to define work as labour for wages. This excludes some working men and most working women from the figures, although the work of an urban housewife in the Third World usually involves a long day of hard physical labour. In rural areas, the figures are even more out of touch with reality, as micro-studies reveal. For example, national statistics in Egypt in 1970 reported that only 3.6 per cent of the agricultural labour force were women. A sample of rural household wives throughout the country revealed that half the wives ploughed and levelled the land in Lower Egypt, and between 55 and 70 per cent participated in agricultural production activities; in Upper Egypt, between 34 and 41 per cent participated in agricultural activities, and about 75 per cent engaged in milking and poultry activities (UN 1984a, p.41).

Another example of statistical discrimination against women is found in a report on Moroccan peasants that divided the population into five categories: actively employed population, unemployed population, school-goers, housewives, other inactive population (quoted in Mernissi, 1981). As Mernissi noted, the 92 per cent of the women classified as 'housewives' and 'other inactive' would hardly have recognised themselves in this description. Anyone who took a walk through the village could see the women engaged in indispensable tasks. The villagers did not recognise the category 'school-goers' either; children were not encouraged to attend school because, in the villagers' view, this did not prepare them for village life and simply produced unemployable adults.

Often, women subscribe to definitions of work similar to the ones in use by policy makers, and are likely to give a negative response when asked whether they work. The way such questions are usually phrased, one researcher remarked, the women might as well be asked if they are men (Chamie, 1985, p.99). There is a growing awareness of the need to phrase questions differently, as Chamie noted when quoting from a survey on labour-force participation in Syria. In this survey, Syrian men were initially asked whether their wives worked, and a large proportion replied that they did not. When the question was rephrased to 'If your wife did not assist you in your work, would you be forced to hire a replacement for her?', the overwhelming majority answered yes.

For the purposes of this discussion, it will be assumed that most adults in the Arab world work for a living, waged or unwaged, but that Arab women's participation in the wage labour force is still low, without attempting to quantify it. Instead, the question that will be asked is: What are the factors keeping women's participation low?

## Three conditions: need, opportunity, ability

In seeking to answer this question, I have pinpointed three conditions which must be met before women (or men) can be fully integrated into the wage labour force: need, opportunity and ability. If any one of these conditions is not met, then women's participation rates will continue to be low. Further, these three conditions must be met at the state and at the popular levels. At the state level, I use 'need' to refer to a country's manpower requirements; 'opportunity' to refer to official efforts to create the proper environment for employment, through planning and legislation; and 'ability' to refer to the government's efforts to train people in requisite skills. At the popular level, 'need' refers to a family's or an individual's requirements for income; 'opportunity' refers to the social and cultural obstacles to women's work; and 'ability' refers to an individual's possession of the right skills.

In other words, before women can be fully integrated into the workforce in the Arab world, the following conditions must be met: a country must need manpower; it must have the appropriate legislation and other facilities for workers; and it must provide the necessary education and training. Moreover, at the family level, people must feel a real or perceived need for more than one income per family; facilities must exist to enable women to work, as well as supportive social attitudes; and women must possess the right skills.

This may sound like a statement of the obvious, but it needs to be said: too much of the discussion in the literature on Arab women and the modern labour force focusses on social and cultural factors, almost to the exclusion of the others. Many sociologists and economists have a tendency to blame the low participation of Arab women in the workforce on the 'conservative nature' of Islam. Of course social factors are important, but much the same attitudes have existed in many parts of the world for centuries: the strength of family ties; the definition of a woman's main role as wife and mother; unwillingness to see the break-up of the family; the efforts to keep men and women segregated in order to avoid the breakdown of social morals; the stigma attached to a husband whose wife goes out to work and who is seen as having failed in his duty of supporting the family; and the double burden women working outside the home have to bear.

However, in the Arab world as elsewhere, the situation changes with changing need and opportunity; tradition is either cast aside or reinterpreted. Some social scientists have become restive with the continued focus on cultural obstacles to the exclusion of other factors. For example, the 1980 ICRW report on women and work in Third-World countries was critical of the tendency in development literature to over-emphasise 'sociocultural determinants, particularly as these operate to restrict the *supply* of women available for work, and single these out as major causes for the low participation and marginal status of women in the work force of developing countries' (p.25). The report noted that there were a number of structural restraints on *demand* in Third-World economies, and gave examples of cases when the sociocultural restraints disappeared in the face of economic need and opportunity. It argued that planners could no longer use sociocultural arguments 'to avoid planning employment focussed strategies for women' (p.80).

## The cultural thesis: an example from Lebanon

An illustration of the tendency to turn to sociocultural factors when other reasons may be as, if not more, important for women's low participation in the workforce, can be found in some of the recent research on Lebanon. Lebanon was considered, until the civil war of 1975 began a seemingly unending cycle of violence, the most successfully 'modernising' country in the Arab world. The participation of Lebanese women in the wage labour force was one of the highest in the region. Lebanese women were estimated to account for 18 per cent of the total workforce on the eve of the war, with the majority of employed women being between 20 and 25 years of age (IWSAW, 1980, pp.8–9). Agricultural workers accounted for the largest group of working women with 22.6 per cent, workers in domestic service were next with 22.5 per cent, followed by professionals (mostly teachers) with 21.3 per cent, industrial workers with 19.6 per cent and office employees with 10.3 per cent.

By 1985, a decade of war had almost destroyed Lebanon's economy, and hundreds of thousands were killed or maimed. A study was conducted to assess the effect of 10 years of war on Lebanese women (Faour, 1985). Faour estimated that some 30 per cent of the labour force was unemployed, and inflation had soared to 150 per cent during the first three months of 1985. The value of the Lebanese pound was finally undermined, and this factor sapped the will to survive that had kept the country going through the merciless shelling of the civil war, the brutal Israeli invasion of 1982 and the outbreaks of violence since then. In 1985, Faour reported, women in Beirut were selling their jewels, the ultimate last resort, to keep their families alive.

Faour outlined the social and demographic changes in a decade of war. Some 700,000 people had been forced to move from their homes to other places in search of shelter. The destruction of homes resulted in a reversal of previous social patterns; for instance, the number of newly married women who lived with their in-laws had risen, whereas in modernising Lebanon nuclear families had become common before the civil war. The age of marriage had risen and mothers, at least in Beirut, were having fewer children. Surveys in Beirut revealed that female-headed households represented some 15.3 per cent of all households in 1984, compared to 9.2 per cent in 1954.

However, micro-surveys showed that the percentage of women in the labour force in Beirut had fallen from 17.6 per cent in 1970 to 13.9 per cent in 1984. Faour said that this could be partly explained by the fact that more girls were entering the school system and, amazingly enough, the percentage of girls completing their high school education and going on for higher studies was in 1984 twice what it had been in 1970. More significantly for Faour's argument, the number of working women in the 25 to 29 age group showed only a slight rise, and there was little change in the number of women who were unemployed or who were looking for work for the first time.

Thus, Faour concluded that one could not blame adverse economic conditions brought on by war, like the destruction of offices and factories, lack of investment, and so on, for the fact that the number of working women in Lebanon did not rise. Indeed, he went further, and said that Western theories relating women's participation in the labour force to modernisation, economic development, educational attainment and lower fertility did not apply to Lebanon or other Arab countries. In such countries, he concluded, social factors were the key to women's low labour force participation.

However, one could argue the case differently and say that while war conditions created pressing economic need at the family level, they did not change the nature of the demand for women's work; nor were women equipped with new skills to cope. This would seem to be indicated by the types of activity being undertaken by women who were trying to survive in war-torn Lebanon. Chamie said women were undertaking income-generating activities that were difficult to trace, such as sewing and handwork at home, house-sitting for absentee owners and housecleaning (1985).

Moreover, studies undertaken by IWSAW to see what work women could do for economic survival seemed to confirm that the nature of demand had remained unchanged (1980). Women continued to enter traditional and low-paid employment, and employers continued to prefer young, single women. IWSAW surveyed 240 organisations in the greater Beirut area – the only ones that could be located out of the 800 listed by the Chamber of Commerce in 1979. These employed some 20,346 workers. The number of males exceeded the number of females by over two-thirds, and 68 per cent of the employers indicated their preference for employing males. Of the total number of women, 82 per cent were single, and more than half of the employers preferred to employ single women. In fact, employers expected nearly two-thirds of their workers to be between 19 and 30 years old. There had been little change in attitudes towards employing women since the National Manpower Study of 1972, and little change was expected in the near future, IWSAW concluded.

Therefore, in the case of war-torn Lebanon, at least two of the conditions given earlier as necessary for women's integration into the workforce were not met: opportunity, that is, planning for women's work at the level of the state, which would be necessary to change employers' attitudes; and ability, that is training of women in new skills that might better equip them to seek the type of work available.

## Need at the state level – and the phenomenon of labour migration

The first of the three conditions for the full employment of the working-age population set above is need – for manpower at the state level, and for income at the popular level. Need at the state level raises the issue of the manpower requirements and problems of the region. Earlier this decade, a study was conducted by the ILO on manpower problems in the Arab world with a view to setting up a regional Arab Programme for Employment Promotion (ILO, 1983). It was found that the problems varied from situations of acute skill shortages, to ones of chronic unemployment and underemployment. The ILO underlined the need for accurate manpower statistics, as well as for improving manpower assessment and planning, building up regional mechanisms for labour migration, improving vocational training, involving youth and women, and promoting integrated rural development and rural industry. The study left unanswered the question of where the funding would come from to carry out any of its proposals.

The uneven distribution of manpower in the Arab world resulted in the phenomenon of labour migration during the days of the oil boom. The Arab people have historically been fairly mobile. Urban Arabs often travelled in pursuit of trade and of education, and nomads travelled in search of pasture for their herds. The modern phenomenon of migration for jobs began in the 1940s and boomed in the 1970s with the growth in revenue of the Arab oil states (Birks and Sinclair, 1980). Over four million Arabs were estimated to be working outside their home countries in other parts of the region by the early 1980s. There were also hundreds of thousands of Arabs from North Africa working in Europe.

By the 1980s, the oil-rich Arab states began to cut back on projects because of the fall in oil revenues and because some of their needs in construction and in services had been met. Thus labour exporters like Morocco, Tunisia, Egypt, Sudan, Jordan, Lebanon, Syria and Yemen were faced with the need to accommodate hundreds of thousands of returning workers, who had been earning higher incomes abroad than those available in the home country. The heavily populated countries had to face this problem over and above that of the large numbers of young people entering the workforce.

Although labour migration was originally seen as a way to alleviate unemployment problems for the heavily populated countries, the costs to both labour exporters and importers may have outweighed the benefits (Birks and Sinclair, 1980). Exporting countries tended to lose the most skilled workers and professionals during their most productive years, which had a negative impact on their national development. The investment by exporting countries in training the workers who migrated was lost, and was not compensated by remittances from abroad. Much of the income earned abroad was spent on consumer goods, which fuelled inflation. The loss of manpower affected agricultural production in some countries. Egyptian officials described the shortage of agricultural manpower as the major crisis facing that sector. In some cases, labour-exporting countries had to import labour to make up the loss, as happened in Jordan, where some 60,000 Egyptians were working by the mid-1980s, mostly in agriculture.

Nor were the Arab labour importers much happier with their situation, in spite of their need for skilled manpower. They were worried about the impact of large non-Arab populations on their culture and traditions. They were also nervous about hosting thousands of expatriate Arabs, particularly the more politicised Palestinians and Lebanese. Moreover, it became possible for the nationals of the labour-importing countries to avoid skilled or semi-skilled jobs and to opt for white-collar occupations. As the nationals began to move into the workforce themselves, resentment was created between nationals and non-nationals, who feared the loss of their jobs.

## Labour migration and the role of women

Labour migration was one of the factors that created need and opportunity at the state and popular levels for the involvement of Arab women in the wage labour force, although this varied from country to country. In some cases, women were encouraged to join the workforce as replacements for male migrants. The rise in the cost of living, partly the result of migration, created the need at the popular level to do so. In Sudan, for example, officials attributed the increase of women's participation in the workforce, put at 22.5 per cent of the workforce in the 1983 census, to the gap left by the number of men who had migrated to the Gulf for better-paid jobs (reported in the 22 June 1984 edition of *Asharq al-Awsat*). More women were working in unskilled jobs in factories, where the drop in male labour was estimated to be about 60 per cent. Women were also involved in education and training in greater numbers, although both male and female teachers had migrated for jobs.

Another way in which labour migration was seen to have increased women's involvement in economic activity and share in decision-making was in the case of women left behind to care for the family. However, the extent to which this happened was uneven, and depended greatly on the women's position prior to the men leaving in search of work. A newly married young woman would not find her position strengthened. Traditionally, in rural areas, a woman gains in power and status when she has children, particularly sons, and establishes control over her own household, wresting control from her mother-in-law.

A study of an Egyptian village south of Cairo (Khafagy, 1984) where some 300 villagers, or 23 per cent of the population, worked abroad in 1977, found some evidence of change in women's roles. Wives managed the remittances sent back by husbands; they dealt with individuals and institutions outside the household, such as merchants or the village agricultural cooperative; and sometimes they hired workers and negotiated their wages. Although their workload had increased, most of the women did not mind and viewed labour migration in a positive light. The husbands were seen to have become more dependent on their wives' advice, and turned more frequently to them at decision-making times. Khafagy concluded that women were doing more than filling the gap until their husbands' return, and that this was likely to have some lasting effect.

Another study on Egyptian villages in Giza (Taylor, 1984) found that, when migration was of short duration, the change in married women's roles was not too profound. The general pattern was that younger wives did not receive control of the remittances, which were sent to male relatives, while older established wives did. On their return, the husbands resumed their former roles in full and the months following the return were reportedly ones of conflict between husband and wife as he reasserted his position.

In a look at another part of the picture, El Solh studied the lives of Egyptian settlers in Iraq to assess the change in roles of women (1985). Women settlers coming from Lower Egypt had already worked on the land with their husbands before migration, so not much change was evident. With women from Middle and Upper Egypt, however, the change was striking, particularly as the women were involved in marketing activities, which meant mixing with male strangers. The women explained the changes by saying they were in a foreign country where no one knew them, or that their situation differed since their husband could not rely on anyone else. Indeed, the husbands preferred their wives to undertake marketing activities since, if the women were caught selling above the official prices, they were not likely to be given prison sentences. As El Solh noted, when ideal and reality clashed, economic self-interest came first, although the fiction of adhering to customs and tradition was upheld.

There is not yet enough information on the extent of the physical and psychological burden migration has placed on those left behind, or on the migrants themselves. In some cases, women were involved in the wage labour force because the migrant husband broke off contact with the family. Such women entered domestic service or took on low-paid unskilled jobs. In these cases, the family was worse off than before.

### Opportunity at the state level: planning for women

From the above, it is clear that different Arab countries had different manpower needs, which were reflected in the phenomenon of labour migration. Obviously, whether a government needed manpower or not affected its planning for women and its willingness to create opportunity. Most Arab governments were publicly committed to 'integrating women in development', and, where there was a labour shortage, as for example in Iraq, they did follow up their public statements with action.

In fact, the Iraqi government was, along with that of the Yemen Democratic Republic, perhaps the most determined to involve women in the modern sector. Iraq's population was rather small, given its size and its abundant resources, including oil. Iraq's need for manpower was so pressing that it had 'imported' over a million Egyptians for the agricultural sector. The war with Iran in 1980 gave a further, tragic, impetus to integrating women in the modern sector because of the loss of male labour. By the second year of the war, there was a noticeable increase of women in government ministries. By the third year, officials were talking about plans to employ more than a million women in unskilled work in the public and private sectors.

The government made determined efforts to change social attitudes. One example was the effort to employ women in a new pharmaceuticals plant set up in a conservative village north of Baghdad (AN, 1983). Because the village families initially refused to allow their girls to work in the factory, female workers were brought in from Baghdad and housed in dormitories. The villagers resented the intruders, and the buses transporting girls from Baghdad were sometimes attacked. Gradually, the girls from the village began to seek work in the factory, being chaperoned at first, and finally going on their own.

The Iraqi case is an example of forceful planning for women when the need for manpower is great. (This will be examined in more detail in the case study on Jordan.) An example of somewhat ambivalent government planning for women comes from Tunisia. As we have seen, Tunisia has the most advanced personal status laws; in theory, it should have been the most eager to integrate women into the modern sector. However, the serious unemployment problem in the country militated against this.

In 1975, unemployment stood at 14 per cent out of a workforce of some 1.9 million, although the number of Tunisians working abroad was already

261,500. By the 1980s, the number of migrant workers had risen to 450,000. Meanwhile, some 60,000 were joining the labour force annually and unemployment continued to hover at 15 per cent. The Tunisian economy suffered from several problems which hampered the government's efforts to make employment available for all those seeking jobs. Like other Arab economies, the Tunisian economy was poorly integrated and the service and light industries required many imports. The 1982–6 development plan hoped to rectify this by emphasising local production of capital equipment and tools (ILO, pp.93–5).

Tunisia was a state that obviously needed no more manpower but that did not prevent an increase in the number of women seeking jobs. The ILO recorded a stronger demand by women for jobs as a result of declining real family income. Clearly, the country's economic problems were bringing about a change in need at the level of the people. However, this was not taken into account by planners, at least not in the 1972–6 government plan where the main concern was to create jobs for men (Chater, 1975). The plan expected the percentage of women seeking work to remain at the same level in 1976 that it had been in 1972, which it estimated at 24.7 per cent of the labour force. In fact, it was actually estimated to have gone up to 28.3 per cent of the active labour force in 1975.

Chater quoted government planners as saying that 'the majority of women do not actively seek work, but are ready when new opportunities present themselves' and 'for the great majority of women supply is equal to demand' (p.201). In fact, the male unemployment problem the government planners faced was so enormous that they could not afford to consider the needs of both men and women. The government was clearly happy to adopt the traditional view that men were the breadwinners and had to be planned for accordingly, and that women were the economic responsibility of their menfolk. Meanwhile, at the popular level, traditional social attitudes were being abandoned as women sought work for wages because of economic necessity.

Tunisia's problems are dwarfed by those of Egypt, given the sheer size of the country and its population. Of the Arab countries, Egypt has the longest history of women working in the modern sector, as it was one of the first to industrialise. (See Tucker, 1976, for an account of changes in the nature of women's work in the nineteenth and twentieth centuries.) By the 1980s, the Egyptian economy was in serious difficulty as the sources of revenue that had cushioned it during the 1970s – oil income, remittances from workers abroad, Suez Canal taxes and tourism – began to dry up. The unemployment figure was unofficially estimated in 1985 at some five million out of a labour force of 13 million, that is, just under 40 per cent, while the annual number of people coming onto the workforce totalled some 375,000.

As the country's economic condition worsened, some state policies that had been protective of the people were abandoned. For example, the Sadat regime scrapped the government's commitment to guarantee each university graduate, male or female, a job in government, which employed about 75 per cent of the non-agricultural labour force, if they could not find work elsewhere. The Nasser regime emphasised the right and obligation of all citizens to work; the Sadat regime urged women to balance their work and family duties, in accordance with Islamic law. (See Gran, 1977 for a good account of the impact of the Sadat years on Egyptian women.) It is obviously useful for a government facing serious employment problems to emphasise social attitudes that keep women at home as wives and mothers. There is an irony here, similar to the Tunisian case, in that the regime which introduced some amendments into the country's personal status laws, thus improving women's legal rights, adopted other policies that restricted their economic opportunities.

Anwar Sadat's 'open-door' economic policy – which meant opening Egypt up to foreign investment and to foreign goods – was meant to bring rapid prosperity. Egyptian intellectuals blame it for the further deterioration of Egypt's industrial base and for increasing the country's economic and political dependence on the West. After Sadat was assassinated in 1981, the new president, Hosni Mobarak, attempted to juggle some elements of the open-door system with those of the socialist system. He had not, by 1986, managed to solve the country's deep-rooted economic problems.

As in Tunisia, worsening economic conditions increased the number of women seeking waged labour. The writer Farida Nakkash pointed out, 'The economic pressures are so strong that any woman, veiled or otherwise, who lands a job tries to keep it in the face of growing unemployment' (AN, 1983). However, women's opportunities were restricted. It was no longer unusual to see job advertisements in Cairo newspapers saying that women need not apply, a depressing development for a country whose people were among the first in the region to have widespread access to education, which had contributed to the education and training of other Arabs, and where paid employment had long been accepted as a woman's right.

The open-door policy was also blamed for effecting certain negative changes in the structure of the female job market. According to a study by the National Centre for Social and Criminological Research, the number of cabarets in a Cairo district increased by 375 per cent in 1976 and 1977, and the number of furnished flats used for 'immoral purposes' increased by 1,000 per cent. Again, it is ironic that the Sadat regime, which made Islamic law the main source of legislation, apparently presided over a weakening of public morals.

Unemployment is the most serious problem the heavily populated Arab states will have to face for the rest of the century. It was not unusual, in the

1980s, to hear well-meaning officials from the sparsely populated countries remark that their heavily populated 'brotherly Arab countries' could best solve their unemployment problem by keeping the women at home (a 'solution' that has occurred to government officials throughout the world at different times). This was in spite of the fact that, on paper, Arab governments were committed to equality of opportunity for men and women.

## Arab labour legislation on women

The legislation regarding working women in the Arab world is fair by international standards. Labour laws provide for equal rights and opportunities for men and women, and specific legislation regarding women in areas such as maternity leave, time off for child care and protection from dismissal because of pregnancy is also adequate (see Table 6). It should be kept in mind that the legislation was most likely to be applied by public sector employers as there were few checks on private sector employers.

As is so often the case with governments, however, there is something of a gap between intention and implementation. This is perhaps best illustrated by the fate of Arab Convention No. 5 of 1976, on working women. The idea for a convention on Arab working women was sparked off by preparations for the UN Decade on Women. In fact, the Convention is a good example of the somewhat ambivalent response of world governments to the Decade: on the one hand, there were attempts to rise to the challenge of changing women's roles; on the other, the attempts were often half-hearted and lacked follow-through.

Convention No. 5 was adopted unanimously at a conference of Arab ministers of labour in 1976. Indeed, according to an eyewitness account, it did not even have to be voted on: it was applauded into being by the ministers, who seemed to be so amused by the whole exercise that they chuckled as they clapped (AN, 1984). Such conventions need to be ratified by at least three members of the Arab League before taking effect (the Arab League has 22 members, grouping the 21 Arab states and Palestine). Ten years after the Convention was adopted, only two members of the League, Iraq and Palestine, had ratified it. Arab governments were repeatedly urged to ratify the Convention, even if they did so with reservations, but to no avail. Tunisia was said to feel that its laws were more advanced than the Convention and so was reluctant to sign; Jordan was said to be on the brink of signing at several points; and the remaining Arab governments appeared eager to sign when approached, but failed to put pen to paper.

The Convention begins by declaring grandly that 'economic independence is the basis of political independence' and that 'human

Table 6   *Laws and regulations governing maternity protection, 1984*

|  | Maternity leave | % of wages paid during leave |
|---|---|---|
| ILO conventions | 12 weeks | $\frac{2}{3}$ salary |
| ALO conventions | 7 weeks | full salary |
| Algeria | 12 weeks | 50 |
| Bahrain | 45 days | 100 |
| Egypt | 50 days | 100 |
| Iraq | 10 weeks | 100 |
| Jordan | 6 weeks | 50 |
| Kuwait | 70 days | 100 |
| Lebanon | 40 days | 100 |
| Libya | 3 months | 100 |
| Morocco | 12 weeks | 50 for 10 weeks |
| Oman | 45 days | 100 |
| Saudi Arabia | 10 weeks | 50 or 100 according to length of service |
| Sudan | 8 weeks | 100 |
| Syria | 50–60 days | 50–70 |
| Tunisia | 30 days | $\frac{2}{3}$ salary |
| U.A.E. | 45 days | 50 or 100 |
| Yemen A.R. | 70 days | 70 |
| Yemen P.D.R. | 60 days | 100 |

*Source:* Henry Azzam, 1979 and ILO, 1985.

resources are the principal means of achieving economic independence'. Women, representing as they do half these human resources, 'must be involved in development on the widest possible scale, and on the basis of complete equality with men'. Among other provisions, it reaffirms women's right to engage in all fields of economic activity; to equality of opportunity, of pay and of promotion; to equality of access to education and vocational training; and to generous terms for maternity leave.

Even though the Convention's history was unglamorous, a process was set in motion. Alongside the efforts to draw up the Convention, the ministers of labour, working within the Arab Labour Organisation, decided in 1973 to establish the Working Women's Committee. (The Arab Labour Organisation is one of the bodies of the Arab League; it is based on a three-way partnership between governments, represented by the ministers of labour, employers and labour unions.) The ALO Working Women's Committee formally began its work in 1976 from its Tunis headquarters.

The Working Women's Committee was hampered by a small budget and a minute staff. Only one professional was employed, the woman head of committee. Still, it managed to organise meetings for working women and to tackle some difficulties. For example, Arab governments had a tendency to send male delegates to meetings and seminars for working women. In 1981, the Committee was able to organise an annual training course exclusively for women at the ALO institutes for training and workers' information, based in Baghdad and Algiers (AN, 1984). The Committee also conducted studies on subjects like: conditions of Arab working woman; access to information on workers' rights and trade unions; day-care centres in Africa; labour-sharing within the family; eradicating illiteracy; the role of women's federations; and working women and trade unions in the industrialised countries.

## The gap between theory and practice

Thus, while in theory Arab states were dedicated to providing opportunities for women through planning and legislation, this was not always reflected in practice. Differences between theory and practice can also be seen when it comes to the facilities needed by working women, even in the case of countries that seek to involve women in the modern labour sector. The experience of Salma (not her real name), a young woman government official in the Yemen Arab Republic, is a good illustration.

Yemen had lost a substantial proportion of its male labour force through migration to the oil-rich states of the Gulf, and the Government encouraged women to take part in the development process. In the modern sector, Yemeni women were soon active in the Sanaa-based government departments. Although the family network was strong, some women felt the need for child-care facilities. Salma decided to try to establish a government-run nursery to help her colleagues, although she herself was not married. It is worth recounting her experience in her own words, as her story is typical of women entering the newly established government sectors in the Arab Gulf countries.

When I came back to Yemen from my studies abroad, I thought I would have problems as a working woman. I applied for a government job and I was surprised by how quickly and easily I was appointed. I was astonished to find such a large number of women working in my department. My superiors do not treat me like a new graduate; they give me serious assignments and expect me to contribute. They've sent me on training sessions although I have not yet completed my first year; they're really encouraging me.

One of the first women to work in government told us what it was like when she joined some ten years earlier. At that time, not many believed that she had anything to contribute and they used to belittle her efforts. She says there have been big changes. Before, she used to walk from one floor to the next and there was not a

85

woman in sight; now there are five or six girls on each floor. She has reached the level of undersecretary. When we see her we feel we are respected, that we can do what she did; it is always more difficult for the first ones who have to pave the way. I also feel there have been changes. Before, it was considered shameful for girls to drive, now I and my sisters drive. Necessity brings change.

There are only two state-run nurseries in Sanaa, but working women need many more, so I decided to prepare a study on this. Some women are setting up nurseries in their homes here and there, but nobody supervises these to see whether they are well-run. Some women leave their children with their families. My sister works, and she has two children, one in school and one an infant. Every morning she brings the baby to my mother, and picks it up again in the evening. She was working when she married, and she cannot imagine not working. I can't imagine sitting at home either.

I wanted to start with one nursery for a few offices close to each other because we couldn't afford to do more at this stage, although we need a lot more nurseries, even for university students. Several women students who are continuing their education after marriage have babies to take care of, and some drop out as a result. While I was doing my survey, many men expressed interest in the nursery because their wives also worked and they wanted somewhere to bring their children. Often, if you have a project, the government will offer some financing, and you can raise matching financing from foreign aid donors – although it is sometimes difficult to get financing for small projects. At the end of my survey, I presented my project. Unfortunately, it was shelved for 'future consideration', where it sits side by side with a project to revive national handicrafts. (AN, 1984)

As can be seen from the above account, women's integration into the modern sector was fairly trouble-free, and when the opportunity presented itself women both worked and studied – and social attitudes changed. Salma's experience was typical of young, university-educated women in the Arab countries with recently developed nation-state structures. Their job satisfaction was high, and they found that their colleagues respected and encouraged them. It should be recalled that their numbers were too small to be threatening and that there was no unemployment problem. The young woman's experience brought up other issues raised by the type of development often adopted by Third World countries and international development agencies: the focus on large projects at the expense of small, community-oriented ones, although the latter were likely to be more useful and successful. Finally, although the Government enouraged women's entry into the modern sector, there were not yet enough facilities to enable them to do so.

### Need and opportunity at the popular level

As the above discussion has sought to show, if women are to be integrated into the wage-labour force a country must need manpower and must provide the opportunity for workers through planning and legislation. The question needs to be asked at the popular level. Do Arab women avail themselves of the opportunities to work and what sort of difficulties do they face because of traditional attitudes? Some answers to these questions were given by a survey on Syrian women working in the public sector (quoted in Rahmeh, 1985, pp.28–33). The 119 women surveyed worked in mixed surroundings; of the total, 15 per cent were in managerial positions, supervising both men and women, and the rest worked under male supervisors. Most of the women worked because of economic need.

Nearly half the women were married, six being widowed and eight divorced. Questioned as to how they coped with home and career, 45 per cent of the married women and 42 per cent of single women said they found the double burden difficult and exhausting, and that they would welcome the existence of low-priced restaurants and ready-made foods. The majority, 81 per cent of the married women and 88 per cent of the single women, said that the male members of the family did not help with the household chores. Some 80 per cent of the respondents owned labour-saving household equipment, with some 70 per cent owning electrical appliances.

As regards child care, most married women felt that their situation was unsatisfactory. Some 51 per cent left their infants with their mothers or other relatives, 18 per cent placed them in nurseries, and 18 per cent had no fixed place to leave their children. Many of the mothers complained of the insufficient number of nurseries, and the mothers who used nurseries complained of the distance from home and of high fees. The mothers also faced difficulties if their children fell ill; 42 per cent had taken leave without pay in such cases. As regards the two months of maternity leave with pay to which they were entitled, 57 per cent of the mothers found this insufficient; 36 per cent had taken more leave at half pay, and another 20 per cent had taken a third month without pay.

Commenting on their living conditions, 34 per cent of the married women complained that they had to live with their in-laws because they could not find housing; 57 per cent lived in their own homes with their families. The single women all lived with their families or with relatives and neighbours. Few of the working women felt they had enough leisure time. Of the single women, 36 per cent said their families were opposed to their having social or political activities, as compared to 15 per cent of the married women; however, 75 per cent of the total had no such complaints.

In spite of the difficulties, 75 per cent of the working women were in favour of women's work outside the home. Of the total, 57 per cent were content with their work. The majority, 84 per cent, said they felt self-confident as working women, and that they were equal to doing the work of men. The majority also said they enjoyed the respect of their husbands and families, as well as of their colleagues and society at large.

This survey showed that working in mixed surroundings was clearly not a problem, that many women felt they were free to enjoy a social life (which would consist largely of visiting friends), and that the nuclear family living in its own household was considered the norm. The problems these working women faced were by and large the same as women faced worldwide. There were no complaints of harassment on the job or of discrimination. The majority were happy with their work, had a good self-image and felt they enjoyed the respect of colleagues and society.

However, the women in this survey, who came from middle to lower-middle socioeconomic backgrounds, were fairly privileged. They worked in the public sector, which in the Arab world is seen to offer the most valued and respectable careers for women, both in terms of job security and because the nature of the work is non-manual. In this case, women were eager to avail themselves of the opportunity to work to satisfy economic need. This was not necessarily the case for women from lower socio-economic backgrounds, as was shown by Mona Hammam's survey of 148 Egyptian factory workers at a textile plant outside Cairo, which employed 400 females out of a workforce of 1,150 in 1975 (Hammam, 1980). Hammam found that job satisfaction was limited, although the factory was chosen for the survey because it offered various services such as a day-care centre, a consumer cooperative and literacy classes. Of the sample, 65 per cent of the women were single, 25 per cent were married and 10 per cent were divorced. All worked because of economic need.

The working mother's day began at 4:00 am when she woke up, prepared breakfast for her husband and children and then went to catch the bus to work. If the factory worker had no male relatives to accompany her to the bus stop, she was likely to face harassment as it was considered unaccept-able for a woman to be out on her own at that time. After a full day on the job, she would shop – 80 per cent of the workers did not own a refrigerator – cook and care for the children. Not many women liked to use the factory's day-care centre, which was viewed as a last resort. The centre was equipped only with bare necessities; the children were tended by illiterate nannies and were offered no instruction or toys to play with. The workers would have had to contribute about 5 per cent of their wages to use the centre. Finally, they felt it was unfair that the children should be subjected to their gruelling schedule. As one mother put it, 'If we didn't *have* to work, we'd take care of them ourselves' (p.61).

Hammam found that, although the working women took pride in the fact that they were contributing members of society, factory work as they experienced it was not seen as a suitable occupation for women. All the single respondents planned to leave their jobs when they married. However, many women who left the factory on marriage found they had to return because of economic pressure. The married women were determined that their children would have an education so as not to end up like them. They had been forced into tiring, poorly paid jobs because of severe economic need. If they had been able to afford it, they would rather not have availed themselves of the opportunity to work, unlike their Syrian counterparts; this was not surprising, given the burden they had to carry, and the lack of compensations such as job satisfaction and respect from society.

Certainly, the preferred roles for many Arab women are still those of wife and mother, and few Arabs view nurseries and day-care centres as an ideal answer to child-rearing. However, the factory workers' determination to give their children an education indicated that they were not averse to women's paid employment outside the home, but that they hoped their children would have a chance of less gruelling, more respected employment.

## Work and public activity: two sets of attitudes

In fact, there are really two parallel traditional attitudes that coexist under the heading of 'social obstacles to women's work outside the home'. The first attitude is to women's work as such, and this is not a serious obstacle. When there are proper conditions and when there is economic need, resistance to women working outside the home disappears rapidly. The second attitude is to women's unrestricted movement in the public sphere, and this is less easily overcome. This was hinted at in the example of the Syrian women above. All the single women lived with families and friends, rather than on their own, and some 36 per cent of the single women faced restrictions on social or political activities outside their work.

The resistance to giving women complete freedom of movement in the public sphere stems from the social concern to maintain women's honour, which is the key to the family honour, and from the belief that uncontrolled mixing of the sexes will lead to the breakdown of public morals and the social order. If a woman were to take a job that was seen as dishonourable, she would be discouraged from that line of work, but not necessarily from work altogether. In Saudi Arabia, for example, the dominant social attitude is that women working in the same area as men is dishonourable in itself. Efforts are therefore made to create opportunities for women in segregated conditions, rather than to prevent women from working at all.

Women's involvement in paid employment outside the home does gradually lessen resistance to their involvement in public activity. A good illustration of these attitudes comes from the work experience of a young

Tunisian woman, who complained that on the job she was 'treated like a man', and received the same wages and benefits, while in the family she was still treated like a woman, that is, she was not allowed much freedom of movement. (I am indebted to anthropologist Amina Minns for some of the observations relating to this woman's story, and to that of Umm Qassem in the following chapter.) The young woman, Zohra, was 26 years old in 1982, and worked as a nutritionist in a Tunisian clinic in a lower socioeconomic district.

I was a child when my parents got divorced. Traditionally the father keeps the children but my mother fought to keep me and bring me up herself. Our society is conservative, but my mother isn't a rigid woman. She always encouraged me to study and to travel, and she wanted me to be free. She had no chance of an education but she taught herself how to read and write.

Zohra lived with her uncle's family in Tunis, where her mother had gone after her divorce.

I love my uncle's family and am grateful to them, but for some years our relationship has been strained. They don't let me do anything but my work. They won't let me learn how to drive. It's always, 'What will the rest of the family say' and 'What will the neighbours say'. So I do what I want behind their backs. For example, I plan to continue my studies in America and so I am learning English. I've taken up sport and dancing. When I took up yoga, they found out and tried to stop me, but I continued in secret. The family doesn't restrict boys as much as girls; they let them drive for example.

What do I understand by the concept of freedom? Freedom for me doesn't mean going out and having a good time. It means doing what you want when you want. They want me to think like them, to be like them. But we don't share the same ideas about anything. Whenever we start to discuss something, it always ends in a quarrel. Family life is very important, and I don't want to see it break up. But we have lost the warmth in my family. We live under the same roof, but it's like living alone. And I think, if I'm going to live alone, why wait until I'm 40 or 50? Sometimes because of our quarrels they tell me to pack up and go. So one day I said, 'OK, it's fine by me, I'll go', and I began to hunt around for a flat. But then they were so full of remorse I gave up the idea. They need me. I do a lot of things around the house and I contribute part of my salary. Now they are starting to accept the fact that I come home late sometimes and they don't say anything. (AN, 1982)

Zohra's story is typical of the growing number of young women in the urban labour force from lower-middle, middle and upper-middle socio-economic backgrounds. Her traditional family had accepted Zohra's education and employment fairly readily; however, they were much stricter when it came to her activities outside work. Innocuous as these were, they were seen to pose more of a threat to her honour, and therefore to her family's honour, than her work did. Her story also illustrates the growing generation gap, and how compromise is hammered out, with some gains for individual liberty and at some cost to tradition. A woman's work, and subsequent economic independence, does result in some social independence, but traditional attitudes relating to women's involvement in public activities will take longer to change than attitudes to women's work.

## The third condition: ability

Women do join the wage-labour force if the conditions of need and opportunity are met. Opportunity, in the case of Arab women at present, often must include work which is socially acceptable. The third condition affecting women's integration into the workforce, ability – that is, the education and training opportunities governments provide and the skills that women possess – is a problematic area for the Arab workforce as a whole. Even countries with serious unemployment problems also suffer from shortages of skilled manpower in certain areas.

In spite of the advances in education in a country like Tunisia, for example, about 54 per cent of labour force entrants barely had an elementary education and 33 per cent were illiterate (ILO, 1983, p.93). The standard of education in the whole region remains low, with the exception of some private schools. The scepticism of the Moroccan peasants towards schooling reported by Mernissi in the early part of this chapter is not unjustified. Arab schools are not yet really geared to producing people with skills suitable to their environment. In the 1980s, government planners became more concerned about encouraging students to enlist in vocational secondary schools that would give them a better opportunity to find employment after graduation and that would also meet the country's requirements for skilled labour. (Table 3 gives some indication of enrolment by Arab students in vocational secondary schools.)

Most vocational training for women in the Arab world is still in traditional fields like handicrafts, home economics and secretarial skills. There are a few exceptions, here and there, as is shown by a project undertaken by the Moroccan Bureau of Vocational Education and Job Development (TME, 1984). Until 1979, training for women was restricted to courses in commercial studies; it was believed that women lacked interest in other fields. In 1979, classes were opened exclusively for women in electricity, mechanical drawing, electronics, accounting and construction drafting. To recruit applicants, the Bureau changed the wording on posters in high schools to include both the feminine and the masculine forms of the words 'technician' and 'student'. Hundreds of women applied for the 75 places available. The classes were eventually integrated, and a wider range of trades was offered. By 1984, girls represented some 17 per cent of total enrolment. The Bureau also managed to overcome initial resistance from employers to employing women.

A less successful, if well-meaning, training project was undertaken for rural women in the Libyan oasis of Kufra in the Sahara, where farming families from various oases had been resettled (Allaghi, 1981). While the families found the living conditions at Kufra much healthier and easier than in their previous homes, the women had practically no outlets for productive activity although they had been active in the oases of origin, like all rural women, in areas like food processing, breeding animals and weaving.

A rural development centre had been set up to train women. Allaghi found that the young wives who did not attend the Women's Centre believed the Kufra resettlement project had created boredom and excessive leisure time. However, the Centre only offered a nine-month course in skills such as sewing, knitting and cooking. There were some complaints that this was too little time in which to learn skills. There were also complaints that there was no follow-up after the girls graduated; the sewing machines they were given broke down and no one in Kufra was able to repair them; the material they needed to work with was not available in the shops. Most seriously, the training they had been given had no relevance to their surroundings. There was no need for knitted products on the oasis; still, some of the Centre's students were hopeful that they might be able to sell the woollens in other parts of the country.

The majority of parents and daughters interviewed valued education, and a substantial number of them wanted their daughters to go to school when the school was built. In addition, the majority of respondents (88.6 per cent of daughters, 64 per cent of mothers and 68.2 per cent of husbands) supported women's work outside the home, so long as it was respectable and segregated. However, the women were not greatly involved in work on the farm, which occupied only 14.3 per cent of the daughters' time and 16 per cent of the mothers', and there were no other opportunities for women's work outside the home. This project shows that, while some effort had been made by planners to cater for women by setting up a training centre, neither the training offered at the Centre nor that likely to be offered in the school when it was built met the needs of the community. Nor was any provision made for engaging women in productive activities, although most of those surveyed were interested in women's work.

## Need, opportunity, ability

The foregoing discussion has sought to show that social and cultural attitudes towards women's work are just one factor among many impeding women's involvement in the modern sector. Three conditions – need, opportunity, ability – must be met before women can be integrated into the wage-labour force. All three must be taken into account at the state and popular levels in assessing why women's participation in the wage-labour force is low. The situation differs from state to state. In countries like Egypt and Tunisia, for example, men and women need paid employment, but the state cannot accommodate them. Unemployment in the heavily populated, poorer Arab countries is the result of deep-rooted economic problems, and women cannot be fully integrated into the modern sector until these are solved. Moreover, individual Arab countries cannot solve their economic problems within their borders. The Arab world, in common with other parts of the Third World, needs to redefine its broad development strategy, and this means transforming regional cooperation from dream to reality.

As regards opportunity, there is ambivalence at the regional and country levels about integrating women in development, in spite of official declarations. Integration cannot be achieved by half-hearted measures or by projects here and there. This was underlined by the UN in the End-of-Decade documents, when the difference between the concepts of 'self-help' and 'self-reliance' was outlined:

The concept of individual self-reliance cannot be equated, or even directly related, to the concept of self-help, however valuable it might be. Individual self-reliance is geared towards defining broader national development strategies . . . It is precisely in the integration of women in development that the fundamental inadequacy of [the self-help] concept becomes apparent: no partial programmes, such as the manufacture of souvenirs or sewing, can in themselves ensure a genuine social and productive integration of women in development. (UN, 1984a, p.216)

Clearly, more commitment is necessary on the part of governments, within a redefined national strategy, to involve women in the modern sector.

Meanwhile, the region as a whole is weak on appropriate education and skills, something that neither the state nor the individual can afford. The young population places a heavy burden on wage earners at the family level; it also places a heavy burden on the state to produce more in order to reduce imports. A larger, better trained labour force including both men and women is vital and the finance to bring this about must be made available through the reallocation of national and regional resources.

How the factors of need, opportunity and ability conspire to involve women in the workforce – and to keep them out – will be further elaborated in the coming pages through case studies on Jordan and the Gulf states. In the final analysis, the integration of women in the wage-labour force hangs on a solution to the Arab economic crisis. This in turn depends on Arab political will to achieve real national independence and regional self-reliance. If the past is anything to go by, little will be achieved in the foreseeable future.

Chapter 4

# Jordanian women's 'liberating' forces: inflation and labour migration

We need to broaden the base of our employment market by turning every available Jordanian into a skilled worker.

*Jawad Anani, Minister of Labour in 1982*

In the previous discussion, the point was made that cultural tradition is not the main constraint on women's work for wages outside the home, and that attitudes change quite rapidly if the need and opportunity arise. Indeed, three conditions – need, opportunity and ability – must be met at the state and popular levels before women can be fully integrated into the workforce. Jordan makes an ideal case study to illustrate this argument further. It is a labour exporter, and the country's development process has suffered because of the loss of skilled manpower. It is also a labour importer that faces some of the same problems as the oil-rich, labour-importing Arab Gulf countries. Moreover, the Government has pursued policies favourable to women, particularly after the establishment of a woman-headed Ministry of Social Development in 1979. Finally, the country has been better able to provide social services than some other Arab states, and the people are quite highly skilled.

## Need at the state level: from unemployment to labour shortage

Jordan's population was estimated at three million by the mid-1980s. Nearly two-thirds are Palestinians, whose forced dispersal from their homeland swelled Jordan's population in 1948 and again in 1967. In the mid-1980s, the main demographic problems were the high birth rate and the youth of the population – about 53 per cent were estimated to be below the age of 15. Only a quarter of the population was counted as economically active, a small formal labour force because of the youth of the population and the low participation of women.

Until 1973, unemployment was a serious problem, and was estimated at about 14 per cent of the labour force. By 1975, however, the unemployment

94

rate had fallen to some 2 per cent, because of the rapid rise in the numbers of Jordanians and Palestinians moving to the Gulf in search of jobs and better pay. By the early 1980s, the number of Jordanians and Palestinian/Jordanians working abroad was said to be over 300,000, nearly half the labour force. Remittances rose from $22 million in 1972 to $1.2 billion in 1981. The remittances helped to finance Jordan's negative trade balance and provided the banking sector with liquidity for credit. However, labour migration proved to be a mixed blessing since remittances fuelled inflation and contributed to an increase in consumer imports (Keely and Saket, 1984).

Serious manpower shortages began to be felt in various sectors of the economy by 1975, when the proportion of the Jordanian workforce outside the country was estimated at 28 per cent of the total, and at 46 per cent of workers in the non-agricultural sector (Birks and Sinclair, 1980, p.48). For instance, some 1,800 Jordanian electricians were said to be working in Kuwait, leaving almost none in Jordan. Salaries in Jordan rose, a further factor in fuelling inflation. In agriculture, there was a critical shortage of unskilled and semi-skilled labour, which was partly resolved by importing labour from Egypt, Pakistan and other Asian countries. These replacement migrants also worked in construction and other fields needing semi-skilled and skilled labour. They were a source of cheap labour since Jordanians had begun to expect higher wages. The number of migrant workers in Jordan was estimated at 130,000 in the early 1980s.

In spite of the large influx of foreign labour, there were still manpower gaps in certain sectors. In fact, the Government's second five-year plan, 1981–5, forecast that the country would need 254,000 additional workers. After taking into account the male and female graduates who would come onto the market during this period, the Government estimated that a further 70,000 workers would be needed. It expected this labour deficit to be met by increasing women's participation in the labour force, by importing labour from other Arab countries, and by Jordanian migrants returning home (Sharayhe, 1985).

## Ability: the female labour pool

Thus, at the state level, there was pressing need for manpower, partly fulfilling the first of the conditions for women's integration in the workforce set above. To meet this need, the Government made a conscious decision to resort to Jordanian womanpower. There was scope to increase women's participation in the formal labour force, given that some estimates in the early 1970s placed this as low as 4 per cent. Moreover, the pool of female

Table 7    *Development of education in Jordan*

| Cycle | School year | Males | Females | % Female |
|---|---|---|---|---|
| Elementary | 1975–6 | 206,618 | 179,394 | 46 |
|  | 1984–5 | 258,814 | 245,412 | 49 |
| Preparatory | 1975–6 | 67,388 | 48,229 | 42 |
|  | 1984–5 | 108,339 | 96,463 | 47 |
| Secondary | 1975–6 | 25,394 | 16,743 | 40 |
|  | 1984–5 | 49,917 | 46,685 | 49 |
| Secondary vocational | 1975–6 | 4,548 | 1,893 | 29 |
|  | 1984–5 | 18,679 | 10,347 | 36 |
| Higher education institutes | 1975–6 | 7,904 | 3,969 | 33 |
|  | 1984–5 | 30,070 | 23,825 | 44 |
| [University | 1984–5 | 15,875 | 10,054 | 39] |

*Source:* Ayesh, 1985, based on Jordanian Government figures.

labour could be tapped without too much extra expenditure on the Government's part, as there had already been substantial investment in women's education over the years.

Education in Jordan is compulsory for nine years, and is provided by both public and private schools. Table 7 shows the impressive increase in female education: by 1984–5, girls accounted for some 48 per cent of the total school enrolment. Therefore, the third condition set above for women's participation in the workforce, ability, was met in Jordan at the state and popular levels. However, there was still not enough emphasis on vocational training for either men or women to produce all the skilled manpower the country needed, and most vocational training that did exist for women focussed on traditional areas.

Education is not, by itself, a sufficient condition for women's integration into the wage-labour force, although it is a necessary one. Female education was, in the early 1970s at least, pursued on an 'in case' basis: it broadened women's horizons, produced better wives and mothers, and was there 'in case' a marriage ended in widowhood or divorce and the woman had to support herself. As the estimated rate of female participation in the labour force showed, women's work for wages at that time was still very much the exception. Education does enable women to enter the modern sector gradually; full integration requires that other conditions, especially that of need at the popular level, be met, as will be seen later.

Women in Jordan had begun to move gradually into the wage-labour force in the early 1940s and 1950s, when there was a growing demand for

Table 8   *Occupation structure of non-agricultural female labour force*[a]

|  | Female labour force by occupation | | % of females to total labour force | |
|---|---|---|---|---|
|  | 1961 | 1976 | 1961 | 1976 |
| Professional, technical and related workers | 28.7 | 57.7 | 28.1 | 41.4 |
| Administrative and managerial workers | 0.1 | 0.8 | 0.4 | 3.5 |
| Clerical and related workers | 6.9 | 19.4 | 5.0 | 19.5 |
| Sales workers | 1.0 | 2.4 | 0.5 | 1.7 |
| Sub-total white-collar workers | 36.7 | 80.3 | 8.2 | 20.1 |
| Production and related, transport workers and labourers | 40.3 | 11.3 | 3.8 | 3.2 |
| Service workers | 23.0 | 8.4 | 11.2 | 9.7 |
| Total | 100.0 | 100.0 | 5.3 | 11.8 |

[a] Includes armed forces.
*Source:* Mujahid, 1985.

women in office work. In the 1950s, according to Woodsmall, there was 'said to be a strong body of public opinion which believes that women are taking up men's jobs' (p.59, 1956). There had been a ban on the employment of women in government offices until 1947, and married women were not allowed to teach (p.59). Most of the women who had taken up non-agricultural occupations by the 1970s were teachers or civil servants. By the 1980s, it was quite accepted for women, even married women, to work for wages outside the home. Only certain private sector employers, including some prestigious banking establishments, still refused to employ married women.

The figures for female participation in the non-agricultural labour force given in Table 8 are based on the 1961 Government census, the 1975 labour force census and the 1976 household survey. (As noted in the previous chapter, statistics in the region should be treated with caution.) They would appear to indicate that the proportion of women to the total labour force had increased from 5.3 to 11.8 per cent. Analysing the trends, Mujahid (1985) pointed out the shifts in occupational patterns: the proportion of blue-collar and service workers in the female labour force had declined dramatically, while the proportion of white-collar workers had nearly doubled. The increase in female non-agricultural participation had come mostly from the educated sectors of the population.

Government figures showed that the percentage of women working in professions that required university education in the sciences nearly doubled between 1970 and 1975, from 4.9 to 9.3 per cent, with the percentage of men falling accordingly. The percentage of women in professions requiring university education in the arts rose from 9.1 in 1970 to 15.2 in 1975, while the percentage in technical professions that required post-secondary education nearly trebled from 14.3 to 38.7 per cent (Harfoush, 1980). The 1975 survey showed that women earned nearly 85 per cent of the men's salary for the same job, which was high by world standards.

## Creating opportunity: planning for women

Government interest in increasing the number of women in the labour force became clear when the Second Symposium of Manpower Development in April 1976 focussed specifically on the role of Jordanian women. The Symposium adopted some 55 resolutions to modernise labour legislation, enforce universal and compulsory education, expand work opportunities for women, provide training and placement services, conduct research on obstacles and attitudes preventing women's participation, enforce the principle of equal pay for equal work, and involve women at the policy-making level. The 1976–80 five-year plan emphasised the need for a new concept of social organisation, whereby all sectors of the population would participate effectively in development: women's participation in the wage labour force would be significantly increased, and family planning policies would be adopted.

The Government's need for manpower had clearly moved it into meeting the second condition for women's integration into the workforce – opportunity; that is, providing the proper environment for women's employment through planning and legislation. In February 1977, a Directorate of Women's Affairs was set up at the Ministry of Labour to follow up and implement the resolutions of the Manpower Symposium. However, the head of the new Women's Directorate, Inam Mufti, resigned about a year after she was appointed. She was reportedly frustrated by the fact that everything had to pass through time-consuming bureaucratic channels, which made it difficult to implement serious programmes; moreover, the Directorate's budget was quite small.

The Government was still determined to increase and upgrade the level of women's participation, and in December 1979, a Ministry of Social Development was established. Inam Mufti was appointed minister, becoming the first woman minister to serve in a Jordanian cabinet. The Ministry had a budget of $6.4 million in 1980, and a staff of 99 working in its offices in Amman. It had directorates and offices spread throughout the country, and several social service and training centres and institutes were attached to the Ministry. The focus was on development and not on welfare; it was felt that, while economic growth had been rapid, social development had not kept up. The Ministry was responsible for all population sectors, with particular emphasis on women, the poor, juveniles, the handicapped and other disadvantaged groups.

After some effort, the Directorate of Women's Affairs was transferred from the Labour Ministry to the Ministry of Social Development. Mufti's plans included organising programmes around the country and not just in the capital, as had previously been the case, in order to stem the flow of rural–urban migration. She wanted to involve other ministries in areas of mutual concern, and she provided direct support to women by making jobs available through her ministry and by offering flexible and part-time work schedules (Harfoush, 1980). By 1982, Mufti felt she had made some progress in overcoming the problems that had faced the Women's Director-ate: 'The Directorate was limited to the small problems of working women. I felt a much wider responsibility. Now, since I'm the person who decides on policy matters, the role of the department is much wider, and we have succeeded in building a network of institutions to back up the role of the Women's Directorate' (AN, 1982).

## Self-reliance vs self-help

The Ministry's policy outlined above showed an understanding of the difference between the concepts of self-help and self-reliance, to which reference was made in the previous chapter. As defined by the UN, self-help was limited in scope to small projects to assist a particular group of people; self-reliance involved drawing up broad national strategies for develop-ment. Self-help strategies on their own, the UN argued, would not integrate women in development, or indeed achieve meaningful and lasting change for developing populations as a whole. Clearly, the Women's Directorate under the Ministry of Labour had been limited to a self-help approach. Under the Ministry of Social Development, the emphasis was on self-reliance. The Ministry adopted a comprehensive approach to the needs of the country and its people in seeing how best to assist disadvantaged groups, and it involved other government departments in drawing up and implementing strategies.

In 1981, Mufti set up a Higher Steering Committee for Women and Family Affairs, which included four ministers (social development, labour, health and education), the president of a university, officials from the Women's Directorate, and prominent citizens. The Committee's role was to make suggestions, debate and review projects and programmes to integrate women in development. The Ministry was also coordinated with the Jordanian Women's Federation, which was formed in 1981 by some 30 existing women's organisations. There was criticism of the way the Federation had been established, and some of the women's groups complained of more Government influence at the expense of non-governmental organisations.

An example of the type of activity undertaken by the Ministry of Social Development in the early 1980s was a project to train women on the maintenance and repair of household appliances. This was a refreshing break in the pattern of training women in traditional fields such as handicrafts. And, as noted above, Jordan was particularly short of electricians, who all seemed to have found jobs in Kuwait. The project was undertaken with the cooperation of the Ministry of Education and the Vocational Training Corporation, and was financed by the Voluntary Fund set up by the UN during the Decade for Women (which was renamed the 'Development Fund' in 1985). The organisers planned to enable women to earn extra income, as well as to help fill the gaps created by the shortage of skilled manpower by training women in technical fields. This is an example of the difference between a self-help approach, which would have been limited to generating income for women, and a self-reliant approach which took the needs of national and social development into account.

Another Ministry project in the early 1980s was the 'Syrian goats breeding project'. The planners aimed to increase rural women's income-earning capacity, to improve the quality and quantity of food available to rural families (it was noted that families were less self-sufficient in food than they had been in the past) and to improve village living conditions. The Women's Directorate involved the Agriculture Ministry Rural Development and Cooperatives' Section, the Rural Women's Association, and students from the Social Services Institute. Before any action was taken, a study was prepared on two villages selected as pilots for the project. The project was then discussed with local authorities and the women in the two villages so that it would gain community acceptance.

A trial group of 10 families was chosen from the applicants in the two villages. Each family was given some Syrian goats, a breed chosen because they produced two or three kids a year and lived off left-overs. The families thus had dairy products for home consumption and sale; when they had a dozen goats, they were to give two to a family that had not received any on the first round. The project also involved the women and their families in building pens for the goats and hutches for the poultry, planting vegetables and fruit trees, painting village houses and beautifying the area. Information on health care was supplied and anti-illiteracy programmes were provided where necessary. It was hoped, as one member of the Higher Committee summed up, that the project would enable 'the village to be self-dependent economically and serve as a centre of activity as it was in the past, which will curtail emigration to the city' (AN, 1982).

## Legislation and 'consciousness-raising'

In 1981, the Government began to examine amendments to the country's labour law, which had been passed in 1960, so that it would reflect the fact that more women were entering the wage-labour force. In keeping with the pattern in the rest of the region, the majority of women who were already in the workforce were single. Government figures for 1976 showed that in the 20 to 44 age group, some 45 per cent of the women in the formal labour force were single, 30 per cent were divorced, 10 per cent were widowed, and only 4 per cent were married. Clearly, married women were an untapped source of modern-sector labour. Indeed, many of the amendments that were being considered to the labour legislation dealt with improving conditions for working mothers by increasing maternity leave (from six to 10 weeks), increasing pay levels during maternity leave, prohibiting employers from dismissing women during pregnancy, and making it necessary for institutions that employed a minimum number of women to provide day-care centres.

Another element of Government policy was the effort to broaden public awareness of the issue, through opening it up for debate. In this, it was enthusiastically backed by the media, which was not surprising since radio and television were Government-controlled, while the press was indirectly controlled through the Government and other subsidies. Seminars were held regularly on issues relating to working women, and national ceremonies were organised to applaud women's contribution to public life and the economy. Such activities were often sponsored by the royal family and addressed by top officials, thus ensuring lavish media coverage.

For example, a seminar entitled 'Women's contribution to Jordan's labour force' was held at the Amman Chamber of Industry in May 1983 to commemorate International Labour Day. It was organised by the Business and Professional Women's Club, and brought together employers and working women. The *Jordan Times* gave about half a page to coverage of the seminar in its 4 May 1984 edition. A paper prepared by the Minister of Labour estimated that the Government was investing some $131 million annually (including investment on education) to broaden the pool of female labour. He said women's earnings had brought them new economic power, which he estimated at about $145 million annually. (Women's total income was much higher because of income from inheritance and other sources.) There were more businesswomen, whose establishments produced at least $73 million annually. There was also a growing trend to entrust the household budget to women. The Minister estimated that women decided on nearly one-third the total spendable income in Jordan, or about $870 million.

Another example of consciousness-raising was a seminar entitled 'Skilled women leadership' organised by the Women's Directorate in coordination with the Public Administration Institute. According to the 8 September 1984 edition of the *Jordan Times*, women from various professions were invited to the three-day seminar, at which several university professors gave papers. The participants noted that there were still too few women in high posts, and discussed ways to increase their number.

The Jordanian media invariably celebrated Women's Day and Mother's Day with extensive articles on and interviews with working women and female students. 'How do Jordan's women evaluate the progress of women's work in the country?' wondered the 8 March 1982 edition of *Ad-Dustour*, on the occasion of women's day. 'Students argue whether the role, status of Jordanian women can be improved' declared the 9 March 1985 edition of the *Jordan Times*.

The 1982 Mother's Day was celebrated with a seminar on working mothers, under the patronage of King Hussain's wife, Queen Noor, and organised by the Ministry of Social Development in coordination with the Business and Professional Women's Club. Speakers reviewed the draft labour legislation, which was then about to be submitted to the cabinet for debate, and the participants set up a committee to make recommendations for further improvements. On the 1985 Women's Day, 31 Jordanian women from the banking sector received shields for which, according to the 19 March edition of the *Jordan Times*, Queen Noor had chosen the inscription: 'Today, the nation honours each Jordanian working woman and takes pride in her contribution to the community and the country'.

The media was active in espousing the cause of women, but was it doing enough? This was discussed at a two-day seminar on the role of the media in promoting women's integration in the development process in early 1984. The seminar was inaugurated by Information Minister Laila Sharaf, who had just been appointed in a new cabinet, and who was the first female information minister in the region. This was a significant step in Jordan: the post was more powerful than it might be in other countries, as the minister had to be in tune with the King's thinking, which involved having regular access to the main decision-maker in the country. (Sharaf resigned after some months in office as she did not feel she had a free hand in deciding information policy.)

## Attitudes of Jordanian employers

Meanwhile, the Government was also aware of the importance of employers' attitudes to the question of womanpower. In 1981, the Ministry of Labour conducted a survey on female students, to assess supply, and on employers, to assess demand for working women (Malki, 1981). The aim was to propose measures for increased participation by women in the wage-labour force so as to lessen reliance on imported labour. Significantly, the study recognised that 'social values and attitudes are not necessarily the impediments to a woman's outdoor work. Technical factors could be at work in [a] good many cases (lack of transportation, ignorance of available job opportunities, absence of child care facilities, etc.)' (p.2). The study indicated the Government's concern to create opportunity for women, as well as its concern that the labour force, men and women, had the right skills to meet the country's needs. It was carried out in cooperation with the Vocational Training Corporation, a body established in 1976.

The survey recorded the responses of 1,092 female students at the third preparatory level, when students had to choose either vocational or academic secondary education. The students were from different economic backgrounds. Of the total, 86.3 per cent planned to go on to academic secondary schools. When the field researchers explained that vocational apprenticeship programmes would guarantee jobs, the percentage who were interested in vocational training jumped to 75.9, leading the surveyors to conclude that there was greater need for career counselling and information about vocational training opportunities. As many as 46.8 per cent of the students were not familiar with the programmes organised by the Vocational Training Corporation.

The vast majority of respondents (89.3 per cent) supported women's work outside the home, and 81.7 per cent planned to seek a job when they completed their education. However, only 47.6 per cent said they planned to continue work after marriage. About 62.2 per cent said their guardians would approve their working outside the home unconditionally, 13.8 per cent said their guardians would approve if certain conditions were met, and 16.8 per cent said their guardians disapproved. As for the type of work the students favoured, teaching came first on the list (46.9 per cent), followed by secretarial work (18.1 per cent) and nursing (13.9 per cent).

The survey on employers covered 149 industrial and service establishments in the Amman–Zerka area which employed 20 or more workers. Of the total number of establishments, 115 employed women, who accounted for 9.7 per cent of their labour force. Jordanian women were 91.2 per cent of the total number of female employees. The survey found that 40.6 per cent of Jordanian female workers were classified as craftswomen; meanwhile, 46.2 per cent of the non-Jordanian female workers were technicians. Of the

Jordanian women, 22.4 per cent were married. The highest proportion of married workers was employed by the services sector, and the lowest in manufacturing. The female employees were found to enjoy nearly the same wages and training and promotion opportunities as the men; however, some establishments still employed only single females, which was against the labour law.

The majority, 92.2 per cent, of the establishments that employed women said they were satisfied with the overall performance of their female employees; 27.8 per cent said women's performance was better than men's and 59.2 per cent said their performance was as good as men's. The 4.3 per cent that said they were not satisfied with the performance of their female employees, complained of absenteeism, the cost of special facilities needed for women, and high turnover. As for employers who did not employ women, 43 per cent indicated they would not be employing women in future as they believed women did not have the same skills and would not perform as well as men, and they feared absenteeism and a high turnover.

Employers were asked whether they would meet certain conditions in order to employ females. Of all employers, 91.2 per cent said they would offer the same wages as men. (This was already the practice of 91.3 per cent of those who employed females.) About 94 per cent of all employers said they would offer the same training and promotion opportunities as for men. (94 per cent of those who employed females already did so.) Some 70 per cent said they would provide maternity leave. (75 per cent of those employing females already did so.) Only 2 per cent said they would provide a nursery (and only 2 per cent of those employing females already did so). The survey concluded that labour legislation should be more strictly enforced as regarded maternity leave, which was guaranteed by law, and as regarded nurseries. (Establishments with over 30 women employees had to provide a nursery or face a fine of 50 dinars.)

On the whole, the attitudes of employers to women's work was favourable, and 84 per cent of those who already employed women said they were willing to hire more women, while 43 per cent of establishments that did not employ women indicated a willingness to do so in future. The survey noted that the reasons that made some establishments unwilling to employ women stemmed from 'purely economic considerations and not from deep-rooted social attitudes and values except in very rare cases' (p.68). No jobs were found to be the exclusive domain of men. It was pointed out that many non-Jordanian female employees were technicians, and that apprenticeship programmes should be set up in areas not covered by the Vocational Training Corporation, which tended to be somewhat traditional in its approach to training.

The most serious problem revealed by the survey concerned the vocational training programmes. Like the women students, only half the employers were aware of the existence of such programmes. Clearly the Vocational Training Corporation had to organise a more active information campaign in schools, at the work place and in the media to help match graduates to the needs of society.

## Need at the popular level

During the 1970s, therefore, the Jordanian Government made determined efforts to integrate women in the workforce through legislation and planning. In its hour of need for more womanpower, the Government found an enthusiastic response from the people. Inflation, partly fuelled by worker's remittances, had begun to erode family incomes. Inflation was estimated to have soared to 36.7 per cent in 1977, according to the International Monetary Fund; it had already been a problem in the early 1970s. The Jordanian family was still rather large, with a national average of seven persons per household, and breadwinners began to find that one salary was no longer enough.

There were two ways for a family to earn an extra income: one of its members could migrate to work in the Gulf, or more of its members, including women, could join the local labour force. As researchers found, the entry of females into the wage-labour force helped to stem the flow of migration: the extra salary increased the family's income and reduced the need for men to migrate (Basson, 1982). Women's integration in the workforce also had a positive effect in terms of family ties, since studies on migration had shown that it could increase strains between family members.

A vivid picture of how people's need for more money brought about change in the position of women is given in this story of the life of a Jordanian woman and her family. Although the family come from a lower-middle socioeconomic background, their attitudes and methods of adapting to change are representative of a majority of the population. Their story shows how need affects opportunity, increasing the willingness to have women seek work outside the home, and influencing social attitudes.

The Jordanian woman, Umm Qassem, was in her forties at the time of writing, and lived with her husband and seven of their children in a two-bedroom apartment on the second floor of a two-storey house that they had built (AN, 1982). The husband's unmarried sister also lived with them. Two of Umm Qassem's daughters were already married and lived in other parts of Amman with their husbands. Her eldest son, Qassem, who was also married, lived on the ground floor of the house. Umm Qassem's first name was Naima, but, as is common throughout the Arab world, the father and mother are no longer called by their own first names once they have a son, but become Umm (mother of) and Abu (father of) the eldest son, in this case Qassem. (In Iraq, this applies to the eldest child, son or daughter.) The enmeshing of parents' lives with their children in this way is an indication of the importance that the family is given at the expense of the individual.

Umm and Abu Qassem had plans to enlarge the house they lived in, so that the rest of their boys could have flats of their own in the parental household once they were married, 'so we can watch over them'. When Umm Qassem was a child, parents and their children would share the same living space with their married sons, wives and children, until the sons set up establishments of their own. This had become increasingly rare, as Umm Qassem's story shows; it was more usual for married offspring to set up their own establishments immediately, either close to their parents or within a reasonable distance.

Married daughters became the responsibility of their husbands, but still kept close ties with their family. As one of the daughters put it, 'The married ones bring their husbands to see the family and will in future bring their children. Even when a girl marries, she does not give up her family.' It is a holy duty: 'the Quran says we should maintain family ties', said another daughter. The close ties were economic as well as social. At the simplest level, when the parents stocked up on food products, they kept their married children in mind. As Umm Qassem put it, 'Whatever they need – thyme, olives or cooking fat, and soft white cheese – we give it to them'. Her daughter commented, 'They seem to forget we are married and still think of us as part of the family'.

Umm Qassem and her husband had moved to Amman from their native village near Irbid some two decades earlier. (Nearly 65 per cent of Jordanians now live in cities.) In keeping with the common practice when she was young, Umm Qassem had married her cousin. They were betrothed when she was 13, and married when she was 17. (By the 1980s, 20 was the average age of marriage for women in Jordan.) As she recalled, 'I hadn't the sort of awareness to know what marriage meant. They came and said, "Will you accept your cousin?", and what did I know whether I accepted him or not? I did and that was that. At that time, if a father promised his daughter to somebody, he couldn't go back on it.'

Things had changed by the 1980s. A mother still tried to play her traditional role in arranging marriages, and in checking out prospective spouses' families 'to find out if it's a suitable family. We want a good, respectable family that will be on our level, not people who are better than us and not people who are worse. A person has to marry in his own class.' However, Umm Qassem said, 'These days they go their own way. But then you find them divorcing after a few years' time. The proper way is for them to accept the advice of their elders. If the boy and girl are determined to have each other, then good luck to them. If they get on, well and good. If not, it's their life, it's nobody else's business.' Indeed, one of Umm Qassem's daughters said she had become engaged to the man of her choice, but had broken off the engagement some two years later; the parents had supported her decision in both cases.

When Umm Qassem moved to Amman, Abu Qassem worked as a carpenter with the government. Meanwhile, the family grew rapidly. A family of 10 children was not uncommon in Umm Qassem's day. (She had five sons and five daughters.) By the 1980s, however, the average for lower-income families was six to seven children, and for middle to upper-income families, three to four children. Umm Qassem coped without any of the labour-saving machines that were to become more common later, such as a washing machine or refrigerator. 'I had to prepare the food, and keep the house clean, and from sunset onwards I'd wash the children's clothes and hang them out to dry. I would have one baby before the previous one had started to walk.'

Would she have used family planning methods to space out her pregnancies or to limit the size of her family, had these been available? 'After I had had four or five children, there was something available. I tried to tell Abu Qassem that we had had enough children. He used to say it wasn't right from a religious point of view. You won't be forgiven if you prevent children coming into the world. I used a method after I had the ninth, but [laughs] it didn't work out right and after five years I had the tenth. It's God's will.'

Attitudes throughout the region are still in favour of large families, although a typical family is likely to have four to six children, rather than 10 and more. Research has shown that, not surprisingly, mothers prefer a smaller family than fathers. It is not unusual for women to resort to traditional or modern methods in order to limit the size of their families without informing their husbands of the fact if they expect opposition. Interestingly, Qassem and his wife planned to wait five years after their first child to decide whether they wanted another, which was somewhat unusual.

Umm and Abu Qassem's family grew larger, prices rose and the purchasing power of the single income dwindled. As Umm Qassem put it, 'I used to go down to the market with a dinar in my hand and fill my basket to the brim, and when I'd finished I'd still have change left. Now, even if you go out with 10 dinars, you come back with no change.' Being an enterprising lady, Umm Qassem decided to undertake some income-earning activity. The 'career' she chose was unusual, but in fact it was far from unusual for married women to find some way of making money on the side, by raising poultry and other animals, or through sewing and handicrafts. This was the practice in normal times throughout the region; war situations accelerated the trends, as happened in the case of the Palestinians.

Umm Qassem found an economic outlet by dealing in antiques – textiles, jewellery, brass, wood. She soon became an expert on 'all the things connected with the heritage of the ordinary people'. She collected pieces from villages and refugee camps, and resold these at a substantial profit in the city. 'If I didn't have the cash, I'd go to someone and say, "Have you got any piece you want to sell?", and they'd say how much they wanted for it. I'd agree with the seller that I would give them the money after I had sold the piece, or I would return it to them. I'd also agree on the share they would give me if I sold it for them, say two or three dinars; I would also get two or three dinars from the buyers, and so I ended up with around five dinars. That's how I started out in trade, back in 1971. I'd pay part of the fares for my trips around the country out of the advance I would get from the seller. They all know me and trust me in the villages and the camps.'

Umm Qassem's knowledge about the value and history of various items enabled her to collect material for national heritage exhibitions and museums. By the 1980s, a little room on the ground floor of her house served as a showroom for clients. She had become so established that villagers and refugees came to her to sell their goods. Things were much easier than when she had first embarked on this career, when the first hurdle she had to overcome was her husband's opposition to her working. 'He said it would bring disgrace on us. It's not the custom in the family for women to work. It wasn't acceptable. People would say that he was not able to provide for his family.'

A women who did not believe in wasting much time in argument, Umm Qassem had begun buying and selling antiques without her husband's knowledge, while keeping up her role as wife and mother. 'As soon as he would go to work, I used to go and get the things and go to the museum. I sold them there and got back before he came home. Before he got back, the food was ready and everything was as it should be.' This went on until he found out and then, 'Well, you know life is expensive and one needs more money. People should help each other. I am not educated; I cannot go and teach somewhere. This business is a clean and honest job. In the end he joined me, and we started going to the villages and conducting our business together, and now it's a family business.'

Umm Qassem had been determined to find the extra income to ensure that her children, sons and daughters alike, had a good education and were able to stand on their own feet: 'My one aim is to make sure that they are happy and not in need.' All her children had gone or were going to school, and one of the sons was in university. There was no longer any need to engage in subterfuge to earn a living: two of her as yet unmarried daughters, who had completed high school, were working in a bank and in an office. Indeed, the only person in the household who was not at work or at school was her son's wife, who was pregnant at the time; it was not clear whether she did not want to work, or if her husband did not want her to. As other family members pointed out, however, if the son and his wife had not lived on the ground floor of their parents' property, thus saving on rent, it was doubtful whether they could have afforded for her to remain out of work.

## Change in the village, too

The changes in attitudes to work reflected the change in attitude to education. Village girls did not go to school when Umm Qassem was young; there were few schools around for either boys or girls. As a girl, Umm Qassem thirsted for education but her parents would not allow her to go to school. 'My father said no, our daughters don't go to school, it's only for boys. They believed girls would go wrong if they went to school, that they'd start writing notes to boys.' However, she was determined to attend the only school in the area, and this she did for a few days, telling her parents that she was visiting her aunt. Soon enough, her parents discovered her little stratagem, and put an end to her school days. Later on in life, Umm Qassem enrolled in a literacy class but was unable to continue beyond the fourth year because of her heavy household schedule.

Umm Qassem's father, who was already reckoned to be over a hundred years old in 1982, still lived in the village with one of his sons. He was asked why he had not allowed his daughter to go to school. The old man replied simply, 'It was not her destiny. There were no schools, neither for Umm Qassem nor for anyone else. You would find the boys learning the Quran, with one teacher teaching 160 or 170 boys, all sitting on a mat on the floor.' In fact, when the formal school was opened, one of Umm Qassem's brothers was sent. Asked what he thought about Umm Qassem being a career woman, the old man replied, 'These days, men, women, children, they all work for a living.'

The house where the old man lived was home to 14 people; another of his sons lived just down the road. The main difference between village and city, in the eyes of the villagers, was that people had more time for each other and cared more in the village. Umm Qassem's father said people had been even kinder in the old days, and more generous with their goods. 'Now everyone is too busy minding their own interests. In the old days, there was no such rush to build houses or secure jobs and high positions.'

There had been changes in attitude to women's roles in the village: Umm Qassem's brothers sent all their children to schools in the village. Education was important, one brother said, because 'a person who is not educated will not be able to live decently. He might end up as a labourer carrying concrete blocks. I want all my sons to be educated. My daughters must be educated, too, because today a girl who is not educated has far less chance of marriage; she might only find a shepherd or someone like that to marry her.'

It is noteworthy that there was distaste for manual labour even in the village, a common reaction throughout the Arab world, partly because vocational labour is under-rewarded. Education for boys was seen as important so that they would not have to become builders carrying 'concrete blocks', although Umm Qassem's father was a builder, and was said to have built most of the houses in the village. Men and women throughout the region prefer careers in the professions and the civil service, a bloated creature in the Arab world, although Arabs are not in a position to indulge in false pride.

Women's education was seen by the villagers as a new prerequisite for marriage imposed by the modern age. Asked if they would allow their daughters to work or continue their education, one of Umm Qassem's brothers said it depended on how well they did in school. Suitable careers for girls were teaching, followed by nursing and the civil service, although in other circles nursing is seen as too close to domestic service to be 'respectable'. One of Umm Qassem's brothers remarked, 'These days girls no longer listen to you. Every one of them wants to have a job; no sooner does she finish her education than she finds the job she wants.' Even allowing for exaggeration, this was an indication that attitudes had changed.

The same change in attitude was noted with regard to marriage. Fewer families married their children to cousins. The old man remarked, 'It thickens the blood.' Although one brother had 'married one of his girls off' to a man of his own choosing, the match had the girl's consent. Parents seemed to accept that a girl could have more say in the matter of her marriage, and could refuse to accept her father's choice even if he had 'given his word on it'. It was also accepted that, once engaged, a couple could go out on their own, whereas previously they had to be chaperoned.

## New avenues open up

With the opening up of education and career opportunities, people had more choice about what to do with their lives. In Amman, Umm Qassem's two working daughters were in no hurry to get married. They felt that, while in some ways they would have more freedom of action when they had their own homes, in others they would be more restricted, 'because your husband is no different. Being an Arab, he is like anyone else in your parents' home and he could say that this was forbidden or that was alright.'

At this stage in the country's social development, working outside the home did not entail living alone outside the home.

Going out alone in the evenings or travelling alone was generally allowed by parents in upper income groups, but not by families like Umm Qassem's. If their daughters were to travel, they would have to have one of their brothers along as guardian/chaperon. This, Abu Qassem insisted, was provided for by the religion. An example of a most unsuitable career for a woman, from the family's point of view, was that of air hostess. As one of the brothers put it, 'a girl should be in her parents' home when the sun rises and when the sun sets'. As noted in the previous chapter, the social obstacles to women's work outside the home disappear fairly rapidly when the need and opportunity arise, but the strict attitudes to women having other activities in the public sphere are more difficult to overcome.

Umm Qassem's sons were expected to be responsible for their sisters' welfare, should they remain unmarried. As mentioned earlier, Abu Qassem's sister lived with the family. With women working for wages, the brothers' economic responsibility could be expected to diminish. However, the brothers also shared responsibility with the parents for their sisters' social conduct. In addition to keeping a watchful eye on their sisters, the brothers helped them live a more active life, by accompanying them on outings and organising parties, which the sisters would not be able to do on their own. The three unmarried brothers acknowledged that young people had more freedom to meet each other than during their parents' time. Boys and girls could meet at university (most schools were segregated), and came to know their brothers' and sisters' friends. The three brothers agreed that this should be kept 'within the limits of what is permissible and what people accept. If you're a girl, you want to be like other girls, to be decent.'

Two of the brothers expected their wives to work when they got married, and both wanted to marry an educated girl so that the couple would be able to build a sound understanding based on mutual respect. One brother said, 'Of course I'll let her work. I'll gain and she'll gain. Life is difficult here, you know, because the cost of living is high.' Marriage was a partnership between husband and wife, who had to help one another. By contrast, the third brother declared, 'I wouldn't allow her to work. One marries someone to look after the house, not to get herself dressed up to go out to work. Inside the home – that's what marriage is all about.'

As can be seen from the above account of one family's life across three generations, there have been substantial, though not uniform, changes in attitudes during the past 20 years. First, a widespread belief had developed in the need for women's education, even if it was only to prepare them better for marriage. Secondly, young people had come to have more choice in selecting marriage partners and careers, which increased their scope for personal freedom. Thirdly, there was a widespread, though not universal, belief that it was acceptable for a woman to work outside the home, given the rising cost of living. The type of work a woman could do depended on the socioeconomic background, with a strong preference for work that was 'respectable' in the middle to lower income groups.

The family's story illustrates the ways people could find around obstacles erected by customs. It also shows how tradition could be pushed aside to allow for change when necessary, as in women working outside the home to satisfy economic need. Family ties were still strong, even though not all members lived under the same roof. Umm Qassem and her children described the family as 'the most wonderful thing about Arab life'. Umm Qassem's strength and power, so clearly illustrated in this story, are not unusual for an Arab woman. In Umm Qassem's family, the husband appeared to be in charge, but in reality she took many of the major decisions and her husband eventually abided by them. Her only failure seems to have been in the area of limiting the family size.

## The pendulum swings

To sum up, by the early 1980s, all factors conspired to integrate women in the workforce. The conditions of need, opportunity and ability were met at the state and popular levels. The country needed manpower, and families needed an extra income; the state provided opportunity through planning, legislation and consciousness-raising, while social obstacles to women's work outside the home melted away; and the state provided educational facilities and sought to improve vocational skills, while at the popular level education was seen as a right for all.

There were certain issues that were not completely resolved. Society still expected women's major role to be that of wife and mother. For example, 46.7 per cent of female students in the 1981 Ministry of Labour survey planned to give up work altogether when they married. Umm Qassem had undertaken work that enabled her to carry out her household duties as well. Meanwhile, her two single daughters worked, but not the married ones. Moreover, employers still tended to discriminate against working mothers. Still, a rise in economic activity by married women seemed to be indicated from the fact that the 1976 household survey found that only 4 per cent of married women between ages 20 to 44 worked, whereas married women accounted for 22.4 per cent of women workers in the Ministry of Labour's survey of employers in 1981. As was noted earlier, married women were seen as a major source of untapped labour by the Government, and the proposed labour legislation amendments, seminars and ceremonies focussed on keeping mothers in the workforce.

While women's integration in the workforce had positive results for the nation in that it reduced the need to import labour, and for the family in that it increased income levels, it was not without its negative side. For instance, women's work for wages, particularly in the rural areas, reduced their economic activity within the home, as Basson's survey of families in Irbid in northern Jordan showed. Food grown or processed at home had to be purchased from the market by women who worked outside the home. Moreover, women's assistance as 'family helpers' on the farm or in other family concerns was also lost if they joined the workforce, and labour sometimes had to be hired in their stead.

There was another serious problem at the family level: thousands of foreign nursemaids were being 'imported' to help bring up the children. According to Jordanian officials, there were some 12,000 domestic workers from Sri Lanka alone by 1985, a substantial proportion of the country's total imports of foreign labour. Officials said their studies had shown that most of the domestic workers had been brought in to carry out the home-based work of urban Jordanian women who had gone to work outside the home. The domestic workers were estimated to be sending some $30 million back to their home countries, which was a drain on the country's hard currency reserves.

The foreign family-help phenomenon was an indication that the services offered by the extended family where, for example, grandmothers or aunts could babysit children, were becoming less available, as modernisation imposed more nuclear family structures. Clearly, if women's entry into the modern sector was to be trouble-free, it had to be accompanied by more equal sharing of household and child-care duties within the 'modern' family. In theory, as women expanded their roles by taking on work for wages outside the home, men too should accommodate change by taking on more work inside the home. In practice, this has yet to happen on a major scale, and women's work for wages may continue to have negative repercussions on the nation in terms of a higher import bill for consumer goods and manpower, and on the family in terms of bringing up the children.

How these problems will be solved, it is too early to tell, particularly as the pendulum had begun to swing back by about 1982. With the recession in the Gulf, more workers were returning home than planned for, and not as many had the opportunity to migrate. Far from having a labour deficit of 70,000 workers, as had been predicted in the 1981–5 plan, the country found itself facing a serious unemployment problem again. This was officially estimated at between 5 and 9 per cent, or about 50,000 people, by 1985 and was one of the major issues addressed in the 1985–90 plan. Planners expected the flow of returning migrants from the Gulf to reach 15,000 workers a year, double what it had been. And, with over half the population under 15, large numbers of school leavers were expected to increase the pressure on the country's job-creating capacity.

The economic outlook was bleak. One of the mainstays of the Jordanian economy, for instance, was Arab aid, which dropped because of the recession in the Gulf. Other economic avenues that had opened, such as the transit market to Iraq during the early part of the war with Iran, also petered out as Iraq's cash dwindled. Naturally, the flow of remittances was affected by the lower number of migrants. The Jordanian Government began to revise its budget to reflect the need for austerity in 1982; it cut back on the money supply and reportedly succeeded in bringing inflation down to 5 per cent. There were proposals to lessen the dependency on foreign workers, particularly in agriculture, and to revive this sector as a major employer. Various development schemes and incentives were mooted to encourage Jordanian businessmen and incentives to encourage Arab investors.

Not unexpectedly, the drive to integrate women in the workforce seemed to slow down as the economy slowed and as the Government's need for manpower disappeared. By 1985, there was 'almost an official policy', a high-ranking official admitted, to encourage married women to stay at home (AN, 1986). The policy was implicit rather than explicit, but it was said to be widely discussed in government circles. No publicity was believed to be necessary because public and private sector employers 'would know what to do' without a government directive: in case a man and a woman applied who had equal qualifications, the man would be given priority. Meanwhile, in 1984, the Ministry of Social Development had been merged with the Ministry of Labour, thus placing the national policy-making body for women back where it had been in 1977; the new minister appointed was a man. By mid-1986, the labour legislation under consideration (which would have, for example, increased maternity leave from six to 10 weeks) had not yet been passed.

Would Jordanian women be treated in their own country as the migrant workers were treated by labour-importing countries, and be pushed out when they were no longer needed? Not altogether, because some of the conditions for women's integration into the wage-labour force still functioned in favour of women's work in 1985: ability at the state and popular level, as women were still being educated and trained; and need at the popular level, given the rise in the cost of living and the new tastes created by a decade of consumerism.

Against this background, it is not enough to say that women must organise in order to push themselves into the wage-labour force so as to fulfil their needs and abilities. For women to be fully integrated into the workforce, economic conditions have to change. That, in turn, involves changing the mode of development pursued, in this case drastically reducing the country's dependence on outside sources of income which gain control of it rather than being controlled by it, and creating sustainable indigenous wealth. This can only be achieved when enough people question the nature and purpose of economic development, and insist on having the major say in decisions regarding the political and economic future of their country. The changes that are necessary are not ones that women can carry out alone.

# Chapter 5

# The Arab Gulf states: demand but no supply

We consume what we do not produce, and produce what we do not consume.
*Criticism of development often voiced by young Gulf Arabs*

In Jordan, the conditions for full integration of women in the modern sector
– need, opportunity and ability – were met at the state and popular levels,
albeit briefly. In theory, the same should have happened in the Arab Gulf*
states, where the need for manpower was even more pressing than in
Jordan. In practice, it did not. Throughout the 1970s and early 1980s, Gulf
women's integration into the modern sector was a gradual process. It is
tempting to turn to tradition and to conservative social attitudes to explain
why women held back, particularly as the veil continued to be conspicuous
in the Gulf, especially in Saudi Arabia. This does not, however, tell the
whole story. As will be shown below, the conditions of need, opportunity
and ability were not met at the state and popular levels.

## A flood of foreign manpower

The impact of oil wealth on the Gulf makes for one of the most dramatic
stories in recent Arab history. Oil was discovered during the early part of
this century, although production and export operations only reached
appreciable levels in the '40s and '50s. In the early days, the revenues were
largely pocketed by foreign oil companies, so the change in the people's way
of life was fairly slow at first. The area was one of the poorest in the world,

* The term the 'Arab Gulf' is being used to refer to the six states of Saudi Arabia, Oman,
Bahrain, Kuwait, the United Arab Emirates (UAE) and Qatar. They share the same
characteristics – small populations, oil-dominated economies, and monarchical systems of
government. In 1981, they established the Gulf Cooperation Council to coordinate their
policies. 'Arab Gulf' is sometimes used to include Iraq and the two Yemens, which, with the
GCC states, could be said to form a natural geographic and cultural entity within the Arab
world. Indeed, Iraq was a member of many regional bodies before the GCC was set up.
However, while Iraq is oil-rich, it has other resources, a much larger population, and a
different system of government; and the two Yemens are among the poorest countries in the
world, as well as having different systems of government.

and the harsh climate and paucity of natural resources added to the rigours of desert life. A mainstay of the economy, pearling, was hard hit when the world market was flooded by Japanese cultured pearls in the 1930s, which further impoverished the region.

Perhaps the pearl divers had the most difficult lives, going out to sea for months at a time while their wives undertook all the tasks needed to keep society running, sometimes diving for pearls themselves if they were very poor (Al-Rumeihi, 1975). In the farming and nomadic communities, work was also shared between men and women; in fact, the labour of both was essential for survival. As elsewhere, it was only the urban upper-class, mostly pearl merchants and traders, who could afford to keep their wives in seclusion.

The oil boom of the 1970s brought almost overnight change. It was like drawing the winning global lottery ticket: from being among the poorest countries in the world, the Gulf states found themselves among the wealthiest. But the windfall brought mixed blessings. On the one hand, the oil producers were able to build nearly everything from scratch – housing, schools, hospitals, industry. On the other, nearly everything had to be imported from abroad to do so – the materials, the skilled labour for construction, the professionals to run the administration, the technology and the technicians. Expatriate advisors drew up plans on how best to spend the oil producers' money, which often had more to do with creating jobs for the expatriates than with the real needs of the oil states. The salesmen of all nations swooped down on the Gulf, peddling everything from paper clips to fertiliser plants.

For the people of the Gulf, the most unwelcome result of over-rapid development was the influx of foreigners, who outnumbered locals by more than two to one in some states. Many of the non-nationals were Arabs from the rest of the region, who, in spite of certain tensions, at least shared the same culture. It was official Gulf policy to prefer Arab over non-Arab labour. However, Gulf officials also feared that too many overly politicised Arabs might be a destabilising factor, and, in any case, their labour had become more expensive than Asian labour. Thus, the number of Asians in the Gulf workforce began to increase rapidly, first from the Indian subcontinent, historically a close trading partner, and then from southeast Asia.

The Gulf Arabs suddenly felt like strangers in their own land, and in private conversation expressed themselves in somewhat dramatic terms. A young woman from the UAE, where the ratio of locals to foreigners was the lowest of the Gulf states, put it like this:

What is happening to us is exactly what happened to the Palestinians. They are pulling our country out from under our feet; one day we will wake up and find ourselves homeless. Nobody asked us if we wanted to build all those industries that we don't know how to run and to bring in all those people to run our countries for us. (AN, 1981)

Given the sensitivity of the issue, it was difficult to estimate the proportion of locals to foreigners. According to Birks and Sinclair (1980), the number of non-Gulf Arabs working in the Gulf by 1975 was around 935,000, while Asian workers were estimated at 347,420. The overall migrant population in the Gulf states in 1975 totalled 2,808,735. (Many white-collar workers were allowed to bring their families along.) Already by 1975, the share of Arab, Gulf and non-Gulf, employment in the total labour force had dropped to 68 per cent from 82 per cent in 1970 (p.75). Between 1975 and 1980 the number of non-national workers increased rapidly, and the number of Asian workers increased more rapidly than that of non-national Arabs. In the UAE, for example, Asians made up more than 70 per cent of the labour force in 1980 (ILO, 1983). Indeed, labour officials in the UAE warned in the early 1980s that, unless a solution was found, nationals might make up only 2.5 per cent of the population by the year 2000.

By the early 1980s, recession, plunging oil prices and the fact that some major construction projects had been completed, dammed the flood. Gulf governments began to send thousands of expatriate Arab and non-Arab workers home. However, hundreds of thousands of migrant workers remained in the Gulf, and will doubtless continue to be there for some time to come, given the small indigenous population and the time it will take to train enough local people to fill the positions. Indeed, according to the 9 September 1985 edition of the Paris-based weekly *Al Yom Al Sabe*, the Kuwaiti Government had been shocked to find, in the 1985 census, that the proportion of nationals in the population had actually dropped to 40 per cent of the total, from 41.7 per cent in 1980. The Government had been expecting it to rise, given the drop in the number of labour migrants.

As can be seen from the above, the Gulf states were clearly in need of all the skilled national labour that could be produced. Gulf governments were determined to reduce their dependence on foreign manpower and to indigenise the labour force, a policy that became known as 'Saudiisation', 'Qatarisation', and so on, and jobs for male and female graduates in the civil service were practically guaranteed. In theory at least, Gulf women should have been as active in the labour force as men because the need at the state level was so great. Moreover, they had at least the same ability to participate since they were fast catching up with men in schools and universities (see Table 3), and had shown a thirst for learning perhaps unrivalled throughout the region. However, women's participation in the wage labour force was a slow and gradual process through the 1970s and early 1980s.

## Opportunity knocks, not too loudly

Was the low participation of women during this time related to state policies? Did Gulf governments encourage women's entry into the work-force actively enough? In the UAE, for example, officials made frequent statements urging women to join the labour force, pointing to the various possibilities that were in keeping with Islamic values and traditions. In Oman, the 1985 yearbook was quite blunt on the subject: 'Ignorant women cannot bring up free men, and women who are neglected cannot take care of others. Unless she is trained and qualified for her task, a woman will be a liability to the progress of others' (p.142). Kuwaiti Government officials both made supportive statements and backed women's groups when they organised conferences and meetings for working women.

Saudi Arabian Government plans took into account the number of women graduates that would be arriving onto the labour market, but a major concern was to ensure that, where women did work, they did not come into contact with men. In 1983 King Fahd 'reinstructed' public and private sector employers not to employ women in jobs where they would mix with men. (The fact that it was necessary to 'reinstruct' people was a sign that the effects of such circulars wore off with time.) Another example of the concern to keep the sexes segregated was the statement by the top Saudi religious authority, Shaikh Abdel-Aziz Bin Baz, in 1984, which urged women to study medicine in greater numbers so that male doctors would not have to treat women patients except in cases of extreme necessity.

On the whole, the governments of the Gulf were long on supportive statements, but short on specific action to boost the integration of women into the workforce on a large scale. None could be said to have matched the aggressive approach of the Jordanian government which, when it found itself lacking skilled manpower and faced with rising numbers of foreign migrants, went so far as to set up a ministry to help integrate women in development, with the possible exception of Oman, where there were echoes of the attitudes and actions of the Jordanian Government.

It is difficult to come to accurate conclusions without the figures to work with, but it is probably safe to say that the state where local women were most active in the wage-labour force during the 1970s and early 1980s was Bahrain. The Bahraini population was the first to enjoy the benefits of education in the region; a girls' school was opened there in 1928. More importantly, Bahrain was the second poorest relative of the Gulf family in terms of per capita income. Bahrain's oil was exploited early and, since it started off with small reserves, began to run out early. The per capita GNP of the Gulf states in 1983 stood at $6,250 for Oman, followed by Bahrain's

$10,150, Saudi Arabia's $12,230, Kuwait's $17,880, Qatar's $21,210 and the UAE's $22,870.

At the national level, Bahrain simply could not afford to finance imports of manpower on the same scale as its neighbours, although it did have a sizeable foreign community. The need for local womanpower at the national level was matched by a corresponding need at the popular level: incomes in Bahrain were not very high and in many cases more than one family member had to work. Indeed, the Government was said to be worried about unemployment among women graduates in areas such as commercial studies in the 1980s and to be planning training programmes in other fields where jobs were more readily available.

In effect, in spite of their apparently pressing need for local manpower, the Gulf states did not have to adopt an aggressive policy on women's participation in the workforce because they had the cash to finance their imports of foreign manpower. Nor, by the early 1980s, did the people in these states feel a strong need for more than one salary per family, with some exceptions in the less well-off states like Bahrain and the more populous ones like Oman and Saudi Arabia.

Obviously, not all Gulf Arabs are millionaires, but the extent of the wealth available can be gauged from the fact that even Oman's per capita income of $6,250, which was the lowest for the Gulf states in 1983, was of an entirely different order from that of poor Third-World countries like neighbouring Yemen, where it was estimated at $550, or Somalia where it was $250. It is too soon to tell whether the recession of the early 1980s forced the pace of Gulf women's integration in the modern labour force, although in theory, with less easy money around, it should have done so.

The lack of need at the family level certainly meant that women did not have to go out to work unless they wanted to. And there were state policies, well-meaning in themselves, that actually further reduced people's need to work, and made it less necessary for women to avail themselves of the opportunity to work. The Gulf governments provided a wide range of social services, creating welfare states that rivalled those of Europe. It was not socially acceptable for men to remain out of work, so the only men covered by social security were old age pensioners or those too disabled to work. However, in the case of women, changes in life situation, such as divorce or widowhood, which might push women into the wage-labour force, could also be covered by social security.

The effect was shown by a study on women and social security in Kuwait (Al-Rujaib, 1982). According to Kuwaiti regulations, social security covered widows below the age of 60, at which point they came under the category of old age pensioners, divorcees under 60, *all unmarried girls over 18,* and prisoners' families. This meant that many working age women were eligible for social security, although the country badly needed workers. The study noted that the proportion of those receiving social security in 1980 was 3.2 per cent of the population, of which 51.1 per cent were working-age women.

The study surveyed 298 women, of whom 38.6 per cent said that the social security they received satisfied their needs. The unmarried girls were most satisfied with the amount they received; 67.9 per cent of unmarried girls found it enough. (The same percentage of girls were found to be living with their families.) The least satisfied were the prisoners' wives, of whom 85.8 per cent found it was not enough, followed by 66.4 per cent of widows and 59.2 per cent of divorcees. The women were asked whether they wished to work and to be trained for employment. The highest positive response came from the prisoners' wives, 81 per cent of whom said yes, followed by divorcees with 31.5 per cent. The overwhelming majority of unmarried girls (92.9 per cent) and widows (94.1 per cent) said no. Thus, some of those with the most pressing economic need were willing to work, while those with the least pressing need (unmarried girls) were among the most unwilling.

## Social attitudes and opportunity at the popular level

What of social attitudes that might create barriers to women's work outside the home? These were certainly more of a factor in the Arab Gulf than they were in other Arab countries. However, attitudes to women's work and education were not negative, as was demonstrated in several studies. A survey was carried out in 1973–4 on the attitudes to women's education and work among 341 families in Kuwait (Al-Thaqeb, 1975). Questions were put to 526 parents, with men and women questioned separately; women made up 48 per cent of those surveyed. Of the total, 96 per cent favoured women's education, with 71 per cent supporting higher education for women, 23 per cent secondary education and 6 per cent elementary schooling. Al-Thaqeb noted that the proportion of men that wanted women's education limited to the secondary level was twice that of the women. As for employment, 69 per cent supported women's paid employment, while 30 per cent did not. The idea of paid employment for women was supported by 82 per cent of women, compared to only 58 per cent of men, despite the fact that the majority of women were housewives whose education was below university level.

A survey of Kuwaiti employees and students was undertaken by the Ministry of Education (Al-Khaled, 1982). The survey's respondents numbered 1,100 Kuwaiti men and women from all walks of life; 700 worked in the public sector from the top ranks down, or in sports clubs, trade unions and social service groups, while 400 were university students. The respondents were almost equally divided between men and women (557 men and 543 women), although there were variations according to category, with more working men (429) than women (271), and more women students (272) than men (128). The survey found five major trends in society on the question of women and work.

*First,* 46 per cent of the total believed women and men should have unlimited education and employment opportunites. (Of those expressing this view, 64 per cent were women and 36 per cent were men.) *Secondly,* 29.27 per cent believed women should be educated to university level in certain fields like medicine, social services and education, and work in those fields that suited their nature (38 per cent of women, 62 per cent of men). *Thirdly,* 9.82 per cent believed women should have access to all fields of education, but work in those fields that suited their nature (56 per cent of men, 44 per cent of women). *Fourthly,* 4.27 per cent believed women's education should be limited to secondary level and to preparing them for married life, while their employment should be limited to looking after the home and raising the children. (All of this group were men.) And *fifthly,* 3.55 per cent believed women should be educated up to technical-college level in fields such as nursing or secretarial skills, and work in these areas (79 per cent of men, 21 per cent of women).

It is immediately obvious that women were much more in favour of equal opportunities in education and work than men. Throughout, the major factor that affected attitudes to women's roles was the sex of the respondent rather than levels of education, marital status, etc., with women in favour of greater opportunities. Unexpectedly, the percentage of students that favoured unlimited opportunities for women in education and work was lower than that of employees – only 35 per cent of students compared to 47 per cent of employees. In her policy proposals, Al-Khaled urged that this information be made use of by educational institutes and women's groups to increase awareness among youth of the need for women to study and work in all fields. Since the majority of students interviewed were women, it would seem that not all women were convinced that they should study and work in all fields; indeed only 51 per cent of women students were convinced that they should (with an even smaller proportion of 27 per cent for men students).

While a large proportion of respondents, 46 per cent, supported equal rights to education and work for women, Al-Khaled noted that this meant that the majority, 54 per cent, did not. Since she had defined work and education as the most important factors enabling an individual to participate in the development process, Al-Khaled did not feel that the result of the survey was positive. She remarked that the division of labour between man and woman on the basis of outside the home and inside the home had made sense when the society was based on a subsistence economy. However, 'the new social balance is much more complex and more integrated into the market economy. Thus all human resources, men and women, must be allowed to take on the challenges of development, and must be prepared to participate effectively and productively' (p.281).

Al-Khaled was also worried by the fact that the results of the survey were in broad agreement with two earlier surveys (Al-Thaqeb, 1975; Al-Qutb, 1975), that is, there had been no movement forward although more than six years had passed. She feared that a type of citizen was being created that consumed the benefits of material prosperity, without contributing to the national economy. This could only mean increased dependence on more advanced societies, a dangerous development.

It should be noted, however, that 88.64 per cent favoured at least some form of employment for women, which was far more than the proportion of Kuwaiti women actually in the workforce in the 1970s and 1980s. This would appear to indicate that social attitudes were not a main factor preventing women's work outside the home in the Gulf. Other factors, such as the lack of economic need at the family level, were just as, if not more, significant.

## Colonisation in reverse, and the question of identity

However, there is no denying that social attitudes were more conservative in the Gulf than they were in other Arab countries, although the same religious traditions and customs were to be found in all, with a considerable difference in degree of adherence. A major reason was that social change as a result of 'modernisation' – formal education systems, industry, growing urban centres, nation states – took place much more quickly in the Gulf than in the rest of the Arab world, where in any case it happened more rapidly than in Europe. The process of modernisation had begun gradually in Syria, Palestine, Jordan, Iraq, Egypt, Sudan and the Maghreb states in the nineteenth and early twentieth centuries, so that, when mass education became available in the 1950s, there was already a base to build on. In the Gulf, the whole process was compressed into two decades. (See Graham's highly readable account of social change in the Gulf in *Arabian Timemachine*, 1978.)

In such a rapidly changing world, customs and tradition provided the only fixed and comprehensible elements, for governments and people alike. Even when the younger generation expressed its frustration with restrictive customs, it supported a slow approach to change. Moreover, the people of the region had a living example of what could happen as a result of rapid modernisation. 'We don't want to be like Iran' was a comment often heard in the Arab Gulf, where it was widely believed that the Shah's frenetic modernisation programme was responsible for the violence of the revolution in 1979. Thus, economic slowdowns, like that of the early 1980s, were welcomed in some Gulf circles, because they would force a reevaluation of policies and programmes, and slow down the pace of change. (Indeed, recessions were sometimes engineered to force a slowdown. This was a favourite tactic of the Qatari government: since most money in the country was earned through Government contracts, it had simply to postpone paying the bills for a few months for an overheated economy to cool down nicely.)

Another main reason for slower change in social attitudes was the large influx of foreign manpower, which the Gulf Arabs saw as a threat to their character and identity. This resulted in a reaction similar to that in countries that had been colonised, except that in this case the 'colonised' were in the dominant political and economic position. For example, one of the steps most Gulf states took in order to preserve their character and identity, was to try to cut down on marriages between locals and non-locals. In some Gulf countries, special permission from the state was required before a mixed marriage was allowed.

In a 1982 discussion with Saudi students, King Fahd answered a question on the subject. He explained that only Saudi soldiers and diplomats were actually forbidden to marry foreign women, and that this was similar to the policy of other countries. It was true that the ordinary citizen had to go through difficult administrative procedures to marry a foreign woman, but this was because of the state's concern to protect the Saudi woman, he said; the state believed the Saudi woman was a better mate for the Saudi man, as she understood the customs and traditions of his society. This did not mean, the King said, that Saudi Arabia did not wish to become linked to brotherly Arab and Islamic states through ties of marriage, but simply that its present circumstances imposed the need to protect its sons and daughters from problems they were better off without.

The Gulf states were not alone in such reactions. Libya, which is similar to the Gulf in having oil wealth, a small population and a large foreign workforce, passed legislation forbidding men employed by the state to marry non-Arab women. The 14 January 1984 edition of the weekly English-language paper *Al-Zahaf Al-Akhdar* (the green march) explained:

The rationale behind this is the fear that a non-Arab woman would find it harder to integrate into Libyan society. She would as a result eventually segregate herself and her children from the society, rendering herself and her children a disservice. She would fail to participate with her husband in this vital stage of development in modern Libya. These are unusual times for Libya. It must make up for centuries of oppression.

It will be recalled that colonised Algeria clung to its Arab and Islamic traditions as a reaction against domination by foreigners, a reaction that continued in post-revolution days when even the women's union took an official stand against mixed marriages. 'So!' wrote the Algerian feminist Fadela M'rabet sarcastically, '... we must divest ourselves of all foreign elements . . . clean ourselves up, disinfect ourselves', and 'since foreign culture is so "depersonalizing", we must take care not to read too much, among others, from the works of . . . Frantz Fanon' (1977, pp.328–31).

## Social alarm bells and foreign nursemaids

On no subject was the Gulf reaction so alarmist, and the threat to character and identity believed to be so great, as on the issue of foreign nursemaids. The foreign nannies, who were mostly Asian, were found not just in families where the wife worked; they were often employed in homes where the wife did not work, and were a sign of affluence and consumerism. In fact, the domestic workforce in the Gulf – which included cleaners, drivers, gardeners and cooks – accounted for a sizeable proportion of the migrant labour force.

The media coverage of the question of foreign nannies, as of other issues related to foreign manpower, sometimes had racist overtones. The headline of one article on foreign nursemaids shrieked, 'The yellow peril is here – we ring the alarm'. In the UAE, information ministry officials once called in newspaper editors and told them to tone down the press campaign against foreign workers (TME, 1983). In a more measured approach to the problem, a 1982 meeting of Gulf ministers of labour and social affairs charged four GCC members with conducting surveys on the impact of foreign nursemaids on children in their country.

The results of the Oman Government study on the issue were published in 1984. It noted that the total number of migrant workers in the private sector had jumped from 14,500 in 1972 to 186,821 in 1982, and that 95.83 per cent of these workers were Asian. It said that foreign nannies were a fairly recent phenomenon in Oman, compared to other Gulf states, as they began to be employed around 1978. The number of nannies was still small, at 1,350 in 1983. To assess the impact of foreign nursemaids on Omani children, the study surveyed 160 families in various parts of the Sultanate. The total number of children between the ages of two and six (the target group) was 272. The children were equally divided among a test group of families that employed foreign nannies, and a control group of families that did not. The main reasons given by families for employing nursemaids were, first to help with the housework, secondly because the wife worked outside the home, and thirdly because of the large number of children. (There were other reasons, like looking after old relatives.) Clearly, the families conceived of the nursemaids' primary role as that of household help.

The survey reported on the characteristics of both the families and the nursemaids. Of the latter, 33.8 per cent were Muslim, 58.8 per cent were Christian, and 5 per cent were Buddhist. About 20 per cent were illiterate, 23.8 per cent could barely read and write, 23.8 per cent had elementary schooling and 28.7 per cent had secondary schooling. Of the total, 25 per cent knew no Arabic and 48.8 per cent could speak a little Arabic; over 95 per cent could neither read nor write Arabic. Most nannies saw their task as a combination of household work and caring for the children.

To assess the impact on children's development, several tests were conducted. It was found that children's ability to remember events was higher among children in the control group (which did not employ nursemaids); they scored 70.9 per cent in the age group four to six, compared to 54.1 per cent of the test group. The percentage of children that could tell a story using words that made sense was 57 per cent in the control group, and 45.9 per cent in the test group. Children were more inquisitive in control-group families, and scored 50 per cent for ages two to four, than in test-group families, which scored 27.4 per cent. Nearly 50 per cent of children in test-group families did not communicate with the nanny in Arabic; about a third used English and some 20 per cent used the nanny's language. The speech patterns of about 20 per cent were influenced by the nanny's accent, and speech defects were more likely to be found among test-group children.

From these and other indications (the study also examined children's reactions to fear and pressure), the survey concluded that the employment of foreign nursemaids had an appreciable impact on children. Among other recommendations, it proposed that nurseries and day-care centres employing trained personnel be set up, since, it noted, nuclear families had become more common than extended families who could help care for children. More women were working and contributing to the country's development, thus lessening its reliance on foreign labour; therefore, proper facilities had to be provided.

It is significant that this survey concluded that, since reliance on foreign nannies had an adverse impact on children, more facilities had to be made available to enable local women to go out to work, and not that women had to be sent back to the home. More conservative circles would have concluded, rather, that the only way to protect the social fabric of society and the family would be to keep women at home.

## Changing attitudes to marriage

Whether it was welcome or not, social change was being brought about by the rapid material development of the Gulf states, and it was affecting basic institutions like marriage. For instance, more men were marrying women from other Arab states or Asia because they could not afford the high dowries that girls' fathers wanted. In the UAE, it was estimated that about 50 per cent of marriages in 1984 were to non-local girls. The issue of high dowries was often the subject of television series and magazine articles. Although the Quran specified that the dowry was the bride's property, some Muslims followed the custom whereby it was paid to the father. In some cases it was spent to cover the costs of marriage and of outfitting the girl and her new home; in others it was used to help a girl's brother with his dowry on marriage; and sometimes it was simply pocketed by the father, who was naturally keen to charge the highest amount possible.

The cost of marriage for a young man could rise to $30,000 or more for the dowry alone, which still left the problem of finding money for housing, furniture, and so on. Governments like Kuwait and Qatar tried to help out by offering a marriage 'allowance', while Oman acted to limit dowries. The cost of marriage also rose in other Arab countries, partly as a result of inflation and partly because of the wealth made available through work in the Gulf; the high cost of marriage was the subject of complaint in countries as diverse as Syria, Yemen and Egypt.

There were also changes in attitude to marriage, as was shown in a survey conducted by the Women's Charitable Association for Social Services in Dammam (reported in the 28 February and 7 March 1983 editions of the London-based Saudi weekly women's magazine *Sayidaty*). From the responses of 260 single men and 292 single women, it was clear that marriage was no longer accorded the prominence it had had: it came in third place after work and education for 58 per cent of men and 44 per cent of women.

As to what the respondents expected from married life, 28 per cent of men and 15 per cent of women said it was a duty one had to undertake. Most men (59 per cent) viewed marriage as a source of love and affection, as did most women (66 per cent). However, most women (73 per cent) saw marriage as a partnership between man and woman, compared to only 45 per cent of men. Asked why they had not married yet, 68 per cent of the women replied that no suitable suitor had come forward, while 39 per cent said they wanted to continue their education, and 18 per cent said they had not been able to select their own partner. Responding to the same question, 44 per cent of the men said they could not afford it, while 39 per cent mentioned the difficulty of making a personal choice.

It was significant that so many single girls appeared ready to postpone marriage until they completed their education, even at the risk of remaining spinsters. Some Gulf girls said frankly that any woman going on to do post-graduate work knew she was taking the first step to spinsterhood. Another serious problem for men and women was the difficulty of selecting a partner. They might not want an arranged marriage, but they did not have many possibilities of meeting suitable partners (although there were usually ways of getting information on potential mates through friends, and even of arranging clandestine meetings). Further problems were likely to arise because most women saw marriage as a partnership, compared to less than half of the men.

Thus, many young people were marrying later, in spite of the fact that Gulf governments favoured high birth rates, in some cases withdrawing contraceptives from the market, as one way of lessening the dependence on foreign labour. Governments like the Kuwaiti Government increased the loans given to nationals for marriage, to encourage earlier marriages and larger families, and tried to ensure that the housing offered to low-income groups could accommodate large families. This is an indication that the Government did not intend to depend on the contribution of women in development: a high birth rate policy would, if successful, shrink the pool of existing labour by lessening women's availability to the workforce.

## The young professionals

It was not unusual, however, for many couples to study and work at the same time, and to share the task of raising their family. The growth of a sizeable young professional class in the Gulf was one outcome of access to education and modernisation; husband and wife frequently assisted one another in coping with the restrictions imposed by customs and by a changing lifestyle. Take the story of 'Noura' and 'Saif', a young Saudi couple from Mecca who were typical of the young Gulf professionals. By 1982, they had been married eight years. Both were studying abroad on government scholarships: Saif had previously worked as a teacher and was then completing his PhD; Noura had completed her BA and wanted to do post-graduate work before finding a job. They already had one child, and another was on the way (AN, 1982):

Saif: We had an arranged marriage. My sisters met Noura, who is a distant cousin, liked her and saw that she shared my way of thinking, so her hand was asked for in marriage on my behalf. I then went and met her. It was unusual in those days to see one's wife before marriage. I liked her, so we got married. I was 22 and Noura was 20. It is difficult to find a suitable marriage partner. Many men go to study outside and get Western ideas, and when they come back, they want to get on with their careers and marriage is not top on the list of their priorities.

Noura: And boys who stay at home to study only want to marry girls of 16; they find the girls who have finished college too old. But girls want to finish their studies before they get married. A cousin of mine in medical school does not want to marry until she gets her degree although when she was in high school she thought differently. All the members of my family were educated; one of my sisters graduated in the social sciences and is now working with a social welfare organisation; the other is at university and is about to complete her degree in geography. My father loved learning, and wanted his girls to go out to study and work. He taught us to be self-confident.

Saif: My sister got married at 17. She is a very bright girl and should have continued her studies rather than getting married so young. That was my opinion. But the sisters of her prospective husband convinced her. Another of my sisters married while she was studying medicine; she later divorced and returned to complete her studies. There is a gap between the expectations that men and women have from one another – and if you add the parents' expectations, you can understand why marriage has become more difficult.

Noura: I'm still a student now, but since I'm used to going out of the house, I wouldn't want to stay at home when I finish. I spent one year at home once, and I nearly went out of my mind.

Saif: I don't think there will be a sudden, drastic change in women's roles. Of course, the situation is not as it is described in the Western press – they picture it as unbearable. But if one does not know any other way of life, it does not matter so much. There are many working women, even in companies, where Saudi women have insisted on being hired. Aramco [the oil company] is packed with female secretaries, including Saudis. Women work in radio and television, and work in the hospitals is mixed. My sister always complains about the hypocrisy of it all; she says that as a doctor in the hospital she carries out her duties like anybody else, but once outside she has to veil. Certain professions are still not respected, to the extent that my father wrote in his will that he would not approve of his daughters working as nurses, stewardesses or secretaries.

Noura: Still, a nurse's school has been opened in Riyadh and many Saudi girls are enrolled. My friend started to study there, but stopped after she got married because her husband didn't like it. As for veiling, in Jeddah you don't have to cover your face if you don't want to, and I don't; when I go to Mecca, I do. I can adapt. It does irk me to cover up, but not to the extent that I would want to go and live abroad. It's usually the men who are sensitive to social stigma, not women. Even conservative women think it's alright to drive, so long as you're well covered up.

Saif: A friend once said to me, 'You're very brave – you let your wife go out of the house without a veil on'! One of my sisters and her friend are not looking forward to coming back after they finish their studies. Imagine, after eight years of studying for a career and driving your own car, to go back to a place where your younger brother can force you to put on a veil if he wants to. But the situation really is not that bad, and slowly there will be change. In the meantime, I thank God I wasn't born a woman!

## The women professionals

The variety of attitudes to education and work can be seen in the above account, as well as the ways people are finding to cope with tradition and modernity. Meanwhile, a great many of the young professionals are women. Research has shown that, in the Third World, the professions are the area where there is least resistance to women's employment. Most working women in the Gulf are to be found in the services sector, with a large proportion of these in the professions.

It is a source of pride in the region that women occupy so many senior posts. While there are no women cabinet ministers in the Gulf, there are women under-secretaries in Kuwait and the UAE, and women can be found as heads of sections and departments in ministries everywhere, mostly in the fields of education, social affairs and information. An idea of their experience on the job is given in the story of Lulwa, who headed a section of a UAE ministry (AN, 1984):

This was my first job after graduation. All the other employees in my section are men. There is great demand for more women to work, and officials are always calling for it, but the customs do not allow it. Do I feel discriminated against as a woman? In my job, since the men are foreign or other Arab workers, they cannot afford to refuse the work I ask them to do. There is a tendency to belittle you if you're a woman with a remark like: 'a national – and a woman too?' [Some Arab and foreign employees tended to look down on nationals of both sexes; a subconscious reason was fear for their own jobs when the nationals were ready to take over.] But in the end it depends on the woman. The way I'm viewed now is very different from when I first started.

The real problem at work is sensitivity between foreigners and nationals: even foreign women resent a national woman. There are two laws, one for nationals and one for immigrant workers, and there is discrimination in favour of nationals in promotions and salaries, which the foreigners find hard to accept. For instance, one of the men in my section has been doing his job for many years; he is now 40, and here I am as his head although I have only been working at it for one year. Still, now they respect me as a person; if a girl respects herself, people respect her.

There are different attitudes to women in the ministry. One of the top officials is so conservative he does not want to admit that there is such a thing as a woman! You can't go in to see him on your own, and if you're not wearing Islamic dress he won't process your paperwork! On the other hand, the minister is very accessible and easy to talk to. If there is a formality to complete in some department and you go yourself, they will complete it quickly for you because you're a woman, putting you before the most important man. But the thinking behind this is that a woman is a poor, weak thing who needs to be protected.

There is some discrimination against women, but they do it in a diplomatic way because they're not allowed to by law. You're getting along quite happily and then you realise they didn't pass a certain task on to you or send you on a study mission because you're a woman. To be fair, sometimes parents don't allow their daughters to travel or to go about the country on their work, and employers get fed up and are put off hiring women. Our customs are difficult. People don't like a girl to stay on after office hours, or to take a cab by herself. No one really is to blame, it's the social customs that are to blame.

I wanted to work to make use of what I had studied, to keep abreast of new material, to make contacts. Secondly, I wanted to stand on my own two feet and guarantee my own future; this gives me a reassuring feeling. If I get married, my husband should not impose any conditions about me working or not working. Anyway, now parents cannot force you to marry; they can point out advantages and make suggestions, but not force. They did not use to force marriage in the old days either, but then it just would not occur to the girl to refuse to do what her parents wanted.

My parents are not typical: they gave us every freedom to study and work. My mother especially wanted us to study and to get experience at work; she feels we know more about some things than her now, and consults us about them. But other families still don't understand why a girl should go out to work and be 'humiliated' in this way.

This young woman's story is a fair description of work in government ministries and of tensions between national and non-national workers. It shows the different attitudes to be found among colleagues and in society, the variety of which gives people some leeway in finding more room to manoeuvre. At this stage, most working women in the Gulf would cite personal interest, rather than economic need, as the first inducement to joining the workforce, but it is clear that economic independence gives the working woman a little more freedom of choice *vis-à-vis* parents and prospective husbands.

Although most women did go into traditional professions such as teaching or the civil service, there were some who opted for more unusual careers in science and technology. Khadija was a civil engineer, who had found a job in a bank's industrial project department:

We're always told that this or that profession is unsuitable for women, but as far as I am concerned any work is suitable – engineering, law, even cleaning the streets. It's how you prove yourself that counts, and civil engineering is an area where there will always be work in developing nations.

My family encouraged me to study. My father was more supportive than my mother; she was more worried about maintaining customs and tradition. My work involves evaluating industrial projects that are submitted to the bank for financing. We have to go out to check the design and structure of buildings, factories etc., and assess their mortgage values. My family does not object to my going out on the job, so long as I wear my abaya [light black cloak] over my long dress; imagine, in all that heat! And I drive, so I can get around. Sometimes, applicants for loans don't take me seriously. You can see it in their faces. One of them, a Gulf national, called me up once to apologise for his attitude. He hadn't said anything outright, but he had not taken me seriously and had shown it in his manner.

What helps me is the people I'm working with. They are the best – all highly educated people who have studied in the US, and who are very broadminded. They are all nationals, and they're always pushing me to achieve more. I am the only woman in the engineering department. My direct boss is from Pakistan, and he is really good. Whenever I make a mistake he advises me. The director is also very good; he has introduced computerisation in the bank and is urging us all to learn it. I had taken a couple of computer courses at university, but now I'm really good at it.

Marriage and children? Yes, well I wouldn't get pregnant for the first two years, and then I hope it's twins so I can get it over with! I won't have anyone else bringing up my children, so I will take at least four years off to care for them, then go back to work. I would try my best to do both, but if I felt my work was threatening my family life, then I might work part-time or stop altogether. (AN, 1984)

## Tug of war on women's work

Obviously attitudes do not all change at one and the same time, and, in the Gulf as elsewhere, range from the very liberal to the arch-conservative. As mentioned earlier, nearly all Gulf nationals prefer slow change in social attitudes, to compensate for rapid change on the material level. Whenever social change appears to be moving too fast for comfort, conservative calls for the reinforcement of traditions and customs become stronger. The tug of war between conservatives and liberals in the Gulf is a regular feature: although both favour a measured approach to change, they differ as to the pace.

Two examples will serve to illustrate the battle between conservatives and liberals on women playing an equal role in the development process. The first example comes from a novel by a Saudi writer, Issam Khokeir, called *The Whirlpool*. According to the 16 April 1984 edition of *Sayidaty*, this novel had gone through several editions since it was first published in the early 1980s. The main character in *The Whirlpool* was a Saudi woman who left her home and children in the care of domestic servants to go out and work. Khokeir told the magazine that the idea for the novel had come to him when he read that female university graduates were complaining that they could not find suitable jobs. He had begun to ponder the purpose of women's education: what was the point of so many years' hard work? Simply to hang a framed degree in the living room? Or should women do something more with their education? He said he had failed to come up with an answer.

The novel was meant to provide the answer, and here he clearly had had no trouble defining what was best for society. The heroine, who has left her children to the care of the nanny, is hurt to discover that they do not ask after her when she falls ill. There are frequent arguments between the heroine and her mother, who urges her to care for her children. By the end of the novel, after many traumatic experiences, the working woman decides to give up her career and to look after her children. Her husband is surprised that she should decide to leave her job after so many years' service. But her mother's caustic comment is that, by having gone out to work, her daughter had behaved just like the housewife who did not feel like cleaning her own home but ended up cleaning the neighbours'. One of the characters in the novel compares women who work outside the home, leaving their children to another's care, to the farmer who abandons his fields for the excitement of the city, but who ruins himself and society.

The second example comes from an article by Kuwaiti lawyer Badriya al-Awadhi, a specialist in maritime law, who frequently wrote for the daily press on issues as diverse as pollution of Gulf waters, social conflicts and international affairs. In an article in the 23 April 1978 edition of *Al-Watan*, she sought to rebuff the views expressed by the Ministry of Health and the Ministry of Awqaf (Islamic trusts) on the question of women's work.

The Awqaf Ministry put out a memorandum in which it did not object to women's work as such; it simply wanted women to work in areas suitable to their 'nature', where they would not be humiliated. The Health Ministry and the Awqaf Ministry both warned that women's work was leading to an increase in the divorce rate, in the number of spinsters, and in the cases of juvenile delinquency as well as to the 'masculinisation' of women. In view of the gravity of this situation, the Health Ministry memo proposed that official and popular forces should strive to emphasise the concept of motherhood, introducing courses into the curricula and preparing programmes for the mass media. The Health Ministry appreciated that many women wanted to work outside the home for economic reasons, but felt that the adverse impact on children was too high a price for society to pay. It therefore proposed that working women with children under six should be paid a salary to stay at home and care for the children; by the same token, women with children under six should not be permitted to work.

Al-Awadhi pointed out that neither memo had based its conclusions on facts. She had checked the figures and found that, for instance, juvenile delinquency was higher among families where the mother did not work outside the home than those where the mother did. Only two of the 61 juvenile delinquents in Kuwait had working mothers, and the rest came from families where the mother did not work. And only two out of 59 youths in the care of the Youth Welfare Home had working mothers.

The officials, she declared, seemed to find it easier to put the blame on women instead of examining the multi-faceted causes that led to such problems, as though men had nothing to do with the problems afflicting society. What about the responsibility of the state towards youth, and the importance of providing facilities to help the young spend their free time productively and well? In fact, she said, the two memos touched on an issue that was more serious than whether women went out to work or not: they were indirectly questioning women's right to work at all. She drew attention to the fact that the Kuwaiti constitution and laws protected working women's rights as did international law.

## Ability: the need for skills

The previous discussion looked at the conditions of need and opportunity at the state and popular level, and at how these affected women's entry into the workforce. The third condition, ability, raises the question of appropriate education and skills. There was massive investment in education in the Gulf during the 1970s and 1980s (see Table 3). Student enrolment nearly doubled between 1970 and 1980, and the percentage of women to the total rose sharply. All the Gulf states have their own universities now, the most recent being in Oman. As in the rest of the Third World, however, the quality of education was uneven, and most students continued to opt for the arts and humanities rather than science and technology. Gulf officials criticised what they described as a trend to pursue PhDs for their own sake, and to see the degree as the end of human endeavour rather than the beginning. Meanwhile, the vocational training programmes on offer were low in quality and relevant skills.

There was also a pressing need for post-employment training. Since the days when the first graduates, men and women, returned from universities abroad, the pattern has been to appoint graduates to high-level positions to replace foreign manpower. This created problems of its own, since it meant that young graduates started close to the top of the ladder, without necessarily having the skills or ability for that position. Frequently, the foreign professionals had to be kept on anyway. As the top posts were filled; the younger graduates were aware that their prospects for promotion were limited, in view of the fact that their superiors were so close to them in age, and this was a source of resentment.

These problems were, on occasion, discussed quite frankly. For example, the need to train new appointees in management skills was the subject of a paper by a young female Saudi lecturer (Al-Hussaini, 1982); many of the points she raised applied to men and women alike, while some applied only to Saudi women. Al-Hussaini noted that the number of Saudi women in the workforce did not reflect their numerical weight in the country, and argued that this could not be ascribed to the fact that most women went into fields like education, medicine and social welfare, since the government still had to depend on many foreign women for skills in these same fields. The reasons for the low numbers, she said, were, first, because Saudi women did not face an economic need to work, and, secondly, because society still viewed their work with a conservative eye.

She pointed out that the area where Saudi women employees most needed training was in management skills, especially at leadership levels. There was also a need to train managers in accounting, administration and legal affairs. Saudi women lacked sufficient skills in these areas because they were relative newcomers to the labour market, and because they had had to take on responsibility in top administrative posts without the appropriate background. Moreover, the central departments of administrative affairs in ministries or universities were run by men. Thus women heads of department had to communicate with administrative directors by phone if they had problems to discuss. This meant that the director could not properly assess the problem, and that the woman acquired no administrative experience.

There was one positive aspect to segregation, she remarked: the struggle over leadership positions that took place in other countries did not exist in Saudi Arabia. Women were able to reach top administrative positions without facing male competition or opposition. (The separation of the men's and women's worlds in Saudi Arabia has also led to the creation of certain woman-specific facilities like all-women banks, which provided further opportunities for women to work in finance.)

## Work for work's sake

Although they were joining the wage-labour force in increasing numbers, Gulf nationals were not necessarily engaged in productive employment. They shared with other Arabs a preference for white-collar work over technical and manual labour, and a large proportion of nationals worked in the public sector, where both locals and foreign workers were underemployed. Kuwari noted that the number of public-sector workers in Kuwait totalled 110,000 in 1975. This accounted for some 45 per cent of the labour force. In fact, the number of public-sector jobs was greater than the number of Kuwaiti nationals in the labour force, which stood at 77,000, mostly employed by the public sector. The number of public-sector jobs in Qatar was about 35,000 and in Bahrain about 30,000. Kuwari noted that Luxembourg, which had a population of 400,000, had only 7,000 public-sector employees (pp.253–4).

The Gulf was not unique. Egypt, for instance, was burdened with an elephantine bureaucracy, partly thanks to Nasser's promise of public-sector jobs for graduates who could not find them elsewhere. One might just

conceivably argue that, given the massive population and serious unemployment problem, this was one way to keep people above the poverty level.
The Gulf states, on the other hand, were forced to import labour, and in
theory could afford a large civil service even less than Egypt. But the Gulf
bureaucracy was bloated too. This is best illustrated by the remark of an
employee in a Gulf ministry: 'When I started work here in the 1960s, we
were only 90 employees and we all worked very hard. Now we are over
1,000 employees. The original 90 are still working very hard, and the rest
are creating work for them!' (AN, 1979).

There were other ways of working without producing, because of state
policies to distribute the area's new-found wealth. Gulf governments often
paid inflated prices for property owned by nationals as one way of spreading
largesse. Moreover, no non-national could go into business without having
a local partner who had a majority share; that is, nationals could 'lease' their
names to non-nationals for a share in the business. Many Gulf women also
set themselves up in business. Gulf women enjoyed control of their own
wealth, and this was made more substantial with the rise in dowries and
amounts of money to inherit. It was estimated, in the early 1980s, that
women controlled a third of the personal wealth in Saudi Arabia. An insight
into the extent of financial activity undertaken by women was revealed by
the stock market crash in Kuwait: of 89 persons whose assets in Kuwait
were frozen by the government, 26 were women.

Such speculative activities further distanced men and women from
productive labour, although in theory they 'worked'. Many Gulf nationals
have contributed to their countries' development, and have worked long
and hard, but the ways of recycling money made it possible for others to opt
out of productive labour altogether. The problem, as one Saudi national
explained caustically, 'is not how to get women to work, it's how to get the
men to work'. So long as the cash exists, Gulf governments are unlikely to
end policies that discourage productive labour, particularly as any moves in
that direction would have political repercussions.

The Gulf economy cannot, even in the short term, afford the luxury of
paying people for unproductive labour. Oil and gas reserves, practically the
only resource in these states, will not last for ever. In spite of the appearance
of wealth, the Gulf states are quite poor, in terms of a self-sustainable
economic base, particularly as there is no guarantee that the industrial
diversification policies of the 1970s and 1980s will end the dependence on
oil. Unfortunately, so long as the cash is there to finance the imports of
foreign labour, the Gulf states will not be forced to demand productive
labour from under-employed nationals or non-nationals.

To sum up, the acute Gulf labour shortage did not lead to women's
integration into the wage-labour force in the numbers and at the pace one

might expect, because the conditions of need, opportunity and ability were not met at the state and popular levels. Oil wealth meant that need at the popular level was not pressing enough for more than one family member to go out to work – with exceptions, especially in the more heavily populated, less well-off states. Oil wealth also meant that the state could afford to finance foreign manpower imports, in spite of the fact that this was felt to be a threat to the social fabric. Moreover, the rapidity of social change reinforced attachment to tradition, particularly as this related to women's roles as mothers, and served to limit, to some extent, the opportunity for work outside the home.

However, many of the Gulf men and women who already work in the modern sector are not really engaged in productive activity. The bulk of the national labour force is concentrated in the service sector in areas where under-employment is high, as is the case in the rest of the Arab world. The issue is not therefore simply to get more women in the workforce by lobbying for legislation or for change in social attitudes or for more facilities like day-care centres. Any attempt to tackle the question of women's integration in the wage-labour force must include a redefinition of the nature of work, and of the overall political and economic development process in the Gulf. And this is not a task that women can shoulder alone.

Chapter 6

# Power past and future

If a woman participates only in the national struggle, she'll have to start at square one after liberation.          *Palestinian woman under Israeli occupation*

The Arab debate on the roles of women is part of the effort to define the role of religion in society and what constitutes a 'modern' Arab identity. It is also part of the quest for economic development and national independence. I have argued that all the soul searching might have been cut short if there had been an urgent need for women's participation in the modern workforce. This has not happened, in my view, because the mode of development in the Arab world has not resulted in real economic opportunities for men or women. So the vicious circle continues: Arab women can only be truly liberated when Arab society is liberated politically and economically; and Arab society can only be truly liberated politically and economically, when it is liberated socially, which involves equal rights for women.

How much of a part can Arab women play in the process of reshaping the Arab world and in improving their own conditions? How do the existing women's groups function, and what are the alternatives? Radical change in any sphere is difficult, if not impossible, to achieve without the power to impose it. What power do Arab women have? What power are they likely to get?

## Defining power

In the literature on the subject of women in the Middle East up to the 1970s, Arab women were assumed to be fairly powerless. Three factors were usually used to assess how much power women had: first, participation in the democratic process, that is having the right to vote, to be elected, to be a member of government, etc.; secondly, the legislation on matters of personal status; and, thirdly, women's access to education and paid employment. Using these indicators, women were believed to have low status and little power in the Arab world: there were few representatives in parliament or the government, although women have the right to vote and to be elected more or less throughout the region; piecemeal amendments had been made in personal status laws which still did not provide for equal treatment of men and women; and women's illiteracy was still high, although many more people had access to education, while female participation in the wage-labour force was still low.

Women in Europe and America were seen to have nearly achieved equality in the last two areas by the 1980s: in matters of paid employment, for instance, the burning issue of the mid-1980s in America was no longer one of access, or even of equal pay for equal work, but of equal pay for comparable work. In terms of personal status, the law was almost completely equal on men and women; Switzerland was in 1985 one of the last European countries to amend its personal status laws. As for the political level, women in the West were still trying to increase representation in parliament and government beyond the 'token woman' level. By comparison with women in the industrialised nations, Arab women seemed to be quite badly off.

Another reason for the pervasive assumption that Arab women were powerless was the fact that much of the literature until the 1970s had been produced by social scientists who were usually Western and male. This meant further reliance on the three factors above, without recourse to field research: Western men were unlikely to meet Arab women from traditional sectors of the population, that is, from the majority of the population. Naturally, the reliance on incomplete statistics or on religious texts to form a picture of the daily lives of the people produced a distorted image. (See Tucker, 1983, and Keddie, 1979, for an analysis of the problems of existing research on women in the Middle East.) Even readers of this book might, if they were to read only passages from chapter 1 on the personal status laws, or selections from the chapters on women in the wage-labour force, form the idea that Arab women had little power since the formal structures seemed to indicate that this was the case.

During the last 15 years, however, Western women have established a strong presence in the social sciences. While some carried in-built cultural and theoretical prejudices into their writing, many others did not. Most importantly, being women, they at least had easier access to other women and to examining their actual situation. At the same time, an increasing number of Arab social scientists, men and women, entered the field, with the advantages of access and, obviously, of a better understanding of their own culture (with perhaps a disadvantage in some cases of lacking hard-nosed objectivity).

Slowly, the meaning of power was redefined for the study of cultures other than Western. In the Arab world, the new breed of Western and Arab social scientists no longer focussed on access to the formal power structures, which were anyway fairly new to the region and which were usually controlled by a handful of men. They began to examine the informal networks that existed, and how these functioned to protect an individual's interests within the family and society.

They began to see that access to parliaments or to the wage-labour force were insufficient measures of power: low representation in parliaments did not mean that women had no power in their community; low participation in the wage-labour force did not mean that women had no money or no control over income. A good working definition, in my view, is this: power is the extent to which a person or group can exercise control over their situation; in the case of women, the extent to which they can influence factors related to their situation in order to serve clearly defined personal (or family, or community) interests.

With revised definitions of what constitutes power, it became possible to understand how women who were supposedly so powerless appeared so strong and self-confident, as they did even (or rather especially) in the more traditional communities which were supposed to be more restrictive of women. As was noted in the first chapter, Nadia Haggag Youssef drew the distinction between the respect given to women and the rights given to them, two elements which combined to make up women's status. She asserted that women could receive greater respect in societies that gave them few rights on paper, than they did in societies that gave them equal rights. Anyone who has met and spoken to the Arab women of the Gulf, for example, could not fail to be struck by the forcefulness of their person-alities, a fact very much at odds with the image formed by a superficial impression.

Writing of women in Moroccan villages, at the opposite end of the Arab world, Susan Schaefer Davis said, 'A closer look at the women's world will also help solve the paradox of why these apparently weak and statusless females often seem, to the observer who knows them well, to be the strongest members of the society' (1980, p.87). Schaefer Davis analysed women's status within the women's world, and not within the men's world, because this was the only approach that made sense. As she pointed out, this was how the members of the society measured status. To merit high status, women did not compete with men in the formal sector but with women in the household. Moreover, when a woman's position was considered relative to other women, it was found that she, in fact, had more opportunities to achieve high status in the women's world than men did in the men's world.

## Negotiating power

The new approach formed the basis of studies, not just on the more accessible, educated Arab women who had joined the modern sector, but also on the diverse systems in force in the Arab world in lower income urban groups, in the villages, and among the bedouin. For instance, a biographical sketch of a settled bedouin woman in Jordan illustrates the difference between the freedom enjoyed by city women and women in the tribe. Jawazi, the settled bedouin woman, was quoted as saying that

The urban Jordanians were much more protective of their girls, and all the women wore veils over their faces [when she and her husband first moved to Amman in the 1960s]. It seemed that Islam was more demanding, Jawazi said, in an urban society. In the desert, there was a freedom of spirit, she says, that did not exist in the city. Jawazi missed that freedom. (Hazleton, 1977, p.268)

Researchers established similar attitudes in other bedouin communities in the region. For instance Beck, in Beck and Keddie (1978), quoted a tribal woman leader among nomadic pastoralists in Iran as saying, 'Discrimination against women is largely an urban malady and a sign of social decline in the bigger towns. In the countryside and the tribes, women have always been treated as equals of men. The chador [Iranian-style veil] is an urban invention. In the tribe both sexes have to work together in order to allow their society to function' (pp.370–1).

Bedouin and rural women did not always enjoy their full legal rights in terms of inheritance, since some families did not want to fragment land holdings by parcelling them out along the lines provided for in Islamic law, but this was compensated by their having a stronger claim on their natal families for economic and moral support, and they seemed to enjoy more freedom of movement. Vanessa Maher's research in Morocco (described in Beck and Keddie 1978, and in her own book on women and property [1974]) noted the different situations of urban women and country women: the former had an easier life, but were socially isolated, passive and subordinated to male authority; the latter had a far more difficult life in physical terms with a heavy work burden, but enjoyed more independence of action.

Studies of peasant families in Egypt showed women participating in economic activity and sharing in decision-making and power as they had more children (especially boys) and grew older and more established, while studies of women in low economic strata in an urban setting, like Sawsan el-Messiri's study on urban women in Cairo also found evidence of leadership roles among women. El-Messiri wrote of the *mu'allima* (feminine for master), a 'term referring to certain working women, mainly butchers, hashish merchants, coffeehouse keepers, or important merchants in the market. They are usually reputed to have powerful status in the hitta [quarter]. They direct large and successful enterprises. Traditionally the *mu'allima* . . . participates in quarrels like a man and disciplines anyone she dislikes with a beating.' The *mu'allima* also mediated marriages, helped out people with talent but no capital, and reconciled quarrelling parties.

It seemed that when the economy was of a subsistence nature and the labour of both sexes was necessary for the survival of the family and the community, women had power and shared actively and sometimes publicly in the life of the community, especially as they grew older and their sexuality was no longer considered to be a threat to family honour. Women from more comfortable strata of society were not completely powerless, either, although they might be more secluded. The instruments of power women developed in a segregated setting were discussed in Carla Makhlouf's book on the Yemen Republic, *Changing Veils* (1979). One of the major weapons was access to and control over information.

Makhlouf said,

One may go even further, and attempt to turn upside down the commonsense 'truth' which contends that the women are excluded from the male world. One can venture that in fact the men are excluded from the female world, as much, if not more, than females are excluded from the world of men . . . Men's speech is closer to classical Arabic and easier to understand for women and for a non-Yemeni, whereas women speak with a guttural but high-pitched voice and at a higher speed. A number of men have actually told me that they could not understand women's language. (p.28)

The existence of a woman's world from which men were excluded had practical consequences. For example, Makhlouf noted that the birth rate in Yemen was significantly lower than in other developing countries, which could have meant that women were controlling their fertility without the knowledge of men.

The power accruing to women from access to and control over information in a segregated setting was also described by the Saudi social scientist Soraya al-Turki, in her research on elite families in Jeddah (Al-Turki, 1986). In a talk to the seminar on women organised by the Oxford Arab Committee in April 1986, Al-Turki said that the very segregation of the sexes that prevented women from gaining access to positions of authority in the wider society 'creates the conditions of their far-reaching control over a man's destiny'. Through traditional networks of kinship and friendship, women not only controlled the information that was necessary when it came to arranging marriages but they also, Al-Turki maintained, used this information to further their own interests.

Al-Turki described the transition process and how traditional instruments of power were being replaced by more modern ones. Educated young women demanded more of a husband's time, giving the nuclear family priority over the extended family, although extended family ties were still strong, and were acquiring more power at the expense of their mothers-in-law. They had also started to exercise more direct control over their own wealth, whereas previously the male kin used to organise matters on their behalf. The Saudi case showed that the source of women's power in elite families was changing from a collective basis to an individual one.

Thus, women found ways to organise and maintain sources of power in traditional settings. There was no doubt that this power was effective, for, in the days before the nation-state took hold, the day-to-day life of the community was run through informal power structures. With modernisation, traditional structures have weakened and this, for women in the Arab world, has had more serious consequences than for men. Both men and women can still rely to some extent on the extended family for economic and emotional support. Both men and women are effectively excluded from formal political power, which is concentrated in the hands of a small minority of men. However, the laws of the state are increasingly replacing the informal structures that served to control community and family affairs. Here, women have a special problem because they are not equal to men in matters of family law, as was demonstrated earlier.

Thus, in addition to the economic and political problems of the region which affect them as citizens, women have the task of tackling laws and attitudes that affect them specifically as women and they have to find new sources of power to do so. It is not enough, for this purpose, to enjoy more of a say in running the day-to-day life of a family at the nuclear level. It is necessary to have the power of numbers to protect interests, as was the case in the traditional networks. It is from this perspective that women's groups, as they have developed since the early twentieth century, should be examined.

### Early women reformers and nationalism

The debate on reforming the position of women in the Arab world was initiated by men. They had had the earliest access to education, and were the first to have travelled to Europe and to have been influenced by European attitudes to women. It was not long before women joined in the debate. Again, the first women reformers were the ones with early access to education, usually through private lessons at home, and to European ideas. Both women and men came from the upper socioeconomic brackets in the main cities.

At the beginning, women's demands for their rights were as moderate and as carefully phrased as those articulated by men on their behalf. For instance, Malak Hifni Nassif, a contemporary of Qassim Amin's, frequently defended women's rights in the newspapers and magazines of the day under the pen-name Bahithat al-Badiya. However, she did not believe that women should fight for public roles and the right to vote like European women who, she felt, were suffering from 'indigestion' as a result of too much freedom. A 10-point plan to improve the staus of women, which she presented to the first Egyptian Congress of 1911, was far from radical. It proposed, among other things, providing school opportunities for girls, training women doctors so that they could care for women, and restricting polygamy; nevertheless, it was turned down.

The first Arab women's magazine was published in Alexandria in 1892, by a Syrian woman, Hind Noufal. By the 1910s, there were over 15 monthly and fortnightly women's magazines in Cairo and Alexandria, many of which were published by Syrian and Lebanese women. The first women's groups began by opening schools for women and engaging in charitable activities, a pattern which has continued throughout the twentieth century. The services provided by the charitable organisations women set up – orphanages, hospitals, vocational training centres for destitute women – were then sorely needed by society. Afaf Lutfi al-Sayyid Marsot has given an interesting account of how upper-class women in Egypt stepped straight out of the harem to run these large and complex outfits, using management skills acquired in running their households, and using their contacts with Egyptian leaders to keep the organisations going even when the men were at odds over policy (1978).

The nascent women's movement was politicised by Arab nationalist opposition to both Turkish nationalism during the last years of the Ottoman Empire and to European colonialism. The women's response was strongest in Egypt, Lebanon, Syria and Palestine, where the first groups were formed and the earliest magazines published. In Egypt, one woman soon towered above the rest: Huda Shaarawi. By the time of the 1919 nationalist uprising in Egypt, she had already established herself as a reformer by opening a girls' school, the first to offer general education rather than just vocational training.

During the Egyptian uprising against the British in 1919, veiled upper-class women went out on demonstrations, as did men and women from all sectors of society. Putting their image as helpless, protected beings to good use, the upper-class women helped the revolution by, for example, carrying pamphlets hidden in shopping baskets out to the villages. (This pattern was to be repeated by Arab women in other revolutions, particularly the Algerian and Palestinian.) When the nationalist leader Saad Zaghloul was arrested and the British banned all publicity about him, women reportedly gathered at his wife's house and wrote 'yahya Saad' (long live Saad) on all the pieces of paper money they could find, and then put the notes in circulation (Fernea and Bezirgan, 1977, p.197).

Shaarawi supported the establishment of the Misr Bank, by subscribing 1,000 Egyptian pounds to the Bank's capital. She urged her friends to subscribe so that Egypt might become economically independent (Al-Sidani, 1982, p.26). She presented petitions to the British High Commissioner, and to his wife, in the name of Egyptian women, calling for liberty and freedom for Egypt. Shaarawi and her colleagues were less ready than their menfolk to accept, even temporarily, political compromise with the British. In 1924, they sent a memorandum to the Egyptian parliament protesting against compromise. They were insisting, by this time, that women should be given the right to vote and to be elected, as well as equal access to education and opportunities to work.

The women had formed an executive committee within the Wafd party; in 1923, this was dissolved, and the Egyptian Women's Union was set up under Shaarawi's leadership. That year, after attending the International Conference of Women in Rome, Shaarawi took off her veil on her return to Egypt and other veiled women followed suit. The constitution of the Women's Union underlined the need for women's access to education, for social and political equality with men (but in accordance with tradition), for raising the minimum age of marriage and for reforming the practices of arranged marriage and polygamy. Some of the women had personally suffered from the practices they opposed: in earlier times, Malak Hifni Nassif's husband had taken a second wife; as for Shaarawi, her marriage had been arranged when she was about 13. Access to education and some reforms of marriage customs were forthcoming in the 1920s, but political equality had to wait until 1956 when, partly as a result of a hunger strike by the women activists of the day, the Free Officers included political rights for women in the constitution.

Women in Lebanon played a part similar to that of Egyptian women in the Syrian/Lebanese struggle against the French, and contributed to the debate on the roles of women through the press. They had established numerous charitable organisations, as well as successful centres for the preservation and development of Lebanese handicrafts (Al-Khatib, 1984). After independence, they were responsible for many of the country's cultural events; of particular note was the Baalbek Festival, which helped to put Lebanon on the tourist map before the 1975 civil war removed it. By the early 1950s, Lebanese women who, like the Egyptian women activists, came from established upper-class families, were persistently petitioning the government for the right to vote. Educated women were given the right to vote in 1952, and the unqualified right to vote was extended to women in

1953, although it remained optional for women and mandatory for men, as in Egypt.

Lebanese women were thus the first in the region to get the right to vote. Women's groups in Lebanon frequently demanded the revision of the personal status laws. Each religious community in Lebanon managed its personal status affairs based on its own texts and traditions. The women wanted these replaced by a unified law, a demand which went to the root of Lebanon's sectarian problem, and which recognised that there would be no peace for the country until religion and state were separated in fact, not just in form.

In neighbouring Palestine, women began to set up charitable associations to care for children, the needy and the sick, much as the Egyptian women had done. They were soon involved in the country's political problems, taking part in protests. A women's association was set up in 1921 and in 1929, a particularly turbulent year in Palestine, the first Arab Women's Congress of Palestine was held. It was attended by over 200 Palestinian women from various cities and towns, who presented their resolutions and demands to the British High Commissioner. The Congress declared that the 1917 Balfour Declaration, whereby Britain was to help the Zionists to acquire a national home in Palestine, had been the 'sole cause of all the troubles that took place in the country, and which may arise in future. We consider that this country will never enjoy peace and tranquillity so long as this Declaration is in force' (Mogannam, 1937, pp.74–5). The Palestinian women, who, like Egyptian women, came from upper socioeconomic strata, also organised demonstrations in Jerusalem to protest British policies in Palestine.

The Palestine Question was a rallying point for all Arab women. The first pan-Arab women's conference, convened by Huda Shaarawi in Cairo in 1938, was held to support the Palestinian struggle. Meanwhile, Shaarawi travelled to many Arab countries, urging the women to set up unions. The first pan-Arab organisation, the General Federation of Arab Women, was established in 1944, a year before the Arab League was set up. (The women protested that there were no representatives of the female sex in the League.)

While nationalism spurred women to joint public action, the demand for women's rights was soon a major item on the agenda of the new women's organisations. However, although these organisations did involve a number of women in working together, they clearly did not have the power to impose radical change. In Egypt, the personal status laws were amended slightly in the 1920s. The age of marriage was raised, the practice of arranged marriages was ended, and women were allowed more grounds on which to petition for divorce. But Egyptian personal status laws have not been radically reformed to this day. As for political rights, these were extended in the first flush of national independence by new governments that wanted to be seen to be modern.

This is not to say that women's agitation had no impact at all, but simply to point out that it was not powerful enough to be likely to succeed in the face of really stiff opposition. In any case, there was so much to be done in order to provide people with basic needs – education, health care, services like water and electricity – that it is not surprising that the state, and the women, dedicated much of their time to solving problems in these areas. The struggle for rights was less important than the cause of nation-building. The question is, have the women's groups of today been any more successful in tackling the matter of equal rights?

## Women's groups, official and unofficial

From the early days to the present time, two broad categories of women's groups have developed. The first category includes the 'official' women: women in government and in the national women's federations which exist in most Arab countries. The second category consists of women in non-governmental organisations (NGOs) of a cultural and social nature. Women's national federations are in theory non-governmental groups, but they are so close to government policy, effectively acting as an arm of the government, that it makes more sense to place them in the first category.

Over the years, the women in the first category met fairly frequently in national and pan-Arab conferences. If the government was active on development issues, the federations would also be active in the economic and social development of the country. The federations were not, however, likely to take a stand on controversial issues that the governments did not wish to tackle. Like the Arab governments, official women's groups lacked credibility at the popular level. At the pan-Arab level, the federations were grouped in the General Arab Women's Federation. Following the 1978 Camp David accords between Egypt and Israel, Egypt was excluded. The Federation then split into two federations along 'moderate' and 'radical' Arab lines. The larger federation was Baghdad-based and held its meetings in Iraq, Morocco and other 'moderate' states, while the second met in Syria, Libya and other 'radical' states.

Meanwhile, the umbrella Arab body, the Arab League, established a Women and Family Department, which was upgraded from a committee in the early 1980s. This was part of the awareness generated by the UN Decade for Women. The League drew up a plan for more research on women, which was to be implemented during the 1980–90 Arab development decade. The aim of the research was to collect information on subjects like the impact of demographic changes on women, the legal status of women on the books and in actuality, the image of women in schoolbooks, and women's image in Arab media. The League was particularly concerned about the position of rural women and held a seminar on this topic in October 1982. The increased interest in women's issues was reflected in the September 1983 edition of the League's journal *Arab Affairs*, which carried a special section on women, with a lengthy bibliography. The League has held annual conferences at which papers on women in different Arab countries are presented; a meeting was held in Amman in 1984 to prepare the Arab position and documents for the Nairobi UN End-of-Decade conference.

As for women's non-governmental organisations, dozens were formed in the Arab world. Most NGOs were of a social and cultural nature and, like most government bodies, they concentrated on welfare and on improving women's position through literacy campaigns, family planning and vocational training, mostly handicrafts. Many were very effective in these areas, and reference was made to the positive role played by Arab women NGOs in the UN End-of-Decade documents. Women's NGOs were particularly active in areas where there were few other public outlets for women, as in Saudi Arabia. They also flourished in other countries; there were estimated to be some 400 in Jordan alone.

The involvement of women in non-governmental bodies is not a phenomenon restricted to the Arab world. It is an indication of the extent to which women worldwide have been excluded from formal structures, and have found an outlet for their energies in informal ones. By the 1970s, international non-governmental organisations had become numerous and powerful enough to have been a major force behind the holding of the UN Decade on Women, as was noted in the Introduction. Moreover, NGOs could succeed in areas where governments failed. An interesting example comes from the 1985 UN conference on women in Nairobi, where people from around the world brought their political problems, as well as their personal, social and economic problems.

By the time of the Nairobi conference, the political disarray at the pan-Arab level had reached unprecedented proportions. As a result, an American-backed Israel managed to remove the 'Zionism equals racism' equation from the UN conference documents at Nairobi, although this had been included in the Mexico and Copenhagen conference documents. The comparison between Zionism and racism is anathema to the Israelis, who consider it unthinkable that they should be accused of racism when they had suffered so greatly from it themselves. The Arabs argue not only that the creation of Israel was achieved at the expense of the Palestinians in Palestine, but also that the Zionist concept translated into the Israeli state was intrinsically racist: one had to be Jewish to have equal rights, as evidenced by the Israeli Law of Return which applied to Jews whatever their nationality but not to the indigenous Palestinians. The Arab governments' failure at the UN conference was more than made up at the NGO Forum where the Israelis, as they themselves admitted, faced a difficult task. The Zionist message was effectively challenged and dismissed from Forum workshops and meetings as a result of the efforts of Arab women and Arab NGOs, with support from Third-World women.

However, although Arab NGOs usually managed to overcome inter-Arab differences and personal rivalries to function effectively outside the Arab world, this had not yet proved possible within the Arab world, or within individual Arab countries. There are some small exceptions. For example, the 1985 Egyptian family law episode covered in chapter 1 showed women working together across political and socioeconomic boundaries, and in spite of the personality conflicts that so often prevent communal work in the Third World, where loyalty to the family or tribe or sect is strong, but loyalty to the community is weak other than at times of major national crisis.

The Egyptian family law experience was seen by some of the women involved as a victory and as an indication that women had learned to work together more effectively. But it was more of a first lesson in working together than the end of the road. First, the struggle was a short one: the family law was overturned and a similar version was restored in just three months. Secondly, the 1985 version of the 1979 law did not introduce the kind of radical change that the Tunisian code had done; most of the women who worked to restore the 1979 law saw it as a 'step on the right road' and as 'better than nothing', but did not insist on such radical reforms as, for instance, banning polygamy altogether. Thirdly, and most importantly, the Egyptian Government was committed to restoring the 1979 law.

Some momentum for equal rights was generated during the Egyptian family law debate, but once the 1985 law was passed, the momentum died down. Similarly, some momentum was generated during the Algerian family law debate of 1984, but not enough for radical change. There has yet to be an example of Arab women achieving rights in the face of entrenched attitudes and as the result of a persistent campaign. Perhaps the best illustration of how far away this is can be seen in the issue of women's right to vote in Kuwait, a problem which had still not been solved in 1986, after some 15 years of intermittent effort by women's groups.

## The right to vote (when parliament exists)

Kuwait is one of the few countries in the region (others being Lebanon, Egypt and Morocco) where the people enjoy a good deal of freedom, in between bouts of muzzling of political expression. This is reflected in lively debates in parliament and in the press. There are thousands of highly educated women, and the women's societies are among the most active and independent of the Arab world. One of these societies, the Kuwait Women's Cultural and Social Association, has sponsored three major regional non-governmental conferences on women. The first was held in 1975 in response to the launching of the UN Decade on Women, and it focussed on the conditions of Gulf women. The second, in 1981, focussed on Gulf women and development and the third, in 1984, focussed on Gulf women and work. Women from all over the Arab world participated and shared their experiences, and the conferences were important meeting points for debate and networking.

In spite of their educational achievements and the fact that they had reached top positions, such as ministry under-secretaries and deans of university colleges, Kuwaiti women did not have the right to vote. The Kuwaiti Constitution declared that all citizens were equal; but the first article of the electoral law restricted voting to literate male Kuwaitis over 21. Women demanded the right to vote at the first Kuwaiti women's conference held on 15 December 1971. This conference submitted a petition to the Kuwaiti National Assembly, which was passed around various committees, and eventually shelved. The issue came up again in 1973, when there were several discussions about giving women the vote in the Assembly. Again, nothing came of it. Meanwhile, the Assembly itself was becoming increasingly vociferous and, in the wave of unease that swept the region following the Lebanese civil war in 1975, it was suspended by the ruling family in 1976. A decision was made to resuscitate it in 1980, and new elections were held in 1981; but no move was made to give women the right to vote.

In 1981, a deputy presented the Assembly with a bill that would have given women the right to vote, but not to stand for election. As he had not consulted any of the women's groups, they had had no opportunity to lobby for the bill or to prepare public opinion through a media campaign. In January 1982, the bill was put to the vote in the Assembly: of the 50 members of the Assembly, 27 voted against, seven voted for, and 31 abstained, including the entire government. There was an uproar in the press and among women; male and female columnists wrote for or against the decision. Women activists organised a petition and took the thousands of signatures collected to the Assembly. They were invited to sit in on that day's debate by the parliament speaker, to the horror of the deputies who had voted against the bill and who were heckled mercilessly as they walked to their seats in the chamber.

Many of the articles in the press attacked the 'unjust neutrality' of the government for abstaining. It was noted that the Assembly's decision was in fact unconstitutional since the Kuwaiti Constitution guaranteed all citizens equal rights. Many writers, as in the Egyptian debate on family law, quoted from the Quran and gave examples from the early days of Islam to support women's political rights; others did the same to oppose them. Those against women's right to vote used arguments similar to ones that have been used worldwide: women's place was in the home; women were naturally unfit for public duty, being moody and emotional; women would have to mix with men at election time if they had the right to vote, which would lead to corruption; and so on. Those arguing for women's right to vote pointed out that men could not claim to speak in the name of women, who had to be allowed to present their own case; that Kuwaiti women had entered many professions and were politically mature and aware; that women already voted in student elections and were to be found on the boards of professional bodies and in unions; and so forth.

A bill could only be presented to parliament once during its lifetime; thus the women had to wait for the new parliament to be elected so that their case might be presented again. The women's groups were clearly more active on this occasion than on previous ones, and organised seminars and debates on the question of their political rights. When the time for new elections drew closer, the women went to some electoral districts to insist that their names be registered in spite of the electoral law. When they were turned away by the registrars, they went to the police to protest the unconstitutionality of the move; they were also turned away from there.

After the new elections, a group of deputies put a bill forward to grant women the right to vote. The Assembly's legal committee called on the Ministry of Waqf (Islamic trusts) for a legal ruling. The Ministry issued a *fatwa* (ruling) that 'the nature of the electoral process befits men, who are endowed with ability and expertise; it is not permissible that women recommend or nominate other women or men'. (This was the Ministry's ruling, and not that of the Assembly.) This provoked another uproar among men and women. Further action was rendered superfluous when, in 1986, parliament itself was again dissolved, largely because deputies had been too severe with ministers on financial questions.

The issue of the women's vote in Kuwait shows that, in spite of the role women's societies could and did play in consciousness raising, they were as yet unable to mobilise the majority of the population in favour of women's rights – not even the women it should have concerned. An indication of women's attitudes to political rights was given in the study carried out by Al-Qutb on 519 Gulf women students (of whom 362 were Kuwaiti) at Kuwait University (1975). When asked whether women should have the right to vote, only 65.5 per cent of the respondents said yes, 17 per cent said no, and 17.1 per cent appeared undecided: there was no consensus on political rights even among educated women.

Men and women who sought political rights for women had a number of factors to contend with. First was apathy and the feeling that getting the vote was not worth the effort, since parliament could be suspended whenever it seemed to be getting too much power. What was the point of fighting for women's political rights if these would not be meaningful? This feeling is not unique to Kuwait; scepticism about the possibility of peaceful change through democratic means is widespread in the region.

Second was the number and strength of the Islamic groups, which gained ground in Kuwait during the 1970s, although opposition to women's political rights was not uniform. The liberal Islamists were in favour of women's political rights, and were critical of the Waqf Ministry *fatwa*. Ironically enough, conservative Islamic groups made use of the women students' vote to increase the numbers of Islamists in the university student council. Some liberals were even said to be reluctant to give women suffrage because Islamic groups might be able to organise stronger support for themselves in parliament by using the women's vote as they did in the universities.

Third was the attitude of the Government. Several members of the ruling family held views that ranged from liberal to radical, and, for instance in 1980, the Kuwaiti Crown Prince had made a statement in support of women's political rights. In the event, as in the Assembly vote in 1982, the Government preferred to take the safe way out and abstain rather than to antagonise powerful conservative forces within Kuwait and in neighbouring Saudi Arabia.

## Seeking other avenues for change

Thus, women's cultural and social NGOs, even active ones, were unable to mobilise enough support to impose change on a reluctant government. Their credibility suffered, and they often came under criticism from women who refused to join either official bodies or NGOs. While the NGOs' contribution to charity and to campaigns on women's rights was recognised, it was felt that they did not reach out to women widely enough or try to cut across class boundaries. There was also criticism that the leadership of such groups had been in the same hands for years, just like the leadership of the official women's groups (and that of the Arab countries themselves).

Women from a younger generation and from more radical political backgrounds did not find an outlet for their energies in social and cultural NGOs. Some of these women met in small groups at home and tried to spread their ideas for social and political reform slowly and without fuss, stressing the need for democracy and equality for women in their countries. They were wary of setting up public groups so as not to be seen to be threatening established NGOs. They would, in any case, have found it difficult to get government permission. Other women sought to work through political parties and professional or trade unions.

Unfortunately, trade unions also lack credibility in the Arab world. There was some active trade unionism in places like Egypt and Kuwait, while in Democratic Yemen all workers were obliged to take part in union activities. However, in countries where unions had become really powerful, as in Tunisia, they were crushed. Some professional unions had a little more credibility because they were more independent of government policy; but the respect they enjoyed gave them some influence rather than power.

One of the most respected professional unions in the Arab world, the Arab Lawyers Union, took an active interest in women's issues and had a women's committee. The ALU enjoyed consultative status with the UN Economic and Social Council. (The UN grants consultative status to NGOs that are shown to be credible.) Apart from holding the Cairo conference on Arab and African women in 1985 referred to in chapter 2, the ALU had placed the subject of women's conditions in the Arab world on the agenda of its 1984 conference in Tunisia.

Still, some women felt that, while the leadership was radical by Arab standards, conservative elements in the rank and file undercut the ALU's effectiveness in lobbying for women's rights. In a talk at a symposium in Georgetown University organised by Arab women students in March 1985, the Egyptian professor Mervat Hatem described the ALU's efforts as pioneering, but restricted by the conservatism of the membership. At the conference in Tunisia, for example, a woman who had prepared a paper suggesting reform in Muslim inheritance laws was not allowed by participants in the audience to deliver it – and the leadership bowed to the audience's wishes. Some Egyptian feminists accused the ALU membership of employing 'divide and rule' tactics with women members who tried to be more radical on women's issues.

In the early 1980s, other independent Arab groups were established which also had active women members and an interest in women's issues. One such group was the Arab Human Rights Organisation, the idea for which took shape during an Arab sociologists' conference in Tunisia. After a meeting in Cyprus, and then in Egypt in 1984, the headquarters of the organisation was set up in Cairo. A counterpart was established by Arab American academics and activists in Washington. Following in the steps of Amnesty International, the Organisation took up the case of Arab political prisoners, and sought to lobby for their release, either through quiet contacts with governments or by resorting to publicity.

The establishment of such organisations was in itself an unusual political development for the Arab world. It showed that new ways were being sought to bring diverse people together for political action, at a time when serious political opposition to governments had been crushed. Members of such organisations did not have to be in agreement on specific political issues, but only on the need for reform in the broadest sense. This form of networking across political and socioeconomic boundaries to achieve reform has obvious advantages: it does not pose a direct political threat to the ruling establishment; it provides people with a framework within which to meet to consider alternative political systems; and it is a structure within which people may learn to overcome personal and political rivalries.

Moreover, such organisations are an indication of growing cultural, as well as political, maturity in the Arab world. In chapter 2, I mentioned the strength of cultural loyalty in the Arab world. The strength of this feeling makes many Arabs, even intellectuals who should know better, defend Arab practices, good or bad, so as not to embarrass the nation. However, the major weapon at the disposal of human rights organisations is precisely their ability to embarrass publicly those governments which infringe basic human rights. The establishment of an organisation like the Arab human rights group thus shows that people who might previously have remained silent about government practices – not just out of fear but out of cultural loyalty to the Arab nation – had become self-confident enough to use the feeling of cultural loyalty as a political tool. This new development can also be seen in the fact that Amnesty International chapters began to be set up in various Arab countries in the 1980s.

Women were active in these and other human rights organisations, and helped to set the agenda. The head of the women's committee in a human rights organisation in Tunisia, for example, said that the question of women's rights had been put on the agenda, although the Tunisian personal staus code was the most advanced in the Arab world (AN, 1985). For one thing, she said, the code did not yet provide complete equality between men and women, because the man remained the legal head of the family. A more serious problem was that women were still not aware of their rights under the law. And there were fears that a post-Bourguiba government might be less liberal on several fronts. The committee was therefore planning a wide-ranging campaign to inform women throughout the country of their rights because 'If women are aware of their rights no new government or authority can take these away.'

Meanwhile, some women did not believe that organisations which did not have women's rights as a central concern could lobby effectively for women. They thus sought an outlet for action in women's groups of a political rather than a social and cultural nature. An example was the Arab Women's Solidarity Association, set up by the Egyptian feminist Nawal Saadawi. This was recognised by the government in December 1984, making it one of the rare legal, independent feminist organisations. The focus was on women's rights, but political and economic problems were also tackled in the belief that women's rights could not be achieved unless social and economic equality was achieved for society as a whole. By the mid-1980s, it had some 500 members. The membership was small and consisted largely of Egyptian and other Arab professional women.

AWSA soon acquired consultative status with the UN's Economic and Social Council. However, in its early days it seemed as though the group might disintegrate because of personality clashes. By mid-1986, it seemed to have overcome the early difficulties, and held its first pan-Arab conference. It is too soon to tell whether a radical feminist group will have any more success in mobilising women than other groups have had so far, and whether this particular group will be able to translate its ideals – 'active participation of women in the political, social and intellectual life of the country as an essential condition for the evolution of a truly democratic society' – into reality.

There were other feminist moves during the UN Decade, such as the initiative by women professionals in Egypt to set up a resource guide on 'Egyptian women in development: professionals and volunteers'. Eight women began meeting in early 1985, partly in response to the fact that the UN Decade for Women had nearly come to an end, and they wanted to find ways to maintain the momentum it had generated. Several women professionals and development experts were invited to meetings to prepare a roster of women working in development fields like community work, health, civic responsibilities, education, science and technology, etc. The target was 50 names in time for the Nairobi conference, and 300 by the end of 1985. By July 1985, the draft guide was ready and gave the names, addresses and vitae of some 50 women from backgrounds that ranged across the political spectrum.

The draft resource guide explained that the women were bound together by 'our common interest and commitment to the development of women' and aimed to meet the 'urgent need to foster information and communication between women and national organizations, as well as to support the local, national and international search for qualified women candidates to serve as consultants, panellists, researchers, etc' (Atif, 1985, p.2). The roster had other obvious uses, such as facilitating the mobilisation of women in times of need; indeed, many of the women listed had been active during the family law crisis.

A significant element in this approach was the awareness of the importance of networking. Networking, the draft resource guide explained, was
the

age-old skill of contacting people to offer alternatives and options. It is a way of
overcoming impasses . . . It is particularly useful when what is available falls short
of people's expressed needs. Women in Egypt grappling with the real dilemma of
integration into the country's development process feel that our predicament
necessitates a choice between various options. This roster is an attempt to offer a
viable solution for women to find more appropriate options through networking.
(p.6)

## Networking, and cultural maturity

Perhaps the most interesting example of networking, and of maturity at the
cultural and political level, is that of the groups of women fighting against
the practice of circumcision in Arab and African countries. There is nothing
in either Islamic or in Christian texts condoning circumcision, which is
practised mostly in sub-Saharan African countries and in Egypt, Sudan and
Somalia, by Christians, Muslims and animists. There are three types of
circumcision: the removal of the foreskin of the clitoris (the mildest form,
known as the *sunna*, or orthodox method); excision, which involves the
removal of the clitoris and part of the labia minora; and infibulation, which
involves removal of the clitoris, the labia minora and the labia majora
(known as pharaonic circumcision). The practice dates back centuries, and
Egyptian mummies were found to have been circumcised. Present-day
reasons given by those who still have the operation carried out on their
daughters range from controlling women's sexuality to hygiene.

The operation is usually performed by midwives, and the poorer the
region, the less hygienic the operation. Side effects range from immediate
complications (pain, shock, infection and death due to infection or bleed-
ing) to intermediate and long-term medical and psychological problems.
Although it is officially banned in countries like Egypt and Sudan, circumcision is still very much in existence, and it is estimated to affect some 70
million women in Africa. Efforts to end the practice were caught up in the
tangled history of colonialism, as well as in government inefficiency and
unwillingness to tackle sensitive issues. (See Al-Dareer, 1982, and Toubia,
1985 for a history and analysis of the problems of circumcision.)

In recent years, however, there have been determined and persistent
efforts by groups of women in the countries where circumcision is practised
to raise public awareness and to stop the operation being carried out. By the
1980s, the concern to end the practice had cut across national boundaries,
and conferences and seminars brought together activists from all over

Africa. At a meeting in Dakar in 1984, an Inter-African Committee was set up; at another meeting in Khartoum the same year, 26 countries were represented at a workshop entitled 'African women speak out against female circumcision'.

Within each country, field workers organised trips for teams of doctors and social workers to rural areas to inform the people about the unnecessary hazards and pain of the operation. Field workers also invited sheikhs and religious scholars to join the teams of doctors and social workers that went out to rural areas, in order to prove to people that religion did not condone the practice. In many cases, field workers found that women did not know that the medical problems they suffered from throughout their lives were the result of the operation. There were also efforts to train midwives in other income-generating careers, because midwives helped to encourage the practice since performing the operation was a major source of income.

Perhaps the most significant aspect of the Afro-Arab women's campaign against circumcision was the level of cultural maturity it revealed, as could be seen at the Nairobi Forum in 1985 where attitudes were quite different from what they had been in Copenhagen five years earlier. Because some Western women had tended to focus on the subject of circumcision to the exclusion of all else (like the economic and political domination of Third-World countries by the West), women from countries where this was practised had a tendency to react defensively. Some men and women have even been known to defend circumcision, or to say that it didn't exist. Afro-Arab women resented the efforts of 'Western sisters to save them', as they put it, and cultural sensitivities on this subject in fact led to a clash at the 1980 Copenhagen Forum between Western women and African and Arab women.

However, by the time of the Nairobi Forum in 1985, women in African and Arab countries 'owned the problem', as they put it. They organised several workshops themselves to debate the question of circumcision in public and to seek ways to end the practice. This was evidence of real cultural maturity. What Arab and African women had been trying to say at Copenhagen was not that they wanted foreigners to keep out of their internal affairs, but that they wanted to be trusted to solve their own problems, and that any assistance given or received should be on grounds of mutual respect.

The Nairobi conference was noteworthy for evidence of cultural maturity, not only among Third-World women, but among women from other parts of the world as well. Women in the industrialised countries had begun to understand and appreciate why Third-World women could not, and did not want to, isolate the problems they faced as women from the problems their countries faced at the political and economic levels. Meanwhile, Third-World women had begun to understand that they could not expect their problems as women to vanish when their countries' political and economic problems were over: the question of women's inequality was not a Western invention; it existed and had to be dealt with. This new maturity was reflected in the number of books that drew on authors from all over the world (for example, Morgan's *Sisterhood is Global*, 1984). It was important not just for sentimental reasons, but because it spread a global network and gave women an important new source of power: the possibility of assistance from abroad in problems they faced at home. Such assistance, given and received on grounds of mutual respect, would no longer be considered 'cultural betrayal'; it would be vital for cultural survival.

## Social, economic and national liberation

If we accept that women in the Third World cannot isolate their problems as women from the political and economic problems of society, is it possible and realistic to try to function at all levels at once? In the Arab world, some Palestinian women under Israeli occupation provide an example of a growing ability to tackle the question of social as well as national liberation. This did not happen because, as is popularly assumed, women's participation in a national struggle automatically 'liberates' women, an assumption that has been shown to be false. Algeria is frequently given as an example of a country where women were mobilised during the national struggle, only to be pushed into the background once liberation was achieved.

To be fair to the Algerian liberation movement, none of the Arab movements of national liberation, with the possible exception of Democratic Yemen, had developed clear policies of social liberation. The behaviour of socialist regimes, like Nasser's, indicated a belief that social change would come about gradually through economic development and by opening education and work opportunities to both men and women. They might have been proved correct, but the socialist experiment was never in place long enough to find out; economic and political conditions inevitably led to a reversal of socialist economic policies.

In the Palestinian national struggle, there has been a growing realisation by women that national and social liberation have to go hand in hand. This is not because the Palestinian leadership is more mature than that of other national movements. Indeed, the structure and functioning of the Palestine Liberation Organisation (PLO) is similar to that of Arab governments. The Palestinian women's federation is closely bound by official policy, and splits along the same lines as the various PLO groups when there is disagreement on national policy. Women are represented in the Palestinian National Council (the Palestinian parliament in exile) in about the same proportion as other Arab women in parliaments in their countries. By 1986, there was not yet a woman member of the PLO Executive Committee. There was some awareness by Palestinian women members of the PLO of the need for a more developed, and better implemented policy on women. (See R. Sayigh, 1983, for a discussion of the process of self-criticism that women in the PLO engaged in.)

The PLO did have something of a liberating effect on women in the communities in exile, through involving them in unsegregated activities outside the home: in guerrilla operations, in economic production, and in activities in the field of education and health. The PLO also reached women at different socioeconomic levels through its work in the refugee camps. However, the economic need that Palestinian families faced because of the occupation of their country also had a liberating effect on women. It was not unusual for wives and mothers to assist in the financial support of their families, and to become the sole breadwinners when their husbands were killed or disabled. Palestinian parents were as concerned to educate their daughters as their sons, and girls were brought up to expect to be able to stand on their own feet, for no one knew what the future would bring.

A more radical change took place among the Palestinians who were able to remain in Palestine (about a million in the West Bank, half a million in Gaza, and some 700,000 in present-day Israel), and particularly among Palestinians on the West Bank. While they recognised the PLO as their political representative, and many were in fact secretly members of different groups within the PLO, they also needed to develop their own social and economic institutions. As in the rest of the Arab world, charitable organisations had flourished on the West Bank before the Israeli occupation of 1967; the majority were run by women. The occupation led some of these organisations to change their approach. In addition to relief work and activities in the fields of literacy and health care, associations like Inaash al Usra (revival of the family) began to work seriously on vocational training and on income-generating projects for women, which also involved them in marketing. (Giacaman, n.d. gives a good summary of women's organisations and changes in attitude.)

While the women who ran these organisations were highly respected, and indeed were considered symbols of Palestinian steadfastness, they did not break out of the traditional mould. Their aim was more to help Palestinian families stay above the poverty line, not so much to change attitudes to women's roles and social relations. By the mid-1970s, an increasing number of young educated women did not feel that the traditional women's organisations and charities were for them. Not only was the leadership fairly static in these organisations, but some groups restricted membership in order to keep things exactly as they had been before the occupation in 1967.

In 1978, some younger women formed the Union of Women's Work Committees, which had its headquarters in Jerusalem. They decided to set up a committee rather than a charitable organisation to avoid difficulties in getting permission for a formal organisation. The committee approach was also adopted by other bodies in the West Bank, like the Medical Relief Committees and the Agricultural Relief Committees, and is an indication of how important informal structures are when formal structures have been destroyed or coopted. There was some fragmentation of the Women's Work Committees over politial issues, similar to the ones that affected the Palestinian movement as a whole in 1983. Two or three of these, including the core WWC, were still able to function effectively within a well-defined political, economic and social framework.

By 1985, the WWC had some 4,200 members, and aimed for a membership of 6,000 by 1986 (AN, 1985). There were major differences of approach between the WWC and the established NGOs in the West Bank, and in the Arab world as a whole. Although the WWC was begun by middle-class town women, it carried the message of the organisation to women from other socioeconomic backgrounds in the refugee camps and the villages. The WWC did not impose itself on the village women. It began by inviting those who would come to a meeting, and asked them what they thought their problems were. The WWC representatives would then ask the village women what solutions they thought would be appropriate to their problems, and which of the women among them were likely to be able to offer a solution for the community. This was a development model that was likely to create a spirit of self-reliance among the people, instead of offering them welfare and creating a condition of dependency. Eventually, village women established their own committees and sent their representatives to WWC general meetings. By 1983, committees were established in some 33 centres in towns, refugee camps and villages.

The solutions women needed for their problems differed from place to place, and the WWC structure enabled it to respond flexibly, with literacy programmes, health care and education, child-care establishments, and income-generating activities. This was vital as more women in the occupied territories were obliged to go out to work as economic conditions deteriorated, and as the men found themselves under political pressure, in exile or in jail. Throughout, the WWC emphasis was on encouraging the community to help itself by drawing on the resources it already had, for instance by setting up its own child-care centres, or finding its own experts to train others. Where a more conservative attitude prevailed, WWC representatives visited the families to encourage parents to let their daughters attend meetings or take part in activities.

At the same time, the WWC worked to increase the women's awareness of their social rights and responsibilities as well as their sense of national responsibility. Naturally, there was already a strong sense of national feeling among Palestinian women under occupation; indeed, some 3,000 had been put in jail by the Israeli occupation authorities since 1967. Some of the new women's committees were able to make a further impact at the political level. West Bank observers noted that some of these groups were able to bring out more people in street protests than the umbrella political organisations to which they might belong.

There was another key development in the growth of feminist groups in the West Bank – the effective use of networking between groups. Giacaman pointed out that groups like the WWC depended on the established charities when they wanted to hold certain activities, because they did not have licences. The charities prove responsive, although their social ideology was quite different from that of the WWC. Thus, women's groups in the West Bank were able to coordinate their activities across political ideology and class boundaries. They were able to tackle issues that specifically affected women and their families – illiteracy, health, income generation, social mobility – within a broader framework of the conditions affecting the Palestinians at large.

## Information as a source of power

The preceding discussion has looked at the different ways in which women are organised in the Arab world. It is worth looking briefly at an area important to the future development of women in the region: information. As was mentioned earlier, women could exercise quite effective control over information in traditional society. How active a role do they play in disseminating information in the 'modern' sector, and how much information exists about women? In fact, the media is one field in the modern Arab sector where women work in large numbers. Arab women journalists are not restricted to women's issues, but cover general features and economic and political stories.

In the early 1980s, for example, about a quarter of the members of the Journalists' Syndicate in Egypt were women, and in the 1983 elections, a veteran journalist, Amina Shafiq, was returned to the board for the fourth time, with 87 votes more than the next (male) candidate. In Tunisia, the head of the Journalists' Syndicate in the early 1980s was a woman. The first seminar for Arab women journalists was organised in Beirut in 1981 by the Arab Federation of Journalists. Some 50 women journalists from all over the Arab world took part, along with other members of the press establishment, to discuss the problems faced by women journalists. At the seminar, women discussed the difficulties they faced in coordinating their careers and child-bearing roles; the lack of opportunities for women in different branches of the profession; and the lack of sensitivity in the media in the treatment of the subject of women.

Several studies have been produced on the subject of media coverage of women over the years. Not unexpectedly, these showed that women were portrayed in traditional roles and were treated as avid purchasers of consumer goods. Five papers were given on this topic at the second regional Gulf conference on women in 1981. The fact that such studies were being carried out at all was an indication of awareness of the need for change in the role of the media. According to the Social and Economic Commission for Western Asia, there was some indication during the UN Decade of a decrease in the portrayal of women in traditional roles in the Arab media, and an increase in the portrayal of women in new roles, particularly as career women.

The number of Arab women's magazines has multiplied a dozen-fold since the turn of the century. Many 'modern' publications are consumer-oriented, and focussed on fashion and family, but even the consumer magazines often carry serious articles on women. During the UN Decade for Women, more radical publications appeared, such as *8 March* in Morocco, and *Al-Nisaa* (women) in Tunisia. The general-interest press also offered a platform for debate of women's issues in the Arab world, even (or perhaps especially) in more conservative countries such as Saudi Arabia. Here, nearly every daily newspaper had its women's page or women's supplement, and issues like women's work, driving and roles within and outside the home were discussed with a good deal of frankness, and both conservative and liberal pens contributed to the debate.

As for the information on Arab women in articles, in journals and books, an immense quantity of literature has been produced in several languages, although the quality is somewhat uneven. Indeed, 17 Arab women social scientists met in May 1982 in Tunisia in a conference organised by the United Nations Educational, Scientific and Cultural Organisation to review the literature on women in the Arab world (Rassam, 1984). The social scientists noted the trend towards studies based on the actual situation of women, and urged the adoption of a multi-disciplinary approach in future research. They recommended that future research be undertaken with practical objectives in mind, such as to how to increase women's active participation in society, since the Arab world could not afford the luxury of research for its own sake. They listed the priorities for research in each Arab region.

One can expect the interest in research on women to continue, not just because of the number of Arab women social scientists graduating from universities who will want to conduct it, but because the subject has gained respectability in universities. An institute was established at the Beirut University College in 1973 – the Institute for Women's Studies in the Arab World (IWSAW) – to serve as a resource centre and publishing house. A serious concern for women's studies has developed in departments like the Centre for Development Studies at the University of Khartoum, and the Documentation Centre of Human Sciences at the University of Wahran in Algeria, as well as in other departments in other Arab universities. Centres like the National Centre for Sociological and Criminological Studies in Cairo, where many of the researchers were women, have also carried out a good deal of research on women.

Women's roles and the handicaps they faced also became respectable topics for discussion at Arab and international conferences on the Arab world. To begin with, one or two papers were given on the subject here and there; by the 1980s whole conferences were devoted to the issue. The Centre for Arab Unity Studies in Beirut held a seminar in September 1981 on the role of Arab women in the unity movement, and published the proceedings. As noted above, Kuwaiti women organised three major conferences on Gulf and Arab women. At the Centre for Contemporary Arab Studies in Georgetown University, there were three papers on Arab women in the 1985 annual symposium; the 1986 symposium was entirely devoted to the subject. At a meeting of Arab sociologists in Tunisia in 1985, two papers were presented on women. The Oxford Arab Committee held a one-day seminar on women in April 1985. In fact, meetings and seminars were organised by governments, academics, professionals in nearly all fields and subjects related to women in the 1970s and 1980s. At the same time, Arab women began to take a more active part in international seminars and conferences on women. Clearly the interest existed, as well as an awareness of the need to produce material of better quality and more relevance.

In spite of these signs of growing interest in women's issues, it cannot be said that Arab women have yet developed effective sources of power in the modern age. One of the major obstacles all women's groups face is the reluctance of women, even those who are firm believers in equal rights, to take part in a women's movement. A good many professional women feel that enough has been achieved in terms of women's rights (the same argument was used by professional women who did not support the Equal Rights Amendment in the US, which failed to win enough support in the 1980s to become part of the American Constitution). These women believe that the achievement of any outstanding rights should be left to the 'natural process' of social change. Many people also believe that the Arab world's problems are primarily political and economic, such as the conflict with Israel and the struggle for democracy, and that social questions, such as equal rights for women, should take second place.

Meanwhile, even women who do believe that there has to be a serious and persistent campaign for women's rights do not want to segregate themselves in women's groups to do so, and prefer to work through the political parties or professional unions to which they belong. According to this view, women's groups, like 'women's literature' or 'women's art', impose artificial boundaries on people. There is thus no consensus among women themselves about the best way to achieve their objectives, even though they might all agree about the ultimate aims. In this state of affairs, networking as a technique for political change becomes even more valuable.

## Empowering people

In conclusion, while there are several active and articulate people seeking human rights for women, it cannot be said that a strong 'feminist' current has developed in the Arab world, in the narrow sense of fighting for women's rights irrespective of the other political and economic needs of society. This is just as well, because the Third-World struggle for democracy and for political and economic independence is not as yet complete.

If, for instance, Arab women were to fight for equal opportunities in the workforce without trying to reform national economic development policies, they would be engaged in an ultimately fruitless struggle: the present economic structures are simply not capable of providing fair and gainful employment for enough of the men and women who seek it. Similarly, if Arab women were to concentrate their energies on making their way to the top of the political ladder, they would win a hollow victory: the present political set-up offers limited participation.

The process of social and economic change is taking place slowly and unevenly in the Arab world, for the reasons outlined in this book. This need not be a bad thing: a society in transition is one where traditions are still alive, and where many different kinds of social systems are in force. With increasing information available from the work of social scientists, it should be possible to pinpoint those traditions that are valuable, and to accept that these are 'modern' and worth maintaining. The Arab family system, for example, has much to commend it: the warmth it spreads through society, the way people create more time for one another, the sense of security and belonging it provides. Such a system should not be lost, unawares, through 'modernisation'; it should be developed so that the negative aspects are modified and the positive ones maintained. Women's roles within the family must also be developed, so that home-based work is shared between all members of the family, as work for wages outside the home becomes the dominant economic system.

Meanwhile, increasing participation by women in the debate on their roles, and in defining the place of religion, culture and tradition in society, will help to ensure that conservative views do not overwhelm all others. The fact that views other than the conservative were forcefully expressed during the Egyptian family law debate by both men and women who believed in equal rights for women was, in the words of one campaigner, one of the most important outcomes of the debate. All sectors of society need to take part in deciding the shape of modern Arab identity, and all must learn to respect one another's views, even though they do not agree with them. Through the debate, liberals, nationalists and Islamists may find that some basic ideas are shared, and that they can agree to disagree on others without violence. This is essential if the people of the region are to learn to live together as equal citizens of the state, rather than as unequal minorities, whether sexual, sectarian, or national. Learning to differ democratically is also essential if the cycle of coup, counter-coup and dictatorship is to be broken.

However, women should not concentrate on political and economic issues to the exclusion of those that affect them specifically as women, like the personal status laws. The example of the Palestinian women under Israeli occupation is one where activists have learned to work on the political, economic and social fronts at one and the same time, and to network with each other across political boundaries to increase their power by increasing their numbers.

Whether they are active as members of women's groups or in national political parties, Arab women need to find the power to ensure that the question of their human rights is kept high on the national agenda, while ensuring that economic and social questions remain on the women's agenda. This is a tall order, and many years will go by before equality is achieved. Still, in the end, women may succeed in bringing to society a definition of power that excludes domination.

# Bibliography

**Works consulted in English**

Abu Nasr, Julinda, Khoury, Nabil F. and Azzam, Henry T., eds. 1985. *Women, Employment and Development in the Arab World*. Berlin, Mouton Publishers.

Abu Saud, Abeer. 1984. *Qatari Women Past and Present*. Harlow, Longman Group.

Ahmed, Leila. 1984. Early feminist movements in the Middle East: Turkey and Egypt. In *Muslim Women*, ed. Freda Hussain, pp.111–23. Beckenham, Croom Helm.

Allaghi, Farida. 1981. Rural women in a resettlement project: the case of Libya. Paper presented for ILO tripartite regional seminar on rural development and women in Africa, Dakar, 15–19 June.

Allaghi, Farida and Almana, Aisha. 1984. Survey of research on women in the Arab Gulf region. In *Social Science Research and Women in the Arab world*, ed. Amal Rassam, pp.16–38. Paris, UNESCO.

Arberry, Arthur J. 1983. *The Koran Interpreted*. Oxford University Press.

Atif, Nadia, project coordinator. 1985. Resource guide on Egyptian women in development: professionals and volunteers (mimeographed). Cairo.

Ayesh, Husni. 1985. Women's education in Jordan (mimeographed). Amman.

Azzam, Henry. 1979. The participation of Arab women in the labour force: development factors and policies. Population and Labour Policies Programme, World Employment Programme, Working Paper No. 80. Geneva, ILO.

Azzam, Henry and Moujabber, C. 1985. Women and development in the Gulf states. In *Women, Employment and Development in the Arab World*, eds. Julinda Abu Nasr *et al.*, pp.59–71. Berlin, Mouton Publishers.

Barakat, Halim. 1985. The Arab family and the challenge of social transformation. In *Women and the Family in the Middle East: New Voices of Change*, pp.27–48. Austin, University of Texas Press.

Basson, Priscilla. 1982. Domestic productivity in male- and female-headed households of rural Jordan. *Ecology of Food and Nutrition* 12:75–8.

Beck, Lois and Keddie, Nikki, eds. 1978. *Women in the Muslim World*. Cambridge, Mass., Harvard University Press.

Birks, J. S. and Sinclair, C. A. 1980. *International Migration and Development in the Arab Region*. Geneva, ILO.

Chamie, M. 1985. Labour force participation of Lebanese women. In *Women, Employment and Development in the Arab World*, eds. Julinda Abu Nasr *et al.* pp.73–102. Berlin, Mouton Publishers.

Chater, Souad, n.d. *The Tunisian Woman: Citizen or Subject?* Tunis, Maison Tunisienne de l'Edition (in French. Book based on doctoral thesis defended at Paris-Pantheon Sorbonne in June 1975, entitled 'Participation de la femme tunisienne à la vie economique: son évolution et ses limites).

Al-Dareer, Asma. 1982. *Woman, Why Do You Weep?* London, Zed Press.

Davis, Angela. 1985. Sex – Egypt. In *Women: a World Report*, pp.326–48. London, published for New Internationalist by Methuen London.

Fernea, Elizabeth Warnock, ed. 1985. *Women and the Family in the Middle East: New Voices of Change*. Austin, University of Texas Press.

Fernea, Elizabeth Warnock and Bezirgan, Basima Qattan, eds. 1977. *Middle Eastern Muslim Women Speak*. Austin, University of Texas Press.

*Forum 85*. 1985. Newspaper published during Non-Governmental Organisations Conference and UN World Conference on Women.

Giacaman, Rita. n.d. Palestinian women and development in the occupied West Bank. Briefing No. 5. London, Council for the Advancement of Arab British Understanding.

Graham, Helga. 1978. *Arabian Timemachine*. London, Heinemann.

Gran, Judith. 1977. Impact of the world market on Egyptian women. *MERIP Reports* 58:3–7.

El-Guindi, Fadwa. 1981. Veiling *infitah* with Muslim ethic: Egypt's contemporary Islamic movement. *Social Problems* 28(4):465–85.

Hammam, Mona. 1980. Women and industrial work in Egypt: the Chubra el-Kheima case. *Arab Studies Quarterly* 1(2):50–69.

Harfoush, Samira. 1980. An assessment of the status of women in education, labor force, and development: the case of Jordan. Report prepared for ICRW, Washington.

Hazleton, Elaine. 1977. Jawazi al-Malakim. In *Middle Eastern Women Speak*. Austin, University of Texas Press.

Hill, Enid. 1979. *Mahkama! Studies in the Egyptian Legal System*. London, Ithaca Press.

Hoffman, Valerie J. 1985. An Islamic activist: Zaynab al-Ghazali. In *Women and the Family in the Middle East*, ed. Elizabeth Warnock Fernea, pp.233–54. Austin, University of Texas Press.

Hourani, Albert. 1983. *Arabic Thought in the Liberal Age, 1798–1939*. Cambridge University Press.

Hussain, Freda, ed. 1984. *Muslim Women*. Beckenham, Croom Helm Ltd.

Institute for Women's Studies in the Arab World. 1980. *Women and Work in Lebanon*. Beirut, IWSAW Monograph Series, No. 1.

International Center for Research on Women. 1980. Keeping Women Out: a structural analysis of women's employment in developing countries. Report prepared for ICRW, Washington DC.

International Labour Office. 1982. Legislation on working women in the countries of Western Asia (in French). Geneva.

1983. *Employment and Manpower Problems and Policy Issues in the Arab Countries: Proposals for the Future*. Geneva.

1984. Protection of working mothers: an ILO global survey (1964–84). *Women at Work* 2. Geneva.

Keddie, Nikki. 1979. Problems in the study of Middle Eastern women. *International Journal of Middle East Studies* 10:225–40.

Keely, Charles B. and Saket, Bassam. 1984. The Arab region: a case study of consequences for labor supply countries. *The Middle East Journal* 38(4):685–98.

Khafagy, Fatma. 1984. Women and labour migration: one village in Egypt. *MERIP Reports* 124:17–21.

Khattab, Hind Abou Seoud and El Daeif, Syada Greiss. 1984. Female education in Egypt: changing attitudes over a span of 100 years. In *Muslim Women*, ed. Freda Hussain, pp.166–97. Beckenham, Croom Helm Ltd.

Maher, Vanessa. 1974. *Women and Property in Morocco: their Changing Relation to the Process of Social Stratification in the Middle Atlas*. London, Cambridge University Press.

Makhlouf, Carla. 1979. *Changing Veils: Women and Modernisation in North Yemen*. Austin, University of Texas Press.

Malki, Abdalla, project manager. 1981. Training and job opportunities for women in Jordan. Survey for Jordan Ministry of Labour and Jordan Vocational Training Corporation, Amman.

Marsot, Afaf Lutfi al-Sayyid. 1978. The revolutionary gentlewomen in Egypt. In *Women in the Muslim World*, eds. Lois Beck and Nikki Keddie, pp.261–76. Cambridge, Mass., Harvard University Press.

Meghdessian, Samira Rafidi. 1980. *The Status of the Arab Woman: a Select Bibliography*. London, Mansell.

Mernissi, Fatima. 1975. *Beyond the Veil: Male–Female Dynamics in a Modern Muslim Society*. Cambridge, Mass., Schenkman Publishing Company.

1981. Capitalist development and women's perceptions in an Arabo-Muslim society: as illustrated by the peasants of the Gharb, Morocco. Paper prepared for the tripartite regional seminar of the ILO on the role of women in rural development in Africa, Dakar, 15–19 June.

El-Messiri, Sawsan. 1978. Self-images of traditional urban women in Cairo. In *Women in the Muslim World*, eds. Lois Beck and Nikki Keddie, pp. 522–40. Cambridge, Mass., Harvard University Press.

Minai, Naila. 1981. *Women in Islam: Tradition and Transition in the Middle East*. New York, Seaview Books.

Minces, Juliette. 1982. *The House of Obedience: Women in Arab Society*. London, Zed Press.

Mogannam, Matiel. 1937. *The Arab Woman and the Palestine Problem*. London, Herbert Joseph.

Molyneux, Maxine. 1982. *State Policies and the Position of Women Workers in the People's Democratic Republic of Yemen, 1967–77*. Geneva, ILO.

Morgan, Robin, ed. 1984. *Sisterhood is Global: the International Women's Movement Anthology*. New York, Anchor Books.

M'rabet, Fadela. 1977. Les Algériennes. In *Middle Eastern Muslim Women Speak*, eds. Elizabeth Warnock Fernea and Basima Qattan Bezirgan, pp.320–58. Austin, University of Texas Press.

Mujahid, G. B. S. 1985. Female labour force participation in Jordan. In *Women, Employment and Development in the Arab world*, eds. Julinda Abu Nasr *et al.*, pp.103–30. Berlin, Mouton Publishers.

Oman, Sultanate of. 1985. *Oman Yearbook*. Muscat, Ministry of Information.

Philipp, Thomas. 1978. Feminism and nationalist politics in Egypt. In *Women in the Muslim World*, eds. Lois Beck and Nikki Keddie, pp.277–94. Cambridge, Mass., Harvard University Press.

Al-Qazzaz, Ayad. 1975. *Women in the Arab World: an Annotated Bibliography*. Detroit, Association of Arab–American University Graduates.

Rassam, Amal, ed. 1984. *Social Science Research and Women in the Arab World*. Paris, United Nations Educational, Scientific and Cultural Organisation.

El-Saadawi, Nawal. 1980. *The Hidden Face of Eve: Women in the Arab World*. London, Zed Press.

Saket, Bassam K., supervisor. 1983. *Workers Migration Abroad: Socio-economic Implications for Households in Jordan*. Amman, Royal Scientific Society.

Salem, Norma. 1984. Islam and the status of women in Tunisia. In *Muslim Women*, ed. Freda Hussain, pp.141–68. Beckenham, Croom Helm Ltd.

Al-Sanabary, Nagat. 1985. Continuity and change in women's education in the Arab states. In *Women and the Family in the Middle East: New Voices of Change*, ed. Elizabeth Warnock Fernea, pp.93–110. Austin, University of Texas Press.

Sayigh, Rosemary. 1983. Women in struggle: an overview – Palestine. *Third World Quarterly* 5(4):880–6.

Sayigh, Yusif, A. 1984. 1973–83: an unusual decade. In *The Arab Economies: Structure and Outlook*, revised edition, pp.9–31. Manama, Arab Banking Corporation.

Schaefer Davis, Susan. 1980. The determinants of social position among rural Moroccan women. In *Women in Contemporary Muslim Societies*, ed. Jane Smith, pp.87–99. London, Associated University Presses.

1983. *Patience and Power: Women's Lives in a Moroccan Village*. Cambridge, Mass., Schenkman Publishing Company.

Sivard, Ruth Leger. 1985. *Women . . . a World Survey*. Washington DC, World Priorities.

Smith, Jane I., ed. 1980. *Women in Contemporary Muslim Societies*. London, Associated University Presses.

El-Solh, Camillia Fawzi. 1985. Migration and the selectivity of change: Egyptian peasant women in Iraq. *Migrations et Méditerranée – Peuples Méditerranéens* 31–2:243–57.

Stowasser, Barbara Freyer. The status of women in early Islam. In *Muslim Women*, ed. Freda Hussain, pp.11–43. Beckenham, Croom Helm Ltd.

Tabbarah, Riad. 1982. Curbing the growth of the cities. *People* 9(1):9–11.

Taylor, Elizabeth. 1984. Egyptian migration and peasant wives. *MERIP Reports* 124:3–10.

*The Middle East*. 1980. 64:49–50.
  1982. 94:27–31
  1983. 100:29–34.
  1984. 113:46–7.
Toubia, Nahid F. 1985. The social and political implications of female circumcision: the case of Sudan. In *Women and the Family in the Middle East*, ed. Elizabeth Warnock Fernea, pp. 148–59. Austin, University of Texas Press.
Tucker, Judith. 1976. Egyptian women in the work force. *MERIP Reports* 50:3–9.
  1983. Problems in the historiography of women in the Middle East: the case of Nineteenth Century Egypt. *International Journal of Middle East Studies* 15:321–36.
United Nations. 1984a. Report of the Secretary General: world survey on the role of women in development. A/CONF.116/4, 11 December 1984. World Conference to Review and Appraise the Achievements of the UN Decade for Women: equality, development, peace. Nairobi, Kenya, 15–26 July 1985.
  1984b. Report of the Secretary General – review and appraisal of progress achieved and obstacles encountered at the national level in the realisation of the goals and objectives of the UN Decade for Women: equality, development, peace: overview, A/CONF.116/5, 5 December 1984; part one, A/CONF.116/5 Add 1, 5 December 1984; part two, A/CONF.116/5/Add 2–14, 5 December 1984. World Conference, Nairobi, 1985.
  1984c. Report of the Secretary General: the situation of women and children living in the occupied Arab territories and other occupied territories. A/CONF.116/6, 30 October 1984. World Conference, Nairobi, 1985.
  1985a. Report of the Secretary General: review and appraisal of the progress achieved and the obstacles encountered by the UN system at the regional and international levels in attaining the goals and objectives of the UN Decade for Women: equality, development, peace. A/CONF.116/8, 21 February 1985. World Conference, Nairobi, 1985.
  1985b. Report of the Secretary General: recommendations of regional intergovernmental preparatory meetings. A/CONF.116/9, 5 February 1985. World Conference, Nairobi, 1985.
  1985c. Report of the Secretary General: selected statistics and indicators on the status of women. A/CONF.116.10, 3 May 1985. World Conference, Nairobi, 1985.
  1985d. Forward-looking strategies of implementation for the advancement of women and concrete measures to overcome obstacles to achievement of the goals and objectives of the UN Decade for Women for the period 1986 to the year 2000: equality, development, peace. A/CONF.116/12, 6 June 1985. World Conference, Nairobi, 1985.
  1985e. Report of the committee on the elimination of discrimination against women on the achievements of and obstacles encountered by states parties in the implementation of the convention on the elimination of all forms of discrimination against women. A/CONF.116/13, 5 June 1985. World Conference, Nairobi, 1985.

1985f. Review of selected major issues in the medium-term plans of the organisations of the UN system: women and development. A/CONF.116/15, 10 June
1985. World Conference, Nairobi, 1985.

1985g. Status of the convention on the elimination of all forms of discrimination
against women. A/CONF.116/BP1, 4 June 1985. World Conference, Nairobi,
1985.

Woodsmall, Ruth F., director. 1956. *Study of the Role of Women in Lebanon, Egypt,
Iraq, Jordan and Syria 1954–1955*. New York, International Federation of
Business and Professional Women.

World Bank. 1985. *World Development Report 1985*. Washington DC, published for
the World Bank by Oxford University Press.

Youssef, Nadia Haggag. 1974. *Women and Work in Developing Societies*. Berkeley,
University of California.

1978. The status and fertility patterns of Muslim women. In *Women in the Muslim
World*, eds. Lois Beck and Nikki Keddie, pp.69–99. Cambridge, Mass.,
Harvard University Press.

## Works consulted in Arabic

Amara, Muhammad. 1976. *The Complete Works of Qassim Amin*. Beirut, Al-
Muassassa al-Arabia lil Dirassat wal Nashr.

Al-Awadhi, Badriya. 1982. *Selected Issues from the Kuwait Draft Personal Status Law
– Divorce, Polygamy, Custody – a Comparative Study*. Kuwait, Al-Yaqtha
Printing House.

Faour, Muhammad. 1985. Conditions of Lebanese women after 10 years of war.
Paper presented to the regional experts conference on the role of women in
national development, organised by the ILO in cooperation with IWSAW and
the Cyprus Statistics and Research Department, Nicosia, 22–6 April.

Farag, Abdel-Majid. 1985. Woman's role in development in the Arab world. Paper
presented to the regional experts conference on the role of women in national
development, organised by the ILO in cooperation with IWSAW and the
Cyprus Statistics and Research Department, Nicosia, 22–6 April.

Haddad, Yahya Fayez, ed. 1982. *Women and Development in the 80s: Papers and
Studies at the Second Regional Conference for Women in the Gulf and Arabian
Peninsula*, Vols. 1 and 2. Kuwait, Women's Cultural and Social Association (Al
Jamiya al-Thaqafiya al-Ijtimayia al-Nissaiya).

Al-Hussaini, Aisha Ahmad Abdel-Rahim. 1982. Women and administrative
development in the Kingdom of Saudi Arabia. In *Women and Development in the
80s*, ed. Yahya Fayez Haddad, Vol. 1, pp. 430–46. Kuwait, Women's Cultural
and Social Association.

Al-Khaled, Fadda. 1982. The development role of Kuwaiti women: a survey of
social attitudes on women's education and work. In *Women and Development in
the 80s*, ed. Yahya Fayez Haddad, vol. 1, pp.266–372. Kuwait, Women's
Cultural and Social Associatiuon.

Al-Khatib, Hanifa. 1984. *The History of the Women's Movement in Lebanon and its*

*Links to the Arab World, 1800–1975*. Beirut, Dar al-Hadatha lil Tibaa wal Nashr wal Tawziy.

Al-Kuwari, Ali Khalifa. 1982. Modes of socioeconomic development in the oil-producing states of the Gulf. In *Women and Development in the 80s*, ed. Yahya Fayez Haddad, Vol. 1, pp.243–65. Kuwait, Women's Cultural and Social Association.

Mernissi, Fatima. 1982. *Sexual Behaviour in an Islamic, Class-Stratified, Capitalist Society*. Beirut, Dar al-Hadath lil Tibaa wal Nashr wal Tawziy.

Al-Najjar, Baqer. 1984. Arab women and changes in the Arab social structure: the case of the Arab Gulf woman. Paper presented to the third regional conference of women in the Gulf and the Arabian Peninsula, Abu Dhabi, United Arab Emirates, March 1984.

Oman, Sultanate of. 1984. *Study of the Impact of Foreign Nursemaids on the Characteristic of the Oman Family*. Muscat, Ministry of Labour and Social Affairs.

Al-Qutb, Ishaq. 1975. A study of trends among students from the Arab Gulf states and emirates at Kuwait University. In *Studies on Women's Conditions in Kuwait and the Arab Gulf: First Regional Conference for Women in the Arab Gulf, 21–4 April 1975*, pp.202–304. Kuwait, Women's Cultural and Social Association.

Rahmeh, Anton. 1985. Woman's role in national development: a case study of Syria. Paper presented to the regional experts conference on the role of women in national development, organised by the ILO in cooperation with IWSAW and the Cyprus Statistics and Research Department, Nicosia, 22–6 April.

Al-Rujaib, Latifa Issa. 1982. Integrating the Kuwaiti woman on welfare in the development process. In *Women and Development in the 80s*, ed. Yahya Fayez Haddad, Vol. 2, pp.794–812. Kuwait, Women's Cultural and Social Association.

Al-Rumeihi, Muhammad. 1975. The conditions of Gulf women. In *Studies on Women's Conditions in Kuwait and the Arab Gulf: First Regional Conference for Women in the Arab Gulf, 21–4 April 1975*, pp.5–12. Kuwait, Women's Cultural and Social Association.

Sharayhe, Wadi. 1985. The role of Jordanian women in national development. Paper presented to the regional experts conference on the role of women in national development, organised by the ILO in cooperation with IWSAW and the Cyprus Statistics and Research Department, Nicosia, 22–6 April.

Al-Sidani, Nouriya. 1982. *The Arab Women's Movement in the 20th Century: 1917–1981*. Kuwait, Dar al-Siyassa Publishing House.

Al-Thaqeb, Fahd. 1975. The Kuwaiti's position on women's place in our contemporary society. In *Studies on Women's Conditions in Kuwait and the Arab Gulf, 21–4 April 1975*, pp.189–201. Kuwait, Women's Cultural and Social Association.

# Index